COMMON LINES AND CITY SPACES

The **Institute of Southeast Asian Studies (ISEAS)** was established as an autonomous organization in 1968. It is a regional centre dedicated to the study of socio-political, security and economic trends and developments in Southeast Asia and its wider geostrategic and economic environment. The Institute's research programmes are the Regional Economic Studies (RES, including ASEAN and APEC), Regional Strategic and Political Studies (RSPS), and Regional Social and Cultural Studies (RSCS).

ISEAS Publishing, an established academic press, has issued more than 2,000 books and journals. It is the largest scholarly publisher of research about Southeast Asia from within the region. ISEAS Publishing works with many other academic and trade publishers and distributors to disseminate important research and analyses from and about Southeast Asia to the rest of the world.

COMMON LINES AND CITY SPACES

A Critical Anthology on
Arthur Yap

Edited by
Gui Weihsin

INSTITUTE OF SOUTHEAST ASIAN STUDIES
Singapore

First published in Singapore in 2014 by
ISEAS Publishing
Institute of Southeast Asian Studies
30 Heng Mui Keng Terrace
Pasir Panjang
Singapore 119614

E-mail: publish@iseas.edu.sg
Website: <http://bookshop.iseas.edu.sg>

All rights reserved. No part of this publication may be reproduced, stored in a retrieval system, or transmitted in any form or by any means, electronic, mechanical, photocopying, recording or otherwise, without the prior permission of the Institute of Southeast Asian Studies.

© 2014 Institute of Southeast Asian Studies

The responsibility for facts and opinions in this publication rests exclusively with the author and his interpretation do not necessarily reflect the views or the policy of the publishers or their supporters.

ISEAS Library Cataloguing-in-Publication Data

Common lines and city spaces : a critical anthology of Arthur Yap / edited by Gui Weihsin.
1. Yap, Arthur, 1943–2006—Criticism and interpretation.
2. Authors, Singaporean—20th century.
3. Singaporean literature (English)—20th century—History and criticism.
I. Gui, Weihsin,| d1978–
PR9570 S63Y26   2014

ISBN 978-981-4379-90-8 (soft cover)
ISBN 978-981-4379-91-5 (e-book, PDF)

Typeset by Superskill Graphics Pte Ltd
Printed in Singapore by Markono Print Media Pte Ltd

CONTENTS

Acknowledgements		vii
About the Contributors		ix
1.	Common Lines and City Spaces: Introduction *Gui Weihsin*	1
2.	The Transformation of Objects into Things in Arthur Yap's Poetry *Gui Weihsin*	14
3.	"the same tableau, intrinsically still": Arthur Yap, Poet-Painter *Boey Kim Cheng*	42
4.	"go to bedok, you bodoh": Arthur Yap's Mapping of Singaporean Space *Angus Whitehead*	73
5.	On Places and Spaces: The Possibilities of Teaching Arthur Yap *Eddie Tay*	96
6.	Arthur Yap's Ecological Poetics of the Daily *Zhou Xiaojing*	114
7.	"except for a word": Arthur Yap's Unspoken Homoeroticism *Cyril Wong*	133
8.	"a long way from what?": Folkways and Social Commentary in Arthur Yap's Short Stories *Angus Whitehead and Joel Gwynne*	151
Index		191

ACKNOWLEDGEMENTS

This book would not have been possible without Shirley Geok-lin Lim, who initiated the idea and encouraged me to take up the editorship of this collection. Jenny Yap and Fanny Yap have shown us much generosity; not only did they give us permission to reproduce images of Arthur Yap's rarely seen paintings, they also spoke at length with some of our contributors regarding their brother's life and family background. We are extremely grateful to both of them for their time and invaluable assistance. Ho Chee Lick also kindly granted his permission to reproduce some of Yap's paintings currently in his possession, as did Peter Schoppert and William P. Mundy with their own respective images. We would also like to thank Shamsuddin Akib, Irving Goh, Patricia Wong, Angelia Poon, Kevin Tan, James Tan, and Tang Chee Onn, for their help, advice, and support in various ways during the research and writing of the essays collected in this volume. Triena Ong and Stephen Logan at the Institute of Southeast Asian Studies have been most helpful and patient editors, guiding us through the twists and turns of the entire process.

My thanks also goes out to my colleagues at Eastern Illinois University and the University of California Riverside, particularly Miho Nonaka, Charles Wharram, Suzie Park, and Traise Yamamoto, for their encouragement and support during some particularly strenuous times.

Finally, I would like to dedicate this book to the memory of Arthur Yap. Unlike some of the contributors, I did not have the opportunity to meet him either personally or professionally, but I have learned — and continue to learn — so much from his writing and from the meeting of scholarly and creative minds in the process of putting this collection together.

ABOUT THE CONTRIBUTORS

Boey Kim Cheng is Senior Lecturer in the School of Humanities and Social Science at the University of Newcastle in Australia. He is the author of several poetry collections including *After the Fire, Days of No Name, Another Place*, and *Somewhere Bound*. His poetry and critical essays have also appeared in numerous anthologies and journals.

Gui Weihsin is Assistant Professor of English at the University of California, Riverside. He is the author of *National Consciousness and Literary Cosmopolitics: Postcolonial Literature in a Global Moment*. He has also published essays in *Journal of Postcolonial Writing, Journal of Commonwealth Literature*, and *LIT: Literature Interpretation Theory*.

Joel Gwynne is Assistant Professor of English at the National Institute of Education, Nanyang Technological University in Singapore. He has published articles on modernism and contemporary postcolonial literature, and is the author of *The Secular Visionaries: Aestheticism and New Zealand Short Fiction in the Twentieth Century* (2010). He is currently writing a book on sexuality, popular culture and postmillennial women's writing under contract with Cambria Press.

Eddie Tay is Associate Professor of English at the Chinese University of Hong Kong, where he teaches Children's Literature, Reading Poetry and Creative Writing (Poetry). He is the author of three collections of poetry, *Remnants, A Lover's Soliloquy* and *The Mental Life of Cities* (winner of the 2012 Singapore Literature Prize). His research monograph is entitled *Colony, Nation and Globalisation: Not At Home with Singaporean and Malaysian Literature*.

Angus Whitehead is Assistant Professor of English at the National Institute of Education, Nanyang Technological University in Singapore. He has published numerous articles and notes on William Blake, Catherine Blake, Frederick Tatham, Frances Burney, Ignatius Sancho, Mary Seacole, Charlotte Smith and William Cowper. He is currently writing a micro-biography of William and Catherine Blake, 1803–31, based upon unpublished archival research. He is also exploring ways in which the resources of the "William Blake Archive" might be utilized in literature in English lessons in Singaporean secondary schools.

Cyril Wong graduated with a doctoral degree in English Literature from the National University of Singapore. He is author of twelve poetry collections, one novel and a volume of short stories. He is a recipient of the National Arts Council's Young Artist Award for Literature (2005) and the Singapore Literature Prize (2006).

Zhou Xiaojing is Professor of English at the University of the Pacific in California. She is the author of numerous articles on Asian American poetry and two monographs, *The Ethnics and Poetics of Alterity in Asian American Poetry*; *Elizabeth Bishop: Rebel "in Shades and Shadows"*; as well as a contributing co-editor of *Form and Transformation in Asian American Literature*. Her recent monograph *Inhabiting Otherwise: Urban Space in Asian American Literature* is forthcoming from University of Washington Press.

1

COMMON LINES AND CITY SPACES
Introduction

Gui Weihsin

Chances are if you are reading this book, you have already been introduced to Arthur Yap and his work through one of the numerous anthologies of Singaporean poetry and writing, or by way of several critical sourcebooks on Southeast Asian or Singaporean literature in English. Yap's consistent presence in these anthologies and collections suggests that he is an important and influential figure in both national as well as regional English-language literary landscapes, and it is regrettable that, unlike some of his contemporaries, no one volume was dedicated to his multifaceted creative output during his lifetime. The present collection of essays addresses this critical lack by gathering new and innovative work on Yap's prose, poetry, and painting written by an international group of scholars and critics. This introduction briefly summarizes the critical reception of his work and then discusses it in terms of three discursive modes of analysis, or literary and textual methods of examining our lived experience and living environment, both in specific terms of Singapore's history, society, and culture and in more general terms of modern life's concerns and predicaments. Some of our contributors examine, with renewed emphasis, important topics in Arthur Yap's writing that have been the subject of earlier critical essays, such as his erudite wordplay and laconic voice, his apparently reserved and ambivalent attitude towards social and national issues, and his thoughtful treatment of urban space and the cityscape of modern Singapore. In addition, this collection also includes essays that shed new light on Yap's literary transformation of mundane objects into multifaceted things; the connection between his verse and the natural environment as a nascent form of ecopoetry; the powerful stillness and silence in his paintings that resonate with his laconic poetic persona; the desire and affection expressed in his mapping of the queer spaces of the city and in the sheer sensuousness of his travel poems; and the social and cultural commentary of his short stories, which have never before been critically examined. It is hoped that the essays included here will pave new ground for future scholarship on Yap's work in different genres and media, such as his paintings and their exhibition at international venues, his rare but dazzling pieces of short fiction, as well as his own linguistic and literary criticism.

Born in Singapore, Arthur Yap Chior Hiong (1943–2006) attended Saint Andrew's School, and then received an honours degree in English Literature from Singapore University. After that, he obtained a master's degree in linguistics from Leeds University and then a doctorate from the National University of Singapore, where he was a member of the English department faculty from 1979 to 1998. Although he began writing poetry when he was in secondary school, his first published collection was *Only Lines* (1971), followed by *Commonplace* (1976), *Down the Line* (1982), *Man, Snake, Apple and Other Poems* (1988), and a volume of selected poems, *The Space of City Trees* (2000). Among his numerous awards are the National Book Development Council of Singapore's poetry prize (1976, 1982, 1988), the Cultural Medallion for Literature, Singapore's highest award for artistic and literary achievement (1983), the Southeast Asia Write Award (1983), and the Montblanc-NUS Centre for the Arts Literary Award for English (1998). Some of his poems, notably "old house at ang siang hill", have become set texts for the GCE O-level English Literature examination in Singapore. Furthermore, as a painter Yap held seven exhibitions both in Singapore and internationally.

Certainly, Yap's oeuvre requires not only a thorough reading but also constant re-reading and re-evaluation, in part because of his characteristic laconic tone and linguistic playfulness that always imply more than they indicate, suggesting a range of ideas rather than staking a definitive standpoint. A glance at both earlier and more recent analyses of his writing provides a snapshot of the range of responses to his canted and studied voice: he "uses words precisely in order to evoke imprecision", and "annotates glancingly, insinuates fugitively, and he evades closure in order to enable oblique disclosure (Patke 2003, pp. 174–75); his "syntactic complexity and ironic expression" culminate in "highly individualized zaniness, vivid local observations, and indeterminate yet resonant and provocative local timbre" (Poon 2009, pp. 175–76); with expert "knowledge of textual cohesion and generative grammars gleaned from his linguistic studies" he performs a "brilliant managing of some cohesive and other linguistic devices" that results in "amazingly original poetry" (Yeo 1999, p. 138). But, in spite of this penchant for indirectness and the expression of "fugitive emotional conditions in a context of keen awareness of transience", Yap also shows us "the interaction between individual critical perspective and social convention" that "results in satire", "cultural subversion", and a "critique of Singapore social ideology" (Lim 1993, p. 156); furthermore, his idiosyncratic blending of public voices and private thoughts express "a kind of grass-roots nationalism, an informal bonding which takes place at the local level" and "the sense of resignation, acceptance and endurance" one must have in order to face the rapid changes of modern, urban life (Brewster 1995, pp. 109–10). But perhaps the most intriguing description of Yap's poetry comes from a scholar who compares one of his poems to "a Singapore lunchtime specialty, Hokkien Mee, in which a distinctive taste is obtained from slightly fermented prawns" (Gordon 1984, p. 55). Although Gordon does not elaborate on the similarity between Yap's writing and an aromatic plate of stir-fried noodles, his comparison points to something earlier critics may have neglected or passed over — Yap's writing is not only subtly nuanced and urbanely intelligent, it is also vividly sensuous, animating people, things, and places with a language of sound and sense (with the second term implying both *meaning* and *sensation*). The essays in this collection extend the insights of earlier critics mentioned above to discuss Yap's social satire and ambivalent attitude towards history and progress; some of our contributors also focus on the visually and physically sensuous aspects of Yap's work and how he represents the environment and those within it as living things and desiring beings rather than simply a set of facts and figures occupying a designated space. (A longer bibliography of criticism regarding Arthur Yap's work can be found at the end of this introduction.)

Broadly speaking, the essays in this collection approach Yap's writing and painting through literary and analytical methods drawn from postcolonial criticism, urban studies, and ecocriticism. In brief, the first critical framework examines the processes and effects of European conquest and colonization of many regions and peoples around the world during the eighteenth and nineteenth centuries, as well as the various efforts of colonized peoples since the early and mid-twentieth century to break away from their colonial masters and establish their own independent cultures, societies, and nation-states. What is also important to postcolonial critics besides the tension between European colonizers and colonized peoples are the ways in which writers in the independent societies creatively use the culture, language, and literature of the colonizers in powerful, innovative, and unique ways, drawing on but going far beyond the boundaries of (in Arthur Yap's case) Standard English and the British cultural and literary imagination. While some critics may be unenthusiastic about connecting postcolonial criticism to Malaysian and Singaporean literature, given that Yap's poems of social satire have often been contrasted with those of other writers who espouse national responsibility and identity (such as Edwin Thumboo), we think it is illuminating to consider how his work contributes to a specifically Singaporean form of postcolonial critique, especially with regards to national narratives of progress and cultural development. Edward Said, whose scholarship informs much of the work done in postcolonial criticism, argues that literature's relationship to nationalism should not dwell on "remaining trapped in the emotional self-indulgence of celebrating one's identity" or nativism (1994, p. 229). Instead of insisting upon a homogeneous national identity based on a unified culture, we need to remember that in postcolonial situations "we are dealing with the formation of cultural identities understood not as essentializations ... but as contrapuntal ensembles, for it is the case that no identity can ever exist by itself and without an array of opposites, negatives, oppositions" (p. 52). But this does not mean that nationalism and the idea of the nation should be condemned or dismissed as simply oppressive and already obsolete, because "moving beyond nativism does not mean abandoning nationality"; instead, we need to think of the nation as taking shape along a *spectrum* of terms such as "nationality, nationalism, nativism" (p. 229). The first two terms connote political consciousness, social struggle, and cultural assertion, while the third term expresses a belief in and insistence on a pure and authentic cultural identity free of the influence of European colonizers or even other neighbouring peoples. Yap's socially satirical writing can be thought of as nationalist in line with the first and second terms on the spectrum (*nationality* and *nationalism* rather than *nativism*).

He offers a counterpoint to the efforts of both the Singaporean state and other writers to create an essential and affirmative cultural and national identity; he reminds us that our society is composed of a relative or relational ensemble or array of *identities* rather than one core *identity* that can be divided or carved up into essential components. In other words, Yap offers a distinctly artistic and literary perspective on how we imagine the relationships between society and the state and between a nation and its culture in ways other than those written down in official histories of progress and development. As the historian and postcolonial critic Dipesh Chakrabarty observes in his study of Nobel Laureate Rabindranath Tagore, poetry shifts our perception out of the realm of "the historical and the objective" as it can "create a caesura [a break or pause] in historical time and transport us to a realm that transcended the historical" (2000, p. 166). This does not mean that poetry merely offers an escapist daydream, because transcending the historical for Chakrabarty means engaging with one's intellect and imagination through a poetic "moment of epiphany" that can "execute the dissolving shot" on objects, spaces, and identities we take for granted in our everyday lives, composing them afresh and challenging us to see them anew (p. 170). Drawing on the idea of "thing theory", in his opening chapter Gui Weihsin shows us the power of this dissolving shot as it traces Yap's literary transformation of utilitarian objects into multifaceted things and of bureaucratic language into critical commentary, all in the space of a few poetic lines. Similarly, Boey Kim Cheng's groundbreaking examination of Yap's paintings, which he exhibited internationally and reproduced in some of his poetry collections, reveals how Yap's visual creations engage in a formal dialogue with his poems, bringing out an aesthetic of stillness and silence as an abstract counterpoint to the grand and heroic symbols of Singaporean nation building. Boey explores in detail Yap's adaptation of modernist styles of both painting and poetry, in which objects, figures, and landscapes are often placed in paratactical relationships, breaking with any sense of established hierarchy or causality, thereby inviting the reader or viewer to look upon them levelly without a prevailing sense of superiority or subordination.

Postcolonial literary criticism is also closely connected to the two other critical frameworks mentioned earlier: urban studies and ecocriticism. As Said reminds us, "[t]he main battle in imperialism is over land, of course; but when it came to who owned the land, who had the right to settle and work on it, who kept it going, who won it back, and who now plans its future — these issues were reflected, contested, and even for a time decided in narrative" (pp. xii–xiii). In the Singaporean context, questions of land, space, architecture and their relationship to the way people narrate or tell the story of Singapore's culture and history are taken up by Ryan Bishop, John Philips, and Yeo Wei Wei (2004) when they discuss the Marina Bay waterfront as an example of how Singapore's "history involves extended, strategic engagement with the twin enterprises of postcolonialism and globalization, as well as with colonialism" that "is readable in the city-state's architecture and physical environment" (p. 2). The government's decision to renovate rather than demolish British colonial-era buildings in the Marina Bay area "preserves the colonial shell of the building while reworking the buildings from the foundation to better suit contemporary use", thereby showing "a continuation, perpetuation, and multiplication of colonial richness into the present global order" (p. 2). Therefore, Singapore's colonial past remains a kind of spectral presence even in the present time of the independent nation-state, a ghost that haunts the shining new spaces and built-up environments around the island. In his poetry and prose, Arthur Yap reminds us of this spectral presence in a society that is constantly focused on turning the past into a usable present and a profitable future, and in his representations of the physical environment he also makes a distinction between two ways of thinking about the past. First, there is *history*, a narrative or story that is framed as a linear series of developing conflicts and events, thus mapping out a clear course into the future. Then there is *historicity*, which "is not a monumental process" but rather "the indeterminacy that allows any kind of historical determination to come about", and in this indeterminacy or uncertainty there lies "the possibility of" thinking about the past-present-future relationship in different, as-yet-unimagined terms (Bishop, Philips and Yeo 2004, p. 10). In other words, historicity suggests a lived experience of the present in which what makes up our collective past is constantly mixing up with and intruding into the frame of the present, thus opening up different possibilities regarding the future that have not yet been shaped by history.

Our cultural and historical relationship with the environment is also the subject of the third critical field of inquiry, ecocriticism, which is closely related to urban studies. The term ecocriticism is often associated with the conservation and preservation of the natural world, and certainly this sense is important to scholars working in this area. However, along with this eco-friendly concern, ecocriticism also pays attention to how natural and artificial environments actively shape our ways of thinking culturally, historically, and socially. As one critic observes, the root word for environment, *environ*, is a verb (rarely used today) that means to surround or envelop, but "this active sense has been lost" such that "we no longer speak of what *environs* us" (Mazel 1996, pp. 138–39, italics in the original). An ecocritical attitude towards literature means that "we need to focus on the speaker who is environed" so that we can "inquire into not only *what* environs us, but *how* it came to do so, by means of what *agency*" (p. 139, italics in the original). Looking ecocritically at a literary text also requires us to consider its formal and aesthetic aspects, because "the aesthetic experience", as Neil Evernden argues, "lies in the relationship between the individual and the environment, not simply in the object viewed, nor in the mind of the viewer. Rather than a subject-object relationship in which the observer parades before the supposedly beautiful view, we have instead a process, an interaction between the viewer and the viewed, and it is in that joint association that the aesthetic experience lies" (p. 97). Just as historicity offers us a sense of the past as a spectral presence that shapes Singapore's present and informs its future, an ecocritical and environmental approach to Yap's writing shows us that "[i]nstead of a detachment from the environment, we have a subtle diffusion into it", and that "we must deal instead with the individual-in-environment" (Evernden 1996, p. 97). Three chapters in this collection focus on the relationship between historicity, environment, and Singapore's cultural and social identities. Angus Whitehead combines detailed historical research into various aspects of Singapore's urban development with a discussion of identifiable local spaces and neighbourhoods in Yap's poetry to show how Yap uses encounters with such spaces to illuminate important moments in Singapore's past in an active and democratizing way. Eddie Tay gives us a glimpse of the capacity of Yap's poems to environ their readers by offering a personal account of his own encounter with Yap's verse together with his experience teaching Yap's poems in another postcolonial urban setting (Hong Kong). Tay concludes by engaging with the work of sociologist and urban studies critic Henri Lefebvre to examine Yap's representations of alienation from and attachment to Singapore's spatial practices and urban milieu. Zhou Xiaojing makes a case for understanding Yap's poems about nature and the environment as a form of "ecopoetry", a genre of environmentally concerned writing that up till now has included mainly British and American writers. Zhou argues that Yap's ecopoetics challenges the anthropocentrism or human-centredness of European philosophy that has found its way into our modern view of the natural world as a resource for human expansion and development.

Instead of clearly demarcating and opposing nature to culture, Zhou points out that Yap intertwines and interpenetrates nature and culture with each other, showing us an ecological view of the world in which human culture and the natural environment are mutually constitutive and transformative.

Furthermore, Cyril Wong's chapter on Yap's sexual identity, his love and affection for his partner Keith Watson, and his representation of queer spaces in the city that are expressed in several of his poems reminds us that Singapore is not only an urban space we live in, but also an environment alive with and surrounding us with desire and love, dejection and loathing, among other emotions and impulses. The difficulties of identifying oneself as gay or lesbian in Singapore cannot be underestimated; despite Singapore being "probably the 'cruisiest' city in Asia in terms of the sexually motivated and flirtatious eye contact between men", there are extreme legal as well as severe social and familial prohibitions against declaring and maintaining an openly queer lifestyle (Peterson 2003, pp. 78–79). Against these strictures, Yap's poetry illuminates how we are environed by a city that speaks through its physical spaces in a language of sense and sensation, as the cultural critic Roland Barthes (1997) observes: "[t]he city is a discourse and this discourse is truly a language: the city speaks to its inhabitants, we speak our city, the city where we are, simply by living in it, by wandering through it, by looking at it" (p. 168). Wong interweaves personal memories of Arthur Yap as a literary mentor with a concise reading of his poems to illustrate how Yap's characteristic reticence can express "the eroticism of the city", which, in addition to sexual or romantic desire, also carries a wider sense ,"*sociality*", because "[t]he city, essentially and semantically, is the place for our meeting with the *other*, and it is for this reason that the centre is the gathering place in every city" (Barthes 1997, p. 171, italics in the original). The publication of collections such as *People Like Us: Sexual Minorities in Singapore* and *SQ21: Singapore Queers in the 21st Century*, along with annual queer pride events like *IndigNation*, are signs that the queer community is making significant efforts towards creating a sociality — understood as the creation or discovery of social connections that have not yet been imagined by society at large — distinct from but on an equal footing with the dominant conventions of Singaporean society. Contrary to the objection some may raise that a critical consideration of homosexuality and erotic desire goes against the spirit of Arthur Yap's poetry and seems to be driven by an identity politics (since Yap himself never referred to his gay identity), it is precisely in the lines of his poems where we see unmistakable moments of tender affection addressed to a loving partner and a ludic delight in the sheer sensuousness of places and things, all of which Wong highlights through a nuanced and thoughtful close reading of Yap's verse and a deft discussion of queer literary theory. Such a detailed study can hardly be construed as a form of opportunistic identity politics; rather, it is an opportunity to move beyond identifying Yap's poetry as an urbanely ambivalent intellectualism and see instead the intimate play of sexuality and sociality in the work of a pioneering Singaporean poet.

It is also in an effort to develop an increasing awareness and understanding of Yap's other genres of writing that Angus Whitehead and Joel Gwynne attempt the first extended study of his seven works of short fiction, published in various collections and journals over a twenty-year period from 1962 to 1982. It should come as no surprise that Yap found the short story a fitting medium for his creative temperament, because, as the novelist and short story writer Elizabeth Bowen reminds us in her introduction to the 1950 *Faber Book of Modern Short Stories*, "[t]he story should have the valid central emotion and inner spontaneity of the lyric; it should magnetize the imagination and give pleasure — of however disturbing, painful or complex a kind. The story must be composed, in the plastic sense, and as visual as a picture" (1994, p. 260). Besides its similarity to poetry and painting, two other media Yap excelled and delighted in, Bowen also suggests that "[t]he extraverted short story — bare of analysis, sparse in emotional statement — is the formula for, never the transcript of, that amazement which poetry deals. The particular must be given general significance" (pp. 258–59). The choice qualities of the short story Bowen enumerates might well be a description of Yap's spare and enigmatic verse that teases out truths and insights from specific observations of objects, people, places, and the nuances of language itself. The connections between Yap's prose, poetry, and painting have yet to be thoroughly explored, and it is our hope that Whitehead and Gwynne's study, along with Boey's discussion of his painting, will generate further interest and scholarship in these areas of Yap's work.

A conclusion to this introduction would go against the grain of the spirit of this collection, which is to inspire conversations, readings, and interpretations regarding Arthur Yap's life and legacy rather than stamping the proverbial last word on the topics covered in these pages. Therefore, in lieu of a conclusion, the editor and contributors to this collection wish to reiterate the aims of this particular book. First, we hope our combination of postcolonial, urban studies, and ecocritical perspectives extends and opens the door for further investigations not only of Yap's own work but also Singaporean literature as a whole through these interwoven critical frameworks. Given that Singapore is both a nation-state and an island-city that is a historical result of British colonialism, its physical environment and social milieu deserve scrutiny in any analysis of the country's political and literary culture. Second, contrary to received wisdom that Yap was an intensely private poet who shied away from topics of political and national significance unlike, say, Edwin Thumboo or Robert Yeo, our discussions of his work show that he was deeply connected to the social and cultural milieu of modern Singapore and that his laconic and ambivalent voice stems more from a difference in artistic temperament rather than a dearth of political commitment. Arthur Yap was a poet and painter of the first rank, and a serious consideration of his elliptical style might illuminate similar moments in the work of other more "public" poets in which instances of personal and intimate reflection turn out to be as pertinent to Singaporean society and politics as the most overt commentary. As the quotations by earlier critics of his work reveal, Yap's writerly voice often hints towards thoughts of public significance while remaining meditatively private, revealing an introspective mind that asks his readers to follow along but also to look between the lines of his verse. This, perhaps, is Arthur Yap's legacy: a sociality motivated by a thought-provoking tension between his voices — between the private, the public, and the playful, between the lyric, the laconic, and the loquacious — that makes his work both confounding and compelling but always worth reading and rethinking, and that invites us to re-read and rethink his work alongside those of his contemporaries and successors within the larger body of Singaporean literature he helped create. Therefore, we consider it fitting to close, but not conclude, this introduction with two passages that express this sociality, taken from his first and final collections, *Only Lines* (1971) and *Man Snake Apple* (1986), respectively:

> and if you can laugh
> care with some concern
> it is because (like me)
> you need lines
> to add up this same old story
>
> (*Only Lines*, p. 3)

i even understand my own knowledge
of this privacy which is public literary study.

the words will move on more swiftly
than tomorrow will be now. & i will
know, in reading again,
i do not know him
or any other, or myself, or that any poetry
is the public transaction that it must be.
& it must be private ultimately.
(Man Snake Apple, p. 118)

References

Barthes, Roland. "Semiology and the Urban". In *Rethinking Architecture: A Reader in Cultural Theory*, edited by Neil Leach. London: Routledge, 1997.

Bishop, Ryan, John Philips, and Wei-Wei Yeo, eds. *Beyond Description: Singapore Space Historicity*. London: Routledge, 2004.

Bowen, Elizabeth. "The Faber Book of Modern Short Stories". In *The New Short Story Theories*, edited by Charles E. May. Athens, OH: Ohio University Press, 1994.

Brewster, Anne. *Literary Formations: Post-colonialism, Nationalism, Globalism*. Carlton South, Australia: Melbourne University Press, 1995.

Chakrabarty, Dipesh. *Provincializing Europe: Postcolonial Thought and Historical Difference*. Princeton, NJ: Princeton University Press, 2000.

Evernden, Neil. "Beyond Ecology: Self, Place, and the Pathetic Fallacy". In *The Ecocriticism Reader*, edited by Cheryll Glotfelty and Harold Fromm. Athens, GA: University of Georgia Press, 1996.

Gordon, Jan B. "The 'Second Tongue' Myth: English Poetry in Polylingual Singapore". *Ariel* 15, no. 4 (1984): 41–65.

Lim, Shirley Geok-lin. *Nationalism and Literature: English-language Writing from the Philippines and Singapore*. Quezon City, Philippines: New Day, 1993.

Mazel, David. "American Literary Environmentalism as Domestic Orientalism". *The Ecocriticism Reader*, edited by Cheryll Glotfelty and Harold Fromm. Athens, GA: University of Georgia Press, 1996.

Patke, Rajeev S. "Ambivalence and Ambiguity in the Poetry of Arthur Yap". *Complicities: Connections and Divisions, Perspectives on Literatures and Cultures of the Asia-Pacific Region*, edited by Chitra Sankaran, Liew-Geok Leong, and Rajeev Patke. Bern: Lang, 2003.

Peterson, William. "The Queer Stage in Singapore". *People Like Us: Sexual Minorities in Singapore*, edited by Joseph Lo and Huang Guoqin. Singapore: Select, 2003.

Poon, Angelia. "Introduction. Section 2: 1965–1990". In *Writing Singapore: An*

Historical Anthology of Singapore Literature, edited by Angelia Poon, Philip Holden, and Shirley Geok-lin Lim. Singapore: NUS Press, 2009.
Said, Edward. *Culture and Imperialism*. New York: Vintage, 1994.
Yap, Arthur. *The Space of City Trees: Selected Poems*. London: Skoob Books, 2000.
Yeo, Robert. "Parts of Speech: A Speculative Note on Arthur Yap's 'Commonplace' ". In *Interlogue: Studies in Singapore Literature. Volume 2: Poetry*, edited by Kirpal Singh. Singapore: Ethos Books, 1999.

Works by Arthur Yap
Poetry
Only Lines. Singapore: Federal, 1971.
Commonplace. Singapore: Heinemann, 1977.
Down the Line. Singapore: Heinemann, 1980.
Man Snake Apple & Other Poems. Singapore: Heinemann, 1986.
The Space of City Trees: Selected Poems. London: Skoob Books, 2000.

Short Stories
"A 5-Year Plan". *Focus* (1962): 19–23.
"Noon at Five O'Clock". *Focus* (1962): 31–33.
"A Silly Little Story". *Focus* (1964): 15–16.
"The Effect of a Good Dinner". In *Singapore Short Stories*, edited by Robert Yeo. Singapore: Heinemann Asia, 1978.
"None the Wiser". In *Singapore Short Stories*, edited by Robert Yeo. Singapore: Heinemann Asia, 1978.
"The Story of a Mask". In *Singapore Short Stories*, edited by Robert Yeo. Singapore: Heinemann Asia, 1978.
"A Beginning and a Middle Without an Ending". In *S.E. Asia Writes Back! Contemporary Writings of the Pacific Rim; Skoob Pacifica Anthology, No. 1*. London: Skoob Books, 1993. Originally appearing in *Tenggara* 14 (1982): 17–20.

Criticism
A Brief Critical Survey of Prose Writings in Singapore and Malaysia. Singapore: Educational Publications Bureau, 1972.
Thematic Structure in Poetic Discourse. Singapore: Copinter, 1987.

Essays, Interviews, and Criticism about Arthur Yap's Work
Bennett, Bruce. "Yap, Arthur". In *Encyclopedia of Post-colonial Literatures in English*, edited by Eugene Benson and L.W. Connolly. London: Routledge, 1994.
Boey, Kim Cheng. "From the Tentative to the Conditional: Detachment and Liminality in the Poetry of Arthur Yap". In *Sharing Borders: Studies in*

Contemporary Singaporean-Malaysian Literature II, edited by Gwee Li Sui. Singapore: National Library Board, 2009.
Brewster, Anne. "Arthur Yap — Dramatis Personae". In *Critical Engagements: Singapore Poems in Focus*, edited by Kirpal Singh. Singapore: Heinemann Asia, 1986.
———. "Formations of Nationalism: Arthur Yap and Philip Jeyaretnam". *Literary Formations: Post-colonialism, Nationalism, Globalism*. Carlton South, Victoria: Melbourne University Press, 1995.
———. "An Interview with Arthur Yap". *Asiatic* 2, no. 1 (June 2008): 97–108.
———. "Introduction". In *The Space of City Trees: Selected Poems*, by Arthur Yap. London: Skoob Books, 2000.
———. Review of Arthur Yap's *Man Snake Apple & Other Poems*, and Kirpal Singh's *Palm Readings*. *SPAN* 24 (1987): 104–6.
Heng, Geraldine. Review of *Down the Line* by Arthur Yap. *Commentary* 4, no. 2 (1980): 105–9.
Lim, Shirley. "Arthur Yap — 2 mothers in a HDB playground". In *Critical Engagements: Singapore Poems in Focus*, edited by Kirpal Singh. Singapore: Heinemann Asia, 1986.
———. "Sub/versions of a National Poetry: Arthur Yap". In *Nationalism and Literature: English Language Writing from the Philippines and Singapore*. Quezon City: New Day, 1993.
Patke, Rajeev S. "Ambivalence and Ambiguity in the Poetry of Arthur Yap". In *Complicities: Connections and Divisions, Perspectives on Literatures and Cultures of the Asia-Pacific Region*, edited by Chitra Sankaran, Liew-Geok Leong, and Rajeev Patke. Bern: Lang, 2003.
———. "Modernist Poetic Practices in the English Poetry from Southeast Asia: A Comparison between Jose Garcia Villa and Arthur Yap". *Kritika Kultura* 9 (2007): 11–26.
Singh, Kirpal. Review of *Commonplace*. *Westerly* 23, no. 2 (1978): 94–95.
Sullivan, Kevin. "Achievement: The Poet With An Artist's Touch — Arthur Yap Talks with Kevin Sullivan". *Southeast Asian Review of English* 8 (1984): 3–20.
Thow, Xin Wei. "Arthur Yap: Uniquely Singaporean". *Quarterly Literary Review Singapore* 5, no. 4 (2006) <http://www.qlrs.com/essay.asp?id=543> (accessed 14 June 2011).
Wong, Cyril. "Uncertainty and Scepticism in Arthur Yap". *Quarterly Literary Review Singapore* 1, no. 4 (2002) <http://www.qlrs.com/essay.asp?id=212> (accessed 14 June 2011).
Yeo, Robert. "Parts of Speech: A Speculative Note on Arthur Yap's 'Commonplace'". *Interlogue: Studies in Singapore Literature. Volume 2: Poetry*, edited by Kirpal Singh. Singapore: Ethos Books, 1999.

2

THE TRANSFORMATION OF OBJECTS INTO THINGS IN ARTHUR YAP'S POETRY

Gui Weihsin

Like William Butler Yeats and Gertrude Stein, Arthur Yap, whose work is also regarded as modernist in theme and style, expressed a fascination with things. For W.B. Yeats, in his famous poem "The Second Coming", it seems as if all things — social norms, cultural values, political aspirations — associated with European civilization had fallen apart and were ruined in the wake of World War I, as seen in the apocalpytic tenor of the oft-quoted line "Things fall apart; the centre cannot hold" (1956, p. 184). Gertrude Stein, on the other hand, offers a more optimistic outlook on things, claiming that "[c]ontinuous present is one thing and beginning again and again is another thing. These are both things. And then there is using everything" (2004, p. 25); Stein's compositional craft takes up everything around oneself as suitable material for the poetic imagination. And then there is Arthur Yap, whose treatment of things expresses a sympathetic yet critical sensibility, observing how "some things remain / some things pass, / some things are tired" (*The Space of City Trees*, 2004, hereafter *Space*, p. 4), and pointing to how we are often caught up in "a habit by which the world moves" such that "people will not look at the centre of things" (p. 78). In his poetry Yap personifies things, calmly observing how they come, go, or grow weary; at the same time, he calls things out to us, drawing our attention to our habitual distraction and unwillingness to look closely at them. And perhaps, Yap suggests, this unwillingness or inability to pay close attention stems from the way in which Singaporeans have grown used to treating what they have around them as objects rather than as things.

This chapter argues that Arthur Yap's poems take a "thing-like" approach towards the landscape, people, and bits and pieces of everyday life that make up Singaporean society after the country's independence in 1965. By a thing-like approach, I mean that Yap's poetry actively transforms what we would normally think of as common and functional *objects* with a set or defined utility into strange and multifaceted *things*. The representation of things in contemporary literature and culture is a subject on which literary and cultural critic Bill Brown has written at length. After a brief discussion of Brown's thinking and how it can serve as a framework for understanding Yap's poetry, I consider the social and cultural role of the English language and English-language writers in modern Singapore. Subsequently, I look at the general reception of Arthur Yap's work by literary critics who emphasize his trademark brevity and ambivalence as well as his roots in Anglo-American modernist poetry. While I agree with some of these critics' insights, I stress the ways in which Yap's poetic vision turns the English language itself from an objective medium of communication into an opaque thing that, in disrupting the smooth flow of our comprehension, enables a critical imagination to take shape.

Although some may feel that discussing Yap's poetry in relation to thing theory is inappropriate and problematic, more an academic trend rather than a thoughtful analysis, I contend that Yap's own writing advances a critical theory of objects and things through the transformative and interrogative power of poetic language. In other words, I am not trying to shove a square peg into a round hole by reading Yap's verse through thing theory, because Yap himself offers his own version of thing theory, as we see in the opening poem of his first collection, *Only Lines*:

> should i also add:
> here are only lines linked by the same old story.
> the same basic plot in which they are grown
> ...

> and if you can laugh
> care with some concern
> it is because (like me)
> you need lines to add up this same old story
>
> *(Space,* p. 3)

Yap feels, that as a poet, he has "only lines" of language that come to us already defined by "the same old story" and "the same basic plot" of conventional and everyday use. Language is an object we use to communicate efficiently, and we can do this because we assume that words have the "same" and consistent meaning across different contexts. But Yap wants to move beyond this sameness of language and its efficient use; he wants to make us "laugh" and "care with some concern", to look in wonder and with worry at the world around us, and to do so we "need" to learn to see, like Yap himself has, how seemingly innocuous ("only") lines "add up to this same old story". To put it another way, Yap sees poetry itself as a thing rather than an object, and it is a thing that can interrogate and investigate the apparently same old stories we tell about ourselves, our community, our society by illuminating the various, multifaceted lines or elements that go into their making. I suggest that Yap's poetic transformation of objects into things produces two related effects: first, it makes us aware of some value assumptions lurking beneath what appear to be neutral or value-free actions and objects (what we would think of as purely "objective" facts or concepts); second, this awareness also helps us observe some cultural, social, and political relationships that would otherwise have gone unremarked because we have become so familiar with using objects for their designated purposes such that we no longer recognize the effects they have on others as well as ourselves. In brief, Arthur Yap's thing-like approach is an aesthetic perspective that offers social commentary; it urges us to think about how the common places and everyday situations of modern Singapore are subjected to increasing objectification and commodification.

"THING THEORY"

Objectification can be thought of as one part of a larger, rational process of clarification and utilization. To look objectively or with objectivity at the things, people, and places around us is to size them up in all their differences and diversity, then pare them down into manageable form. It is to clear away the ambiguities and doubts surrounding things, leaving behind just a few or (better yet) only one meaning or function that we can safely set aside for reference or take up for general use. Such an objective process of denotation — narrowing things down so that they fit within a larger and logical scheme of facts and information — is both necessary for our modern lives as well as necessarily reductive, a necessity that Yap alludes to when he says that objectification is "a habit with which the world moves" (*Space*, p. 78). Furthermore, this reduction is not always a process that uncovers the essential truth about people or things, for it requires an act of interpretation as much as any other process of definition. Bill Brown, a literary critic who works on poetry and material culture, makes an important distinction between objects and things, arguing that "[w]e look through objects because there are codes by which our interpretive attention makes them meaningful, because there is a discourse of objectivity that allows us to use them as facts" (2004, p. 4). An object is like a window, Brown argues, that lets us look out at the world, but we do not have a free-ranging field of vision because there is always a window frame that limits what we can see. This object-window frame is the set of beliefs and ideas — what Brown calls a discourse of objectivity — that our society erects around us, and this frame both focuses and restricts the ways in which we relate to our world. Objects appear to be transparent, their functions and meanings already well-defined, so that we can use them as tools in our everyday life, but these functions and meanings are neither necessarily hard-and-fast facts nor the absolute truth about the sundry bits and pieces that make up our lives.

It is when objects break down into bits and pieces, Brown goes on to suggest, that their thingness rears its head: "We begin to confront the thingness of objects when they stop working for us: when the drill breaks, when the car stalls, when the windows get filthy, when their flow within the circuits of production and distribution, consumption and exhibition, has been arrested, however momentarily" (2004, p. 4). In other words, when objects' ease-of-use is rudely interrupted, when they cannot fulfill their assigned functions, we become aware of them as things, as tangible parts of our lives that we need to look at more closely because they no longer fit neatly into their assigned roles or "do their jobs". This awareness of things applies not only to tools and appliances, buildings and structures, but to human relationships as well, as Bill Brown concludes: "The story of objects asserting themselves as things, then, is the story of a changed relation to the human subject and thus the story of how the thing really names less an object than a particular subject-object relation" (p. 4). An *object* (whether it is an inanimate substance or a living person) with a defined function is meant to be wielded or commanded by a *subject*, a user or a superior being — this is what Brown means by the "subject-object relation". But a *thing* complicates such direct use or command, either because it can no longer function in its designated capacity, or because it is much more than or exceeds the limits of its defined role. Therefore, the "thingifying" of objects first of all makes us aware of the value assumptions that go into objective definitions of things in our lives, definitions that allow us to use objects without thinking twice about their thingness; second, it raises the question of what other social relationships might be possible or have gone unnoticed, relationships we might not have glimpsed because we have been looking through object-windows framed by our society's discourse of objectivity.

THE ENGLISH LANGUAGE AND MULTIRACIALISM IN SINGAPORE

Discourse, in everyday use, usually means speech, narration, or the language and manner in which one carries on a conversation. At the philosophical and literary level, these meanings are still relevant, but, more importantly, discourse also refers to a set of concepts and beliefs that govern the way in which we receive, process, and disseminate knowledge about the world around us. This idea of discourse is developed at length by the philosopher Michel Foucault (1972). In the context of post-independence Singapore, these two meanings of discourse coincide in the government's national language policy that distinguishes between English as a common administrative language and Malay, Mandarin, and Tamil as "mother tongues" for the various ethnic groups — respectively, the Malays, Chinese, and Indians — in Singapore. As sociologist Nirmala Puroshotam observes in her study of race and language in Singapore, the symbolic associations of these languages are clear and distinct: mother tongue languages are "socially identified with a particular ethnic group" through state policy, and they are regarded as "culture-giving" symbols of Chinese, Malay, and Indian practices and values (1989, p. 509). While the idea that a particular ethnic group should express itself in a given language seems like common sense, Puroshotam suggests that what happens in Singapore is that a discourse of objectivity is at work in the definition of mother tongue languages. In other words, it is the seemingly objective concept of the mother tongue language — specifically, the designation of Mandarin as naturally belonging to the Chinese, Tamil as naturally Indian, Malay as essentially Malay — that creates the ethnic or racial categories Singaporeans identify as "Chinese", "Malay", and "Indian". Therefore, it is not so much that ethnic cultures or races create or express the mother tongue languages; instead, language "is not only a way into 'ethnic culture', [because] language is the ethnicity that it gives" (p. 514). This insight into the Singaporean government's language policy is important because it raises the question of the place and symbolic or cultural associations of English in modern Singapore, and the position of English literature and writers who write in English.

The English language is both a legacy of British colonialism in Southeast Asia and, according to Puroshotam, "the symbol of modernization and economic development" (p. 509); it is meant to meet the "economic necessity for a nation like Singapore in the international scheme of things today, and consequently the language of social and economic mobility within the island" (p. 511). Just as the mother tongues are objectified as culture-giving symbols, English too is objectified with a clear "politically defined purpose: the transmission of information and skills, but not of 'value'" (Gordon 1984, pp. 45–46). The mother tongue languages are meant to ground Singaporeans in their "Asian" cultures and values, to balance out the deleterious or "Westernizing" effects of English. But if English is regarded, objectively, as strictly a language of information transmission and social and economic mobility, then how does this affect Singaporeans who, either by necessity or choice, write poetry and fiction in the English language? How does English, in other words, create and sustain a literary culture in Singapore? The question of whether or not a European language can be a creative language for non-European or formerly colonized cultures has a long history of contention without any definite resolution.[1] My focus here, however, is on the ways in which English-language writers and poetry are situated in relation to political, social, and cultural forces in Singapore. Jan B. Gordon, writing shortly after the publication of a Malaysian and Singaporean poetry anthology in 1976 entitled *The Second Tongue*, finds that in many of the poems by Singaporean writers, "a certain 'Anglo' quality seems grafted on in much the way that the English language itself is in Singapore" (1984, p. 47). Gordon also suggests that "the very weakness is symptomatic of the role of English in the culture itself ... literary history is conveyed as technical information and not at all internalized as part of the country or the emotional life of the poem" (p. 49). One can see that Gordon holds an organic idea of literature and language that goes back to nineteenth-century Britain, where a critic like Matthew Arnold, in his seminal work, *Culture and Anarchy*, argues that literature (especially poetry) provides cultural and spiritual values to counterbalance the danger of anarchy created by social modernization and economic industrialization. This way of thinking, however, is very similar to the Singapore government's official language policy discussed above, where mother tongue languages are objectified as cultural symbols and values while English is promoted for business and technological development. In this manner, English can never become "internalized as part of the country" because it will always be seen as a "Western" language. My point here is that, like the "mother tongues", English too is objectified by Gordon, but objectified as an instrumental and coldly rational language in the Singaporean context.

Shirley Geok-lin Lim, on the other hand, departs from this organic conceptualization of language and literature by focusing on the social and political privileges and problems that come with the use of English as a literary language in Singapore. She agrees with Puroshotam that English is a language that is promoted by the state for purposes of national development because it is regarded as an international language that can promote intellectual exchange and global commerce. Lim, however, feels that English cannot simply be detached from its historical and cultural associations, stating that "the English language carries with it British and Western traditions and ideals; it is a strong transmitter of cosmopolitan values" (2002, p. 40). Writers in Singapore who use English find themselves in a difficult situation because they are "inevitably identified with a colonialist heritage", seen as "alien from Asian identity, and transmitting dangerous Westernised, cosmopolitan, and technological attitudes" (p. 48). These writers have to struggle with a double consciousness: on the one hand, they try "to recover past Asian traditions and cultural values" (p. 48); on the other hand, they are "critical of the encroachment of cosmopolitan and technological attitudes" (p. 49). I agree with Lim's analysis of the dilemma that English-language writers face in modern Singapore, especially given the ways in which the language has been politically designated for economic and technological uses. But, while the project of recovering an Asian past and criticizing Western or cosmopolitan attitudes might aptly describe the vision of a Singaporean poet like Edwin Thumboo (whose work Lim discusses as an example of such writing), I suggest in contrast that Arthur Yap's poetry and his treatment of objects, cultures, and values as things is a critical attitude that takes aim at both Westernized or cosmopolitan ideas as well as ideas identified as Asian or traditional. Arthur Yap's use of English makes a virtue out of necessity: by writing poetry in a language that is privileged in Singapore for its denotative and instrumental uses, Yap makes us aware of the "thing-ness" of English itself by stressing the language's connotative and associative aspects.

ARTHUR YAP AND MODERNIST POETRY

This turn away from denotation and the instrumental use of English towards connotation and the imaginative possibilities of English as a poetic language leads literary critics to argue that Arthur Yap writes in the modernist vein, notably through his humor and irony, linguistic playfulness, mixture of formal and colloquial speech, and unconventional syntax and punctuation. Shirley Geok-lin Lim, for example, suggests that Yap's "combination of low realistic and high lyrical elements" and his "exploitation of registers and tones in spoken English for comic and satirical effect" follow the practices of American poet E.E. Cummings (Lim 1993, p. 137), who in turn was much influenced by the modernist poet and critic Gertrude Stein. Additionally, Rajeev Patke emphasizes that, in Yap's poetry, "modernist attitudes control and drive the tone and syntax: the irony is the principal cognitive instrument; humor the chief antidote to boredom, passivity, and despair" (2007, p. 21). His diction and vocabulary "are drawn from books" and his poetic "rhythms are remote from ordinary speech or song" (p. 17). What Patke underscores here is that Yap's pervasive irony and disarming humour are coupled with words, phrases, and sentences that are drawn from learned, formal speech or allude to other works of English literature. These characteristics are often associated with early twentieth-century modernist avant-garde verse by British and American poets. Furthermore, Yap's connection with William Butler Yeats's modernist sensibility is highlighted by Patke's assertion that the Singaporean poet's "poems demonstrate a sense of integrity in relation to human experience, a reflective and a skeptical cast of mind" (Patke 2007, p. 18). Like Yeats, who lamented how things had fallen apart in the West after World War I but who also felt the need to assert some sort of spiritual or cultural centre, Yap does not cynically reject or sneer at his society and its foibles. In fact, the "integrity" that conjoins Yap's verse to human experience in modern Singapore comes from the thing-like perspective of his poetry. Witness how Patke, in the opening pages of another essay, describes Yap's artistic style:

> His poems move away from the notion of having an intention and then applying meaning to lever it into the reader's lap. Things and persons and events and non-events simply are, like bits of sharp glass that the poem tilts, kaleidoscope-fashion, into momentary shapes laden with the knowledge that they are random, fortuitous, and always liable to fall back into their constituent and unconsoling bits. (2003, pp. 173–74)

Although Patke here does not refer specifically to any of Yap's poems, what he describes is very similar to what I discussed earlier about the distinction between objects and things, and Patke's analysis connects with the two short epigraphs taken from Yap's poetry. The "intention" of the Singaporean state is to use English as an object or "lever" to enforce and apply meaning on its population. However, Yap's poetry works as a kaleidoscope, snatching the objects of everyday life and the objectified English language out of their instrumental contexts, re-arranging them into "momentary shapes" that help us see other possible meanings and relationships. This kaleidoscopic process is described by Yap himself in the three brief lines from "location": "some things remain / some things pass, / some things are tired" (*Space*, p. 4). Things are what "remain" when objects break down, "pass" away, or — if we consider how human beings too can be objectified — grow "tired" and cannot perform their function. Yap's use of anaphora and punctuation here point to connections with the second epigraph. The anaphora (the repetition of the phrase "some things") drives home the importance of things and what happens to them, and the comma slows down the pace of our reading by introducing a caesura or short pause between two brief lines. Both these devices serve, as Yap says in "down the line", to break "the habit by which the world moves" (p. 78). Just as a kaleidoscope focuses our vision on to the centre of multiple and mutable patterns made up of bits and pieces of coloured glass, so Yap's poetry compels us to "look at the centre of things" as they are re-arranged by his craft.

The Transformation of Objects into Things in Arthur Yap's Poetry

The arrangement of words in a poem to reveal unexpected connections or meanings is central to American critic Marjorie Perloff's (1981) idea that one important strand of modernist writing is the poetics of "indeterminacy" (p. 4). By this phrase, Perloff does not mean that modernist poetry is utterly nihilistic or meaningless; instead, she argues that modernist poetry, especially that of Gertrude Stein, "allows for free play, constructing a way of happening rather than an account of what has happened, a way of looking rather than a description of how things look" (p. 85). Perloff elaborates on this way of happening in her discussion of Stein's famously difficult poem "Tender Buttons" by arguing that "the best way to think of a text like this one is to compare it to an X-ray. Words are related so as to show what is there beneath the skin, what is *behind* the social and artistic surface" (p. 108, Perloff's italics). This poetic method is not only limited to words, images, and things, for Stein's writing "seeks to enact the rhythm of human change, to show how a relationship, any relationship between two people who are at once the same and different, evolves" (p. 93). Arthur Yap's poetic style continues this tradition of a poetry of indeterminacy (with E.E. Cummings and Gertrude Stein as his Anglo-American modernist predecessors) but within the context of postcolonial, post-independence Singapore. While one might argue that modernist poetry is a distinctly British and American and early-twentieth century literary movement that has little or no bearing on modern Singaporean society and literature, we must keep in mind that the creative energies and critical force of modernist poetry are not limited to a Western cultural or historical context; they can be and have been adapted by Singaporean writers as a way of asserting their own postcolonial cultural and literary autonomy. In fact,

> poetry enriches the connotations of the "postcolonial" by keeping us close to the energies inherent to language and form, while also showing how postcolonial preoccupations bring the aesthetic dimension of poetry closer to its cultural, political, and ethical implications. The conjunction sharpens awareness of the role played by words, rhythms, idiom, style in the translation of cultural dependency into cultural self-confidence. (Patke 2006, p. 14)

Rather than rejecting the English language and the tradition of Anglo-American modernism, Arthur Yap displays such a "translation of cultural dependency into cultural self-confidence" by taking up the language and literary style of the former colonizer and applying them to the way things happen in modern Singapore, thereby heeding Gertrude Stein's provocative injunction, "and then there is using everything" (Stein 2004, p. 25).

THERE IS USING EVERYTHING: YAP'S THING-LIKE PERSPECTIVE

Arthur Yap developed this poetic approach of "using everything" throughout his entire poetic career. Beginning with his poem "location", published in Yap's first collection *Only Lines* (1971), we see how he constructs (in Marjorie Perloff's words) "a way of looking" at things "rather than a description of how things look" (Perloff 1981, p. 85).

> so this village is still here
> here without change
> and if i stay here any longer
> i am already
> where i shall always be
> here without change
>
> in this village still here....
>
> (*Space*, p. 4)

The poem begins with a declarative sentence that affirms, through the adverb "so", a sense of nostalgia about the preservation of a small community ("this village") against the encroachment of modernity and "change". However, in the third through sixth lines of the poem Yap's poetic speaker appears, and the use of the conditional "if" in line three introduces a degree of uncertainty regarding the immutable nature of the traditional village. Furthermore, the repetition of the phrase "here without change", along with the adverbs "already" and "always", make us think twice about the possible meanings of a life without change: on one hand, it may mean the preservation of traditions and customs of the village community, but on the other hand it may point to stagnation and a lack of growth in the individual. Yap seems to be encouraging change and growth when he creates a stanza break that interrupts the smooth flow of the lines "here without change // in this village still here." What might have been the last line of the first stanza becomes the opening of a new stanza, a new beginning that pushes against the idea of immobility expressed by the line's concluding and end-stopped phrase "still here."

What kind of change does Yap have in mind? The next few lines of the second stanza show us that Yap's poetic "I" fades away, shifting our focus from himself to "things" and what happens to them:

> some things remain
> some things pass,
> some things are tired
> bicycles arriving
> cleaned bicycles departing.
> and if today
> not many people are arriving
> do not change the day
> to bring in yesterday
> riding an old identity
>
> (*Space*, p. 4)

The first three lines of this passage mark a turning point in the poem. The anaphora or repetition of "some things" seems to suggest the continuity and permanency evoked at the beginning of the poem, but the comma after "some things pass" is significant. In contrast to the definite end brought about by the full-stops in lines seven and twelve ("in this village still here." and "cleaned bicycles departing."), the comma introduces a short pause that is more a moment of conscious reflection rather than resolute conclusion. Of course, we cannot miss Yap's pun on "tired", which refers both to a state of weariness and the fact that bicycles, which are about to appear, are vehicles with tires. But the comma draws our attention to and raises questions about how and why things pass and grow tired: where do they go, are they destroyed or demolished (in the sense of "pass away"), and what could possibly tire out an inanimate vehicle that is a means of transportation? By this point the poem has enacted, in both sense and sound, a change in the smooth, seamless enjambement of its opening lines. Yap develops the relationship between the poetic speaker and the village community by paradoxically effacing the speaker and focusing instead on the objective nature of the bicycles that arrive and depart the village in the latter half of the stanza. It is important to note here that the bicycles do not seem to be metaphors or metonyms for people or travellers, nor are they personified and given human qualities, because Yap points out that "not many people are arriving." In other words, we are meant to understand these bicycles for what they are — as vehicles for transportation

— and this draws our attention to the strange fact that the people riding them are absent from the poem. Thus, there is an inhuman atmosphere to this ceaseless traffic of bicycles that have no apparent purpose, although we get a glimpse of the economic nature of this traffic when we learn that the village serves a defined function: to get the bicycles "cleaned" rather than to be a space for forming a community or increasing human socialization. Furthermore, Yap cautions against the instrumental use of nostalgia and history to strengthen or rejuvenate a community. The solution to the problem of "not many people" coming to the village lies not in "bring[ing] in yesterday / riding an old identity" or dressing up the past in order to create a new character for the present. In these lines, "yesterday" is personified as a rider of the numberless bicycles coming to and going from the village, and, following the logic of the earlier lines, this past is "cleaned" like the bicycles, thereby producing a sanitized or manufactured nostalgia.

Against these forms of objectification, Yap does not construct his own social or historical framework and force it upon his readers. Instead, he asks us to become active onlookers in order to scrutinize the objects in our everyday lives, as we can see in the closing lines of "location":

> and if you see a bicycle
> leaning on the grass
> neither tired not cleaned
> then it is just resting
> sufficiently
> to make no sense at all
>
> *(Space*, p. 4)

Here, human contact is re-established in the poem as readers are directly addressed through the second-person pronoun ("you"), but the conditional "if" marks Yap's tone as inviting rather than commanding. Furthermore, Yap seems to advise a degree of detachment, for we are asked to "see" or look at this last bicycle rather than to ride it or set it upright. What is significant in these closing lines is that this bicycle has become a thing rather than an object because, unlike its counterparts earlier in the poem, it has stopped working or functioning according to its defined purpose. As Bill Brown reminds us, "we begin to confront the thingness of objects when they stop working for us" (2004, p. 4). Having reached a state where it is "neither tired nor cleaned", where it has lost its objective function as a vehicle or a symbol for the business in the village, the bicycle begins to take on human characteristics. Personified as someone relaxing, "leaning on the grass", and "just resting / sufficiently", the human qualities of this bicycle emerge along with the re-establishment of human contact by Yap's poetic speaker in his address to the reader. Yap's final line, "to make no sense at all", might be interpreted as saying that the bicycle, in becoming a thing, is now a useless or meaningless piece of machinery. And yet it is precisely the desire to make things mean something definite or sensible — the process of objective denotation — that Yap is asking us to reconsider. If we bear in mind that "the story of objects asserting themselves as things ... is the story of a changed relation to the human subject" (Brown 2004, p. 4), then the story of this bicycle asserting itself as a thing makes no sense if we try to figure it out according to the definitions that are (to recall the beginning of the poem) "still here" or "here without change" in our society. Instead, Yap's poem itself dramatizes the process by which an object (in this case the bicycle) asserts itself as a thing (which no longer performs its defined purpose) and becomes alive to us (through its personification as someone resting). Yap's intentions are reinforced if we consider how the poem's title, "location", is a term that refers not only to a definite place — the village we see at the beginning or the old identity from yesterday — but also to the *act* or the *process* of locating something. What occurs in the latter half of the poem is such a process of locating the thingness of an object or new meanings in a set of old definitions, and through this a possibility of change emerges that was refused or foreclosed when the poem began.

Yap extends and develops his subversive perspective on conventional subject-object relationships in a poem appropriately entitled "things". The poem begins with a simple and spare list of commonplace objects we would find in our home, namely "chair / wall / window / desk / bed" (*Space*, p. 67). However, Yap goes down the list and breaks these objects away from their mundane functions and gives us a closer look at them as things:

> chair makes us fat, upholstered in blubber
> long shot: wall. no one has ever succeeded
>
> in being hung up like a portrait, truly dead.
> medium shot: window. open it.
> let the sun in, let suicide out.

> before hitting the ground, frame it in slow motion.
> reverse repeat, pan it back to window, its source.
>
> (Space, p. 67)

Yap inverts the functional relationship between person and chair and turns the chair into the grammatical subject of his sentence, a subject that makes those who sit it in "fat" and "upholstered in blubber". People who sit in chairs for too long begin to take on qualities of both furniture and corpulent animals due to their inactivity, thereby losing their humanity. Yap's playful tone, however, comes across in the use of the amusing word "blubber", suggesting a degree of humorous detachment that differs from the pensiveness of the earlier poem "location". This would explain Yap's use of filmmaking techniques to focus on the objects in the room; rather than describe them in detail, his visual framing detaches these objects from their usual context and helps us see them in a different light. Yap's "long shot" of the wall, for instance, gives us an ironic take on human ambition and competition. With his signature combination of enjambement and stanza break, Yap suggests that to be immortalized for posterity by being "hung up like a portrait" is not a matter of life after death, but a state of becoming an object with one clear function or meaning: being "truly dead" without any life whatsoever. Yap continues with this theme of objects and death by giving us the "medium shot" of the window, which leads to the dark humour conveyed through neat parallelism: "let the sun in, let suicide out." The shocking succinctness of this suicide is undone by the next two lines in which Yap uses "slow motion" and multiple commas to slow down our visualization of the suicide's fall. What is important here is that Yap stops just "before" he shows us the suicide "hitting the ground", thereby withholding any catharsis or purging of fear and horror we might experience by witnessing the gruesome conclusion of the suicide's plunge. Instead, Yap, using a "reverse repeat", "pan[s]" our gaze "back to the window", which he states is the "source" of the suicide. Yap does not allow us to dwell on the graphic details of defenestration, but instead asks us to consider how a window could possibly be the source of a person's suicide. This inference makes sense if we recall how Bill Brown describes the "discourse of objectivity" using the analogy of a window: "[w]e look through objects because ... there is a discourse of objectivity that allows us to use them as facts" (2004, p. 4). The window in this poem functions as such an objective discourse, for it seems to be a transparent space through which (as Yap states matter-of-factly) the sun comes in and the suicide goes out. Just as the chair turns people into furniture or animals, and the wall and portrait mummify people instead of immortalizing them, the window seems to limit, negate, or destroy what makes people human and human life meaningful. Like his earlier poem, "location", Yap does not offer a set of life-affirming meanings to redefine the objects he scrutinizes in "things"; instead, through his poetic detachment and the overt use of filmmaking techniques, he asks us not just to look *through* objects and see them for what they can do, but to look *at* them as things and examine what they might be doing to us.

But the poetic revisioning of objects as things need not necessarily be a negative or destructive experience. In his 1986 collection, *Man, Snake, Apple,* Yap offers a more affirmative view of things in the poem "tropical paradise". The title bears a pun that is typical of Yap's linguistic wordplay: the poem describes scenes that seem to be set in a rainforest or jungle, which is the most obvious meaning of "tropical"; at the same time, the word can also mean "of or related to a trope", which means a metaphor or any other figurative turn of speech. The poem therefore is a process of troping or turning that is the reverse of what we see in "location" and "things". In fact, the first half of this poem is a celebration of the sensuous twists and turns of language itself, and how its manifold, thing-like nature is "the concrete yet ambiguous within the everyday" (Brown 2004, p. 4). This poetic gesture subtly questions the Singapore government's official language policy that objectifies English as an instrumental language for economic development and social mobility, an objectification which takes place in the second half of the poem. Yap's speaker is self-effacing — there is no "I" who speaks — but we can infer that the powerful, sensual impressions that begin the poem are experienced by this speaker: "the feel of things. textures. the elastic skin, / gently pliant to the touch. the cold metallic shock / of water in a shaded pool, galvanizing all the pores;" (*Space*, p. 107). These opening lines, filled with descriptive appeals to our tactile, thermal, and visual senses, focus our attention on "the feel of things" and how words and texts can become "textures". Language is more than an object or transparent medium of expression through which we receive facts and figures or communicate our intentions; instead, it is a thing through which we experience the world via tangible textures woven out of sense and sound. This is why Yap uses recurring consonant (for example, "elasti*c* s*k*in" and "*c*old metalli*c* sho*ck*") and vowel sounds (for instance, "cold", "shock", "pores" and "water", "shaded", "galvanizing"), as well as synesthesia (the refreshing feeling of cold water is described in terms of gleaming, galvanized metal, thereby combining both thermal and visual senses) to set the tone for the first stanza.

In the third stanza of the poem, the solitary experience of the poetic speaker in the opening stanza now bursts into a vibrant celebration of things that "dance to the thrall of / primeval rhythms" (*Space*, p. 107) Yap suggests that things have something which objects, with their defined meanings and functions, lack: namely the power of "growing so fast" that we can "feel the / heat of their regeneration" (p. 107). What Yap alludes to here is what Bill Brown (2004) describes as one of the characteristics of things, namely "to overcome the loss of other words or [to serve] as a place holder for some future specifying operation" (pp. 4–5). In Yap's poetic paradise of figurative profusion, words turn into things that can regenerate or reveal once more the multiple meanings and relationships that were lost or hidden when they become objects. Furthermore, as Yap suggests in the closing lines of this stanza, "among the green mysteries of / certainty, they consume the decay of aged life" (*Space*, p. 107); the thingness of words also offers the possibility of building on old meanings and relationships in order to create new ones.

The second half of "tropical paradise", however, has a more sinister tone as the sensual, vibrant descriptive imagery of the first half is replaced by a repetitive and incantatory form with allusions to religious sacrifice. The fourth stanza of the poem describes "a stone falling endlessly / & in it the silence of before & after" (*Space*, p. 107). This falling stone suddenly transforms, in the next stanza, into an offering delivered to a distant and impersonal deity: "a head falling. / o lord it is to you it falls" (p. 107). The phrase "before & after" points to the logic of cause and effect, and what Yap suggests here is that once the primeval stone is defined as part of this rationalized relationship, it falls into silence, like a decapitated head offered up to the god-like ideas of progress and modernization. This perspective makes sense if we recall that the English language in Singapore is not only "the symbol for modernization and economic development" but also an "economic necessity for a nation like Singapore in the international scheme of things today" (Puroshotam 1989, pp. 509, 511). This theme is echoed at the end of the poem, where the limb of a tree falls "in the timelessness of before & after", only to become an amputated "limb falling / o lord it is to you it dies". The personification of the stone and the tree limb drives home the contrast between the first half of the poem, in which things are growing and regenerating, and the second half where objects die a symbolic death as they are sacrificed at the altar of modernization and economic growth. Yap alludes to this zeal for economic progress in the penultimate stanza where he describes "a tall tree falling eternally, / & in it the rapidizing of leaves" (*Space*, p. 107). The word "rapidizing" is a neologism — a word invented by Yap — and sounds very out of place in the second half of the poem, which resembles a religious liturgy or prayer. However, if we consider how the word is a combination of "rapid" and "rigidizing", then Yap might be suggesting that the rapid modernization of society may cause it to become rigid and inflexible, requiring too much to be sacrificed too soon for economic necessity.

LOOKING AT THE CENTRE OF THINGS: YAP'S SOCIAL COMMENTARY

The critical perspective enabled by Yap's thing-like approach to language and everyday life can be seen in several of his poems that offer social commentary and critiques of modern Singapore. As some of his readers have pointed out, Yap is adept at switching between different registers or levels of the English language, from the colloquial Singaporean English or "Singlish" of everyday Singaporean life, to his learned and laconic musings, to the clichéd catchphrases of government bureaucracy and the business world (Lim 1993, pp. 144–49; Talib 1999, pp. 122–23). While one might think that Yap's skilfulness in accurately reproducing so many different kinds of speech means that he is trying to reproduce authentic versions of Singaporean life in his writing, I argue that this linguistic versatility is further evidence that Yap wields language like a multifaceted thing rather than a transparent object or medium of commnunication. The multiple levels of language in his poetry suggest what literary critic Mikhail Bakhtin (2000) calls "heteroglossia" — literally other (*hetero*) language (*glossia*) — defined as "the social diversity of speech types" (p. 341). Although Bakhtin was discussing heteroglossia in the modern European novel, his insights on poetry are in accord with my earlier discussion of Bill Brown's thing theory. Bakhtin (2000) suggests that "heteroglossia ... can be introduced into purely poetic genres, primarily into the speeches of characters", and that in poetry, "it appears, in essence, as a *thing*, it does not lie on the *same* plane with the real language of the work: it is the depicted gesture of one of the characters and does not appear as an aspect of the word doing the depicting" (p. 341, Bakhtin's italics). What Bakhtin means is that the mixture of linguistic styles in poetry draws our attention to the discrepancies between the associative or connotative aspect of language that cannot be reduced to its denotative or objective usage. Yap's heteroglossia, thereofore, draws our attention to the discrepancies between words and meanings instead of merely imitating everyday life, just as thing theory shows us the objectification and reduction of things and human relationships.

Such discrepancies are very clear in one of Yap's early poems, "statement", published in 1974. Yap mimics the formal and authoritative tone of a high-ranking official in either the government or a business organization who is talking down to a subordinate. This mimicry is obviously satirical, and the ludicrousness of the speaker's language intensifies as the poem progresses. The poem begins with the official speaking in a seemingly pleasant and breezy tone:

> of course your work comes first.
> after that, you may go for a walk,
> visit friends but, all the same,
> it is always correct to ask
> before you do anything else.
>
> (*Space*, p. 29)

Yet this pleasant opening contains certain phrases such as "of course" and "all the same" and "ask / before you do anything else" that can be interpreted as commands or imperatives rather than suggestions. This underlying voice of command becomes evident in the next stanza, where the speaker absurdly instructs the subordinate to phrase his or her suicide as a request ("please may i jump / off the ledge") in order to receive official permission ("you will be told: start jumping") (*Space*, p. 29). The impersonal side of the organization is further revealed when the offical makes protestations of generosity and broad-mindedness: "no one is in any way / narrow-minded anymore these days. / it is that everyone likes to know / these things way beforehand" (p. 29). The use of indefinite pronouns "no one" and "everyone" underscores the faceless and inhuman nature of the speaker's organization, and the attitude of acceptance is completely undermined by the way the subordinate's suicide is routinized "way beforehand" as though it were an item on a meeting agenda. The sheer senselessness of the situation is conveyed in the poem's conclusion:

> most probably they will say nothing,
> thinking should it legally, morally,

> departmentally be yes/no/perhaps,
> or if it's not too late:
> why don't you come along? we shall bring
> this matter up to a higher level.
>
> *(Space*, p. 29)

The possibility of the subordinate's suicide generates "nothing", or absolute silence; the lack of human reaction and emotional response testifies to the organization's highly bureaucratized thinking — "legally, morally, departmentally" — that cannot cope with answers or situations beyond "yes/no/perhaps". The speaker/superior's final line, "we shall bring / this matter up to a higher level", is a parody of numerous routine phrases used in many workplaces when a problem appears to be outside one's area of responsibility, and suggests that any answers to the subordinate's grievances will be endlessly deferred up the organizational hierarchy. Moreover, and with more sinister undertones, the pun on "higher level" suggests that the subordinate will fall to his or her death from an even higher floor of the building in which the organization is housed. My point here is that Yap adopts a thing-like approach to language by apparently mimicking the clear, courteous, and objective language of a bureaucratic functionary. By taking this manner of speech to an extreme, Yap shows how it breaks down because it is incapable of allowing those who use such language to relate to or understand other people; in fact, those who use this form of language find their thinking and behaviour objectified "legally, morally, / departmentally" and limited to "yes/no/perhaps". Behind the supposedly transparent and efficient ease and politeness of the poem's speaker lies a heartless and highly regulated bureaucracy obsessed with work and success.

This obsession with economic success and the use of clichés from the corporate world is further satirized in "letter from a youth to his prospective employer". Here, Yap emphasizes the bumptious nature of his poetic speaker — an ambitious young man applying for a job — by following Bakhtin's (2000) idea that heteroglossic language creates "the depicted gesture of one of the characters" (p. 341) rather than a seamless representation of everyday life.

> […] i am reasonably qualified:
> quite handsome: my lack of experience compensated
> by my prodigal intelligence: i shall not expect

to marry the typewriter: it's decision-making
i'm after: that's what i am: a leader of tomorrow:
so why don't you make it today?

(*Space*, p. 52)

The young man's only form of punctuation in this poem is the colon, a symbol that is supposed to signal to the reader that what comes after the colon will explain or clarify what precedes it. However, instead of clarifying his credentials, Yap's speaker uses colons to create what he thinks is an impressive list of his own achievements, but his malapropisms thwart his lofty intentions (as seen in his misuse of "prodigal" instead of "prodigious" when talking about his intelligence). The young man's language becomes a chain of objectified clichés and catchphrases taken from corporate terminology and motivational seminars, such as "a leader of tomorrow" who can "make it today". Like the earlier poem "statement", the absurdity of the speaker's manner of speech increases as the poem goes on, until finally we are presented with a senseless chiasmus or transposition of words in reverse order: "all opportunities being equal: / i am equal to any most opportune moment: / any most momentous opportunity" (*Space*, p. 52). Chiasmus is a rhetorical device commonly used in classical poetry and public oration, but its use in the context of a job application is completely inappropriate, highly affected, and humorously points to the ambitious young man's utter "lack of experience" and incompetence. Along with "statement", this poem shows us how Yap's commentary of modern Singapore is performed through an imitation of bureaucratic speech and corporate catchphrases. His imitation of what is meant to be direct and transparent language turns language itself into a thing, for in both poems language no longer allows communication but, instead, creates obfuscation. Yap's satirical humour helps us look past the discourse of objectivity inhabited by both the bureaucrat and the ambitious applicant in order to see the objectification of language and human relationships in modern Singapore. To put it another way, given that English has a "politically defined purpose" in Singapore, namely "the transmission of information and skills, but not of 'value'" (Gordon 1984, pp. 45–46) what Yap has done is to challenge this objective function of the English language by mimicking the tone and terminology used to transmit information and skills. In doing so he has given the language its own value as a versatile medium capable of critical commentary on modern Singaporean society.

This critical commentary, which focuses on the thingness of objects, is not only limited to the government bureaucracy or the civil service and its employees. In two related poems, "an afternoon nap" (1977) and "2 mothers in a hdb playground" (1980), Yap offers a critical look at the social competition rife in everyday Singaporean life as well as the immense pressure placed on Singaporean children as their parents try to make them succeed in a rapidly modernizing society. Shirley Geok-lin Lim analyzes how, in "2 mothers", "the conversation betrays intense social competitiveness, displayed in concerns over academic achievement and material possessions", and how Yap "demonstrates two instances of code-switching" by introducing words in Malay and Hokkien (a Chinese dialect or regional language) to the colloquial Singaporean English dialogue (Lim 1993, p. 148). What is also significant about Yap's style in this poem (in the context of thing theory) is the way in which Yap switches the two speakers around halfway through the poem. Ah Beng's mother's words begin the poem, followed by a response from Kim Cheong's mother that is typographically distinguished by an additional indentation. However, halfway through the poem, between stanzas seven and eight, the lines belonging to Ah Beng's mother become indented, while Kim Cheong's mother's words are now flush with the left edge of the poem. The reversal in no way affects the mothers' conversation, which carries on without interruption. This suggests that Yap is not just recreating "a carefully chosen moment in an encounter" between two women, "with the interpersonal relationship defined through nuances of spoken speech" (Lim 1993, p. 148). Instead, Yap's code-switching — his use of what Bakhtin calls heteroglossia — draws more attention to the language of the poem as "depicted gesture[s]" of his characters than as a faithful representation of everyday dialogue (Bakhtin 2000, p. 341). The dialogue between the two mothers is not really a conversation, as they are talking *at* rather than *to* each other; as Lim points out, their words are "an escalation in social boasting" rather than a meaningful dialogue (1993, p. 148). Furthermore, given that the two mothers suddenly switch places seamlessly, their relationship to their sons becomes questionable — in other words, we begin to wonder if the mothers actually care about their sons as children or if they are more concerned about how the sons can boost their own social status. In the latter case, just as the two mothers change positions in the poem, so Kim Cheong and Ah Beng (the two sons) become interchangeable objects. Yap's heteroglossic code-switching breaks down the objectified speech of the two mothers' social boasting to show the possible breakdown of family relationships in Singaporean society.

This theme also comes across in "an afternoon nap", which is an ironic title since the speaker's repose is interrupted from the outset by "the ambitious mother across the road / [who] is at it again." (*Space*, p. 60) The mother's ambition is not for herself but her son, and her use of language is not meant to communicate with or encourage her son, but to cajole and browbeat him, as seen from the way she is "proclaiming her goodness" and "shouting out his wrongs" (p. 60). In the second and third stanzas of the poem, we witness how the intense pressure to succeed academically in order to thrive socially has transformed what should be a loving and nurturing mother-son relationship into that of a predator and prey:

> she strikes chords for the afternoon piano lesson,
> her voice stridently imitates 2nd. lang. tuition,
> all the while circling the cowering boy
> in a manner apt for the most strenuous p.e. ploy.
>
> swift are all her contorted movements,
> ape for every need; no soft gradient
> of a consonant-vowel figure, she lumbers
> & shrieks, a hit for every 2 notes missed.
>
> (*Space*, p. 60)

The harshness of the mother's voice, which was displayed in the opening stanza, disrupts the harmony that ought to come from "strik[ing] chords" on the piano. Instead, the mother becomes increasingly "strident" as she begins "circling" her son like a predator circling its prey before moving in for the kill. In the third stanza the mother is again likened to an animal: an ape who corners her son with "all her contorted movements" and "lumbers / & shrieks" when he fails to play the piano. In addition to these metaphors and analogies, Yap's use of word sounds and line breaks also underscores the violence and tension between mother and son. The two layered sets of rhymes in the second stanza ("piano lesson" / "2nd. lang. tuition" and "cowering boy" / "p.e. ploy") might indicate that both schoolwork and parental expectations are being layered or piled upon the boy. The third stanza's enjambed or run-on lines also suggest the "swift", "contorted", and unstoppable advance of the mother's wrath towards her son. Finally, Yap inserts one detail that alludes to the Singapore government's policy on mother tongue languages in the 1970s and 1980s when he writes that the mother's voice "stridently imitates 2nd. lang. tuition". "2nd. lang[uage]" is a term used in Singaporean schools to refer to a student's officially designated mother tongue (Chinese, Malay, or Tamil), which is supposed to provide the child with cultural and moral values appropriate to his or her ethnic group. Yap's inclusion of this detail can be read as a two-pronged criticism of this mother tongue policy: first, the mother has to "imitate" these supplementary lessons in the mother tongue, suggesting that she herself is not a fluent or natural speaker of this language; second, the harsh and coercive domestic context in which the child is learning this second language runs counter to the official aims of the mother tongue policy, one of which is to integrate the child into his or her community. Yap breaks the apparent transparency of the term "mother tongue" by using the awkward abbreviation "2nd. lang." in his poem, thereby turning it into a contentious thing rather than an object of government policy, and drawing our attention to the connotations and implications of this term in the context of his poem.

The imitation of different registers of speech is not the only means through which Yap offers his social commentary. His urban poems describe the built-up spaces of Singapore in which society's desire for progress and modernization manifests itself in the physical structures of the cityscape. "old house at ang siang hill", for example, focuses on "the individual's subordination in the city's overwhelming physical weight" and how "the city's unrestrained growth destroys the old and traditional" (Lim 1993, p. 141). What is remarkable about this poem, which recounts someone's brief visit to the house where his or her ancestors once lived, is the speaker's gradual shift from a sympathetic eye to a cold and impersonal attitude. The poem seems to enact or embody the implacable process of how the past is swept aside by the objective need for economic growth and physical change. The poem begins with a decorous, even reverent, description of the house and the visitor's actions:

> an unusual house this is
> dreams are here before you sleep
> tread softly
> into the three-storeyed gloom
> sit gently
> on the straits-born furniture
> imported from china

> speak quietly
> to the contemporary occupants
>
> (*Space*, p. 16)

The "unusual" sentence structure of the first line, with its reversed word order, underscores the signficance of this house for the visitor, and the idea that "dreams" dwell in the house before "sleep" comes suggests that the building is more than just a house — perhaps it holds unconscious but important memories and sentimental, familial attachments for the visitor. Yap's choice of adverbs ("softly", "gently", "quietly") suggests the visitor's care and respect towards both the house and its furnishings (which, being "imported from china", allude to the family's immigrant past) as well as its "contemporary occupants". But by using the neutral and transient word "occupants" instead of owners, residents, or inhabitants, Yap foreshadows both a change in the speaker's tone as well as the impending vacating and demolishing of the house itself.

The change in tone is marked in the second stanza by the speaker's identification with the current occupants of the house and their wish to "dislocate" the visitor's "intentions" (*Space*, p. 16). The occupants are utterly dismissive of the visitor's attachments to this house and the ancestral past it represents: "so what if this is / your grandfather's house / his ghost doesn't live here anymore / your family past is superannuated grime" (p. 16). The gradual objectification of the house can be seen from the way even the ghost (the memories and spectral presence) of the visitor's grandfather has been evicted, along with the use of the cold and unfeeling term "superannuated" to characterize the obsolescence of the visitor's family history. The house is no longer a home but an object made up of "bricks and tiles", and, as we learn at the end of the second stanza, scheduled for demolition by the government's urban "re-development / which will greatly change / this house-that-was / dozens like it along the street / the next and the next as well" (p. 16). The concluding stanza of the poem is a simple, matter-of-fact couplet that sums up the fate of the "house-that-was": "nothing much will be missed / eyes not tradition will tell you this" (p. 16). This aphoristic ending sounds strangely trite, but the imperfect or slant rhyme of "missed" and "this" suggests that something is amiss and does not fit neatly into the scheme of urban re-development. Yap wants us to step back from the impersonal and objective voice of the poetic speaker who now looks only with his "eyes" and sees the past as "superannuated grime" that needs to be scrubbed away by rapid modernization. Instead, Yap asks us to think about the "tradition" evoked by the description of the house in the first stanza, with its "dreams", its "three-storeyed gloom" and "straits-born furniture / imported from china". The tantalizing nature of the house's dreams, its enigmatic gloom, and the transnational history of its furnishings, all suggest that Yap is presenting the house to us as a mutlifaceted thing at the beginning of the poem. The poem then enacts what happens when "an unusual house this is" becomes an object of rapid modernization and urban re-development into "this house-that-was". Yap poses the question of what will happen to Singapore's tradition and heritage (embodied in part by its buildings and urban spaces) if they are treated with such scant regard by society and the state.

Such an eviction of history's ghosts and a declaration that the past is superannuated sounds very similar to how Bill Brown (2004) defines part of the relationship between things and modern society: "To declare that the character of things as things has been extinguished, or that objects have been struck dumb, or that the idea of respecting things no longer makes sense because they are vanishing — this is to find in the fate of things a symptom of a pathological condition most familiarly known as modernity" (pp. 9–10). Yap's poetry draws on some important aspects of modernist verse to cast a cool and critical eye on modern Singaporean society, to ask "how does the effort to rethink things become an effort to *re*institute society" (p. 9, Brown's italics).

In this chapter I have focused on Yap's thematic concerns and stylistic turns that transform common objects into unusual things. Where objects are struck dumb to be used without hindrance, Yap gives them voice as things to be treated with care; where words and speech have become regulated and functional, he revitalizes them through heteroglossia and irony; where people spout corporate clichés and competitive boasts, he satirizes their affectation to remind us of the importance of human affect. Yap's poetry challenges the idea mooted by some critics of Singaporean literature that the English language cannot foster a cultural identity in Singapore, as his work testifies to the power of English in developing a thoughtful and critical intellectual stance and its ability to make us "look at the centre of things" (*Space*, p. 78).

Note

1. For arguments supporting and opposing English as a suitable language for African cultures and societies, see the works by Achebe (1994) and Ngugi (1986) respectively.

References

Achebe, Chinua. "The African Writer and the English Language". In *Colonial Discourse and Post-colonial Theory*, edited by Patrick Williams and Laura Chrisman. New York: Columbia University Press, 1994.
Arnold, Matthew. *Culture and Anarchy and Other Writings*, edited by Stefan Collini. Cambridge: Cambridge University Press, 2005.
Bakhtin, Mikhail. "From The Dialogic Imagination: Four Essays". In *Theory of the Novel: A Historical Approach*, edited by Michael McKeon. Baltimore, MA: Johns Hopkins University Press, 2000.
Brown, Bill. "Thing Theory". In *Things*, edited by Bill Brown. Chicago: University of Chicago Press, 2004.
Foucault, Michel. *The Archaeology of Knowledge*, translated by A.M. Sheridan Smith. New York: Pantheon, 1972.
Lim, Shirley Geok-lin. "Sub/Versions of a National Poetry: Arthur Yap". In *Nationalism and Literature: English-language Writing from the Philippines and Singapore*. Quezon City, Philippines: New Day, 1993.
———. "The English-language Writer in Singapore". In *Singaporean Literature in English: A Critical Reader*. Serdang, Malaysia: Universiti Putra Malaysia Press, 2002.
Gordon, Jan. "The Second Tongue Myth: English Poetry in Polylingual Singapore". *Ariel* 15, no. 4 (1984): 41–65.
Ngugi, wa Thiong'o. *Decolonising the Mind: The Politics of Language in African Literature*. Oxford: Currey, 1986.
Patke, Rajeev. "Ambivalence and Ambiguity in the Poetry of Arthur Yap". In *Complicities: Connections and Divisions*, edited by Chitra Sankaran et al. Bern: Lang AG, 2003.
———. *Postcolonial Poetry in English*. Oxford: Oxford University Press, 2006.
———. "Modernist Poetic Practices in the English Poetry from Southeast Asia: A Comparison between Jose Garcia Villa and Arthur Yap". *Kritika Kultura* 9 (2007): 11–26.
Perloff, Marjorie. *The Poetics of Indeterminacy: Rimbaud to Cage*. Princeton, NJ: Princeton University Press, 1981.
Puroshotam, Nirmala. "Language and Linguistic Policies". In *Management of Success: The Moulding of Modern Singapore*, edited by Kernial Singh Sandhu and Paul Wheatley. Boulder, CO: Westview, 1989.

Stein, Gertrude. "Composition as Explanation". In *Look At Me Now and Here I Am: Writings and Lectures 1911–1945*, edited by Patricia Meyerowitz. London: Owen, 2004.

Talib, Ismail S. "The Language of Singapore Poetry". In *Interlogue: Studies in Singapore Literature. Volume 2: Poetry*, edited by Kirpal Singh. Singapore: Ethos Books, 1999.

Yap, Arthur. *The Space of City Trees: Selected Poems*. London: Skoob Books, 2000.

Yeats, William Butler. "The Second Coming". In *The Collected Poems of W.B. Yeats*. New York: Macmillan, 1956.

3

"THE SAME TABLEAU, INTRINSICALLY STILL"
Arthur Yap, Poet-Painter

Boey Kim Cheng

Despite Arthur Yap's disavowal that there is any symbiotic relationship between his painting and poetry, the similarities between his visual canvases and his written verse are palpably obvious. In an essay about the relationship between poetry and painting, Wallace Stevens (1951) points out that "often a detail, a propos or remark, in respect to painting, applies also to poetry" (p. 160). Stevens elaborates on the parallels between the two practices and concludes that "it would be possible to study poetry by studying painting, or that one could become a painter after one had become a poet, not to speak of carrying on in both métiers at once, with the economy of genius, as Blake did" (p. 160). Stevens' proposition takes Horace's *ut pictura poesis* ("as is painting, so is poetry") a step further. Not only are the processes of poetry similar to those governing painting, a similar aesthetic reflex also binds commentaries on art and poetry.

Stevens' formulation is especially pertinent in the case of dual practitioners — poets who paint or painters who write poetry. With William Blake, Paul Klee, D.H. Lawrence, Hermann Hesse and David Jones, poetry and art are bound by the same aesthetic and thematic concerns, fed by a common pool of impulses and obsessions. Indeed the reciprocity or cross-fertilization between poetry and painting is a key Modernist impulse that is well-documented. William Carlos Williams, Ezra Pound, Gertrude Stein, Paul Eluard and Wallace Stevens all drew inspiration from their artist-counterparts in the quest for new poetic modes and themes, often looking to art for what cannot be expressed in words, while Wassily Kandinsky, Pablo Picasso and Paul Klee aspired to the lyricism of colour, voice, and form that they found in poetry. In the case of poet-painters, art and poetry complement, reinvigorate and reinforce each other. Arthur Yap, as a poet and painter, inherited this Modernist alliance of art and poetry, which can be seen most clearly in his predilection for abstraction in both his paintings and his verse. There are few truly ekphrastic poems in his oeuvre, by which I mean poems that respond to particular paintings; neither are there poems about painters or poems consciously advocating any aesthetic school or movement. But there is a substantial body of poems that mediates between art and poetry, conducting lyric meditations on the aesthetics of perception and compositional issues, exploring the relationship between seeing and making. These are recognizably painterly poems that bind Yap's art and poetry in a poetic or aesthetic of minimalist restraint and abstraction, tilting the poem and painting towards difficulty, stillness, and silence.

Abstraction is the governing impulse in Yap's oeuvre. Although the poems still retain strong figurative traces and offer semblances of objects, landscape, and the human figure, they lean towards a liminal zone where the semantic outlines and narrative resonance that figures of poetic speech usually generate for the reader are on the brink of being erased. In this liminal or in-between space, the poems gravitate towards the non-representational and non-verbal spaces that Yap's paintings inhabit. Conversely, the poems can also be seen as pulling away from this centripetal force of abstraction and providing an ironic commentary on the paintings. Yap the painter is unmistakably present in his poetry, and Yap the poet informs and underpins the visual lyricism of his art.

ABSTRACTION AS RESISTANCE

Yap is characteristically as reticent, ambiguous, and elusive about his art as he is about his poetry. In a 1972 review of his art, he says that "[i]n many ways my painting is an extension of my words and at other times what I cannot put in words, I express through art" (*New Nation*, 17 June 1972). Here his painting forms a continuum with the poetry, extending and complementing it. This affirmation is contradicted a few years later, when Yap says of the inclusion of his black and grey series in *Commonplace*: "There is no direct link between the poems and the paintings. I just wanted to include the paintings as they are visually pleasing" (*New Nation*, 3 September 1977). When asked if there is any relation between his paintings and poetry in a 1984 interview, Yap states: "No. If I can express everything through one medium then I won't have to choose two. My paintings are usually non representational. I explore different things: the relation of space and shapes and forms and so on. In poetry I think — I've been told I'm a little more human in my poetry than in my painting" (Sullivan 1984, p. 6). The categorical denial is characteristically laconic and self-deprecatory, and taken at face value, out of context, it denies any correlation between Yap the painter and Yap the poet. Yet there is a strong hint of irony in the response and in the explication of the difference between his painting and poetry. The distinction Yap makes between the two is important — the absence of the human figure in his art is a salient feature of his abstraction — but the hesitant note in "a little more human" undercuts the categorical assertion at the beginning of his response. Yap's poems reveal a shared abstraction: the qualification "a little more human" concedes that despite the recognizable human presence in the poems, they are driven by the same impulse towards non-representation.

Yap's seeming self-contradiction and reluctance to assert any direct links between his art and poetry is all of a piece with his self-effacing, hermetic temperament, which expresses itself in a poetry that is non-autobiographical, lower-case, or "tentative and conditional" (*Man Snake Apple*, p. 36), and in an art which is non-figurative and non-narrative. It can also be read as evidence of Yap's relentless mediation and negotiation between the two media and creative roles each entails. Yap rejects the view that his poetry is abstract but expatiates on his idea of abstraction as a principle that is operative in both his poetry and painting: "Abstraction is simply the paring away of things that are not essential" (Brewster 1986, p. 3). It would seem that, while cautious to repudiate any overt connection between the two media in his oeuvre, he acknowledges the same aesthetic principle at work in both. Obviously, as Yap points out with a hint of self-irony, his poetry has more human elements and is thus more figurative and representational, but abstraction is an underlying and often governing impulse too, especially in poems that deal with art in direct or oblique ways. Indeed, his poetry mediates between the figurative and the abstract and inhabits a liminal zone between the two. Paul Klee, whose art and poetics are a visible influence in Yap's work, says in a famous quotation about modern art: "Formerly we used to represent things visible on earth, things we either liked to look at or would have liked to see. Today we reveal the reality that is behind visible things, thus expressing the belief that the visible world is merely an isolated case in relation to the universe and that there are many more other, latent realities" (Klee 1968, p. 185). In a review of his solo exhibition in 1974, Yap asserts that his work is not "escapist" (*New Nation*, 15 June 1974). Abstraction for him is not an avoidance of reality and its representation but seeks to perceive and make visible the real.

Studies of Yap have mainly focussed on the socio-political elements in iconic poems like "2 mothers in a HDB playground" and "old house at ang siang hill". However, a survey of Yap's poetic oeuvre reveals a preponderance of poems rinsed of human presence, inhabiting either a liminal or hermetic world of barely recognizable spatial markers. Their abstract tone has more in common with Yap's art than with the tenor of his few social poems. Abstraction in Yap's poems on one level opposes the nationalist poetics of another Singaporean poet like Edwin Thumboo, whose poetry performs an overtly socio-political function in articulating "the macro-narratives of nationhood" (Goh 2006, p. 38). This nationalist aesthetic was a dominant impulse in art and poetry when "the poet in Singapore bears an over-determined relation to the development of the state into nation and painters in the first two decades after Singapore's independence" (Patke 1999, p. 90), to which Yap is a counter-example. Responding to a contrast of his apolitical stance with that of Thumboo and Robert Yeo, Yap states:

> For me, I don't think it's a poet's business to be a spokesman of any kind. I think Robert feels, for example ... I think basically we are on to the same thing, except our concerns are very different. He thinks I am far too private, for example. And my own stand is that I'm not a person who wants to write poems with a political basis, commenting upon society as such simply because that is the way I feel ... if that is really what I want to do then I would rather be a politician or a social worker, or whatever that is. (Sullivan 1984, p. 8)

Abstraction is Yap's rejection of any socio-political affiliation and constitutes a resistance to the pressure to practise nationalist poetics, a significant strategy in the 1970's and early 1980's, when so much of Singapore poetry and visual arts was driven by a postcolonial desire to validate the local and national. In the poem "local colour", from Yap's first collection, *Only Lines* (1971), this non-conformist stance is already much in evidence: "the artist himself is neither here nor there / he mistakes grassroots for his hair / now the strands have sprouted in the air / flanking an attap hut as a cultural stair" (p. 11). The rare rhyming quartet satirizes and critiques through its pun on "grassroots" any artist whose work serves the nascent nation-building agenda by affirming the local through valorization of Singapore's multiracial make-up, iconic images of its birth and formation, and the use of the variety of English called Singlish. Indeed, the more identifiably social elements of Yap's work can be read as fitting into this genre that he derides, like "house at ang siang hill" and "2 mothers in a HDB plaground", but these are few and far between. The primary thematic focus of both his art and poetry is unapologetically abstracted from the social and public realm. He states that "it doesn't mean I have to wear my Singaporean citizenship like a badge all the time, that every poem has to reflect some Singaporean concern, or knock some Singaporean concern" (Sullivan 1984, p. 8). Yap is aware that his hermetic poetics invites criticism from more public poets like Yeo, but he asserts that his work does not shun social responsibility or reality.

Yap's rejection of the public function of art and poetry chimes with the stance of postwar abstract artists who refused the claim of politics and forged "an idiom that belongs to no one country, race or cultural temperament" (Rosenberg 1947, p. 75). Robert Motherwell declares art's autonomy: "art is not national, that to be merely an American or French artist is to be nothing" (quoted in Guilbaut 1983, p. 175). Yap's resolutely detached stance, his minimalist style, his commitment to difficulty and disjunction, constitute an implicit gesture of non-alignment, carving out a liminality committed to the autonomy of art. Abstraction expresses realities that are hidden, and Yap's art and poetry do not replicate what is visible in the world, avoiding the imitative or figurative. His work is more interested in the rhythms of perception, the poetics of process and becoming, the syntax of making and creating, the grammar of composition. By eschewing the merely imitative function of art, Yap creates what Klee calls "poetic painting" (quoted in Aichele 2006, p. 65), which, because it is not bound to observable reality, is endlessly resonant in lyric and symbolic possibilities. His poetry, though considerably more mimetic, shares the same propensity towards abstraction, challenging interpretative efforts and resisting pressures to conform to socio-political agenda. Both Yap's poetry and art push the boundaries and are relentlessly open-ended, committed to a process of becoming rather than a definite state of being. Yap explains his experimental poetics in these terms: "The danger for an artist is to do only one thing and in a way it is good, as an individual style takes time to develop. On the other hand, I do not see myself painting just circles for 20 years" (*New Nation*, 2 September 1977). Abstraction means taking risks, embracing what Yap calls "the accidental / to make it come more fully to life" (*Space*, p. 37). Yap's abstract aesthetics is indebted to Klee (1968), who underscores the importance of "the accidental" (p. 185) in drawing, and to Mark Rothko, another palpable influence on Yap, who sees art as an "adventure into an unknown world, which can be explored only by those willing to take risks" (Gottlieb and Rothko 1968, p. 545).

FIGURATIVE TO ABSTRACT

Mark Rothko shrugs off the label of being "abstractionist" and says of his style: "I do not believe that there was ever a question of being abstract or representational. It is really a matter of ending this silence and solitude, of breathing, and stretching one's arms again" (Gottlieb and Rothko 1968, p. 549). Resolutely refusing to be straitjacketed as an abstract painter, Yap declares that "the line between representational and abstract art is at best thin" (*New Nation*, 2 September 1977). For him, abstraction is not simply an antithesis to the figurative or representational. Yap's art and poetry thrive in the liminal zone between the abstract and the figurative. In *Untitled No. 3*, the tree is on the verge of being metamorphosed into an abstract vertical line that binds the lower bands of earth and the horizontal blocks of landscape and sky. It is one of Yap's few landscape paintings where nature still retains a recognizable form, but only just. The painting fixes a threshold moment, when the figurative is on the verge of transformation into the abstract (see Plate 1). There are no human traces here, and the movement towards abstraction demands that they be kept out. In a poem entitled "landscapes" Yap observes wryly:

> a few trees do not add up to a landscape:
> the sparse foreground needs a few children
> running & chasing each other. one or two

> background isolates touch puffy clouds
> & drain all attention into vague blue.
> 					(*Commonplace* 1977, p. 44)

Though Yap adamantly refutes any connection between his paintings and poems, there are poems that enact the compositional process and engage with aesthetic problems encountered on the canvas. Although the poem "landscapes" is discrete from *Untitled No. 3*, it describes the underpinning philosophy and tension of the painting. It points towards that which is absent, and which is the counterpoint to abstraction — human presence, and in doing so makes that absence a latent part of the landscape. The lack of human figures in the foreground implies a paring back and flattening out of the painting. Yap seems to subscribe to Gottlieb and Rothko's (1968) credo: "We favor the simple expression of the complex thought. We are for the large shape because it has the impact of the unequivocal. We wish to reassert the picture plane. We are for flat forms because they destroy illusion and reveal truth" (p. 545). In resisting the anthropomorphizing of landscape and stripping the picture of extraneous detail, Yap keeps his painting hovering between dimensions, between formal and free, the figurative and abstract. What is foregrounded is the form of the tree, unifying the different planes through its vertical movement.

Both "landscape" and *Untitled No. 3* underscore the process of becoming rather than a state of being; they are tentative statements, sketches or studies that reflect the contingent nature of reality as much as the fluidity of aesthetic perception. A poem from *Down the Line*, "nature study", also comments on the pictorial concerns:

> take away the seeming branches & the real
> you have a trunk that is bidirectional.
> growing upwards, falling downwards
> (confusion).
> you have a trunk that is bilocational,
> pointing to lichfield rd and serangoon garden.
> you have workers acting as if swearing
> were a concrete object they've patented.
> the trunk, moved in installments,
> may come partly to you.
> the frame around the picture
> of trees & idyllic nature,
> of trees & more trees,

of trees & sky.
there is still a choice.
> (*Down the Line*, 1980, p. 41)

The spatial markers "bidirectional" and "bilocational" delineate a threshold moment before the human and figurative become translated into the abstract. It is a visual process or "a form of image-making which is committed to the deletion or erasure of the depicted object at the exact moment when depiction takes place" (Bryson 1995, p. 59). The poem could well be a verbal mirror to the painting used for the cover of *Commonplace* (see Plate 2). The painting is a spatial field that is not just a representation of experience but rather *is* experience itself. It is in this experiential space where Yap ponders compositional principles and possibilities. The painting is a textual map of almost-erased referents, with the ghostly traces of the tree and rocks providing tenuous links between the figurative and the abstract, the visible and invisible. Yap's poetry reveals the same impulse towards abstraction that governs his art. Even when they are grounded in experiential context, the poems shrug off circumstantial and narrative detail and aspire towards abstract lyricism or lyric abstraction. Wallace Stevens' (1951) observation helps illuminate the dominant impulse in Yap's work:

> While one thinks about poetry as one thinks about painting, the momentum toward abstraction exerts greater force on the poet than on the painter. I imagine that the tendency of all thinking is toward the abstract and perhaps I am merely saying that the abstractions of the poet are abstracter than the abstractions of the painter. (p. 601)

TAKING THE LINE FOR A WALK

The key abstract motif that informs Yap's art and poetry is the line, which enacts the liminal mode and moment in Yap's work. The line mediates between the lyric and the narrative, the visual and the verbal, language and silence, the painter-poet observer from the observed, creating a poetic mood of ambiguity and ambivalence. The title poem of *Only Lines* announces the linear motif:

> should i also add:
> here are only lines
> linked by the same old story.

> the same basic plot
> in which they are grown
>
> should add
> little doubt the field is only green
> the sky the same old blue
> in the presence of my eyes,
> your preference
> (though not mine)
> should see for your own eyes
> and if you can laugh
> care with some concern
> it is because (like me)
> you need lines
> to add up this same old story.
>   (*The Space of City Trees*, hereafter *Space*, 2000, p. 3)

The line connects objects or images in a linear movement, creating a pictorial and lyric image in search of its subject. Its improvisatory nature inscribes a liminal space where reader and poet meet, and where the figurative and abstract become wedded. This linear projection is akin to the movement in the untitled painting in Plate 3, where the blue, red, and light grey shapes in the bottom section ascend from an inky foreground, drawn up and backwards into the receding plane by a tenuous line that rides out to the lineaments of coastal cliffs and the hovering band of sea.

The alignment of the shapes and colours illuminates a littoral or coastal landscape that litters Yap's work, suggestive of the island nation bounded by water, its margins eroded, erased, and re-inscribed, reconstituted by land reclamation. Yap's recurrent evocations of the littoral, in his paintings and poems, secrete a critique of Singapore's frantic efforts to remake itself. The poem "& the tide" maps this shifting littoral and reflects the nation-state's uncertain shape and identity:

> & the tide which is being urban-renewed
> at bedok must go on its own tidy ways
> without too much of a fuss
> ...
> & the sum of their margin:
> a littoral of slightly raised sand
> & carefully arrayed litter.
>   (*Commonplace*, p. 39)

Such a state project like land reclamation would have received a more celebratory treatment in the hands of Thumboo. Rather than valorize the city-state's control over nature and its own destiny, Yap's understated deadpan irony stakes out a liminal and ambiguous border zone where nationalist poetic is subverted and the nation's agenda and identity are subject to scrutiny. Like the painting in Plate 3, the poem follows a vertical format that enhances the liminality; the ampersand, the elliptical beginning, the jagged rhythm and syntax mime the uncertain outline of the littoral and undermine the certitude of nationalist politics and poetics.

Yap's use of the line can be traced to the work of German painter Paul Klee (1968), who asserts that "[a] tendency toward the abstract is inherent in linear expression" (p. 182). This tendency can also be seen in Yap's use of vibrant colours and the liminal play between the abstract and concrete. Klee's description of his own art as taking the line for a walk endorses an improvisatory approach that is open to chance and experiment (pp. 182–83). For Klee, the line is not so much a continuous graphic movement as something more errant and unpredictable, a metonymic gesture that delineates the in-between spaces, and which gestures towards invisible or latent realities. When the line is more implied rather than drawn, as in the painting in Plate 3, it comments on the images that it limns and the alignment of objects that makes the line possible in the first place. Thus the receding line vertically slices the landscape into two, while the horizontal line pegs out the sea and sky in the top part of the composition. Together they generate tension and a liminal state where nothing is fixed or certain. Often, Yap's line bisects the canvas into an upper and lower zone, in a way reminiscent of Klee and Rothko. The line creates a counterpoint, with the often brighter, lighter colours and rising shapes in the upper half orchestrating an upward movement while the lower zone with more sombre tones and heavier shapes holds it in check. At the same time, the line suggests a horizon and is thus a reminder of the landscape that the painting refers to. In *Untitled* (see Plate 4), the line is implied rather than drawn, fleshed out where the red and blue panels meet, and the allusion to a horizon and landscape is unmistakable. A clearly outlined circle floats above, drawn in a continuous green brushstroke wrapped by a red line to evoke either the sun, moon, or the *ensō*, the Zen circle, "usually depicted in a single brushstroke" that embodies "the all, the void, and enlightenment itself" (Addis 1989, p. 12). In its vertical format divided into an upper and lower zone, and in the contrast between the near monochromatic upper band and the fluid, indeterminate shapes smudged in the lower half, the composition has strong echoes of signature works by American painter Mark Rothko. Its equilibrium is tenuous and ambiguous: the red could be in the ascendant or the blue could be construed as rising and inexorably drowning out the red. In its ineffability and liminality, it is a tacit affirmation of Rothko's famous dictum, "[s]ilence is so accurate" (quoted in Breslin 1993, p. 387).

The line traces a liminal moment where binaries are held in fleeting equipoise. In *Untitled* (see Plate 5) the black line cuts the canvas into two and creates a tonic and thematic tension. The linear movement of the black and white bands, which resemble a road, in the bottom half is a counterweight to the vertical smudged bands of varied sienna, grey, blue, and the eloquently white circle with smudged outline. The ascending motifs are pegged to the horizontal bands, the luminous white of the circle echoing the white of the linear bands. The round or ovoid shape is a recurrent motif in Yap's work, as it is in Klee's, whose 1915 *Moonrise at St Germain* Yap's painting faintly echoes. The underlying chord of Yap's paintings is essentially tragic, resonating with intimations of death, but there is the counterpoint of wit, irony, playfulness, sensuality, and a subdued joy, ingredients that Rothko, in his 1959 Pratt Lecture, lists as being vital to great art (Borchardt-Hume 2008, p. 91). There is also what Rothko calls "an inner light" (p. 91), a serene glow that comes from the use of contrasts, chromatics, and glazed tones. The painting in Plate 4 achieves this by playing the cadmium red against a transparent cobalt blue, and arraying the hard outline of the *ensō* against the fluid shapes below, generating a luminosity that is contingent and fleeting. The painting in Plate 5 features an ochre glaze that has been scraped back to reveal the underpinning white and blue, creating a subdued glow that seems to come from within and which aspires towards the white halo. Enhancing this light is a playful dark ochre line that slices the inky blotch in the centre-right of the picture, a tenuous thread connecting the ascending movement to the gravitas of the solid bands at the bottom. Rothko's influence is also evident in the division of the painting in upper and lower panels, and in the deployment of soft-edged shapes. Another Rothko influence is the ragged gray seam at the top of the painting. This is one of Rothko's signatures, a ragged band or border that hovers near the top edge of the painting and opens the composition up to ambivalence. In Yap's painting, the grey strip blends the black and white of the road-like bands below, its soft tone and spectral form contrasting with their hard edges. As Yap himself observes, "[h]ard edges are too limiting up to a point. Square and triangles are just too programmed. Soft edges are more flexible to work with and how the picture develops is less predictable. There is, therefore, more ways in which soft forms can develop" (*New Nation*, 15 June 1974). The soft edges temper the linear definition, creating gaps, breaks, fluid areas that induce ambiguity and uncertainty, creating open-endedness and resistance to closure that is a trademark of his poetry.

In Yap's poetry, the linear motif also sets up contrasts thematically and structurally. In "open road" the figure of the road and its linear movement echo the road-like image in Plate 5, splitting the landscape in two — between the sky that "looms, quick capricious illusion" and the cyclist halting "at the sightless road" (*Space*, p. 38). It is an unresolved moment, its ambivalence underscored by the absence of the period at the end of the last line: "the road slices through two lives / which are the quick and mainly, the quicker" (p. 38). This refusal to frame the moment, letting it elide into something beyond the textual boundary, is replicated in Yap's paintings by the liminal motifs and also by Yap's preference to paint up to the tacking edges of the canvas. This, and the fact the paintings are unvarnished and unframed, accentuate the liminality, leaving both the surface and edges "open". Both practices can be traced to Rothko, who painted the tacking edges and exhibited his canvasses unframed so that the paintings overflow and fuse with the wall, extending its reach to embrace the viewer (Mancusi-Ungaro 1998, pp. 290–91). This enhances the paintings' immediacy and expansiveness. In a poem entitled "conceptual art" Yap underscores the resonance of this style of painting that overflows the limits of the frame:

conceptual art

is enough

when a picture is removed
the patch of wall it clung to
shows a contrasted freshness, exactly
the size of the picture.

the resulting afterimage,
to be sure, is precise,
is exact, is clear.
to be sure, it effloresces,

> is out of tone with wall,
> is, strangely, too loud.
>
> is,
> too, enough.
>
> (*Commonplace*, p. 41)

The poem is one of many in Yap's poetic oeuvre that transfers aesthetic concepts, compositional or structural principles relating to painting into the typographical and semantic spaces of the poem. Its title flows on to the first line, enacting a threshold moment and a liminal gesture that erases the visual or printed frame and frees the painting into dialogic interaction with unbounded space and with the viewer. In its typographical miming of the idea, Yap's poem approximates the fusion of form and content in concrete poetry.

Yap's linear motif, while foregrounding the binaries of absence/presence, also unsettles them. In "dramatis personae" the speaker announces: "we're variations of the line". The linear motif continues: "we in public are private figures / humanizing the landscape" (*Space*, p. 27). What underwrites these binaries are a dialectical tension between the abstract and the representational and in-between space where the two merge or coexist: "where does the road end and the beach begin?" The triptych explores the dialectic between public and private, self and communal, a pervasive theme in Yap's work. In the last poem, the public pond fuses the earth and water elements of the preceding lyrics and also conflates the human and the non-human as the "you" of the poem becomes "a still pond" that is "too abstract". The three settings are liminal spaces where the private and the public intersect, where the individual and the community border on each other, but the opposition, as Brewster (1986) notes, "remains unresolved" (p. 32).

The eponymous poem of *down the line* extends the linear meditation on perception, space and art. It is a process poem, enacting the movement of the aesthetic eye, conducting a reflexive enquiry into the nature of perception:

> call is what we will, it is liquid graphics,
> neither statistics nor logistics can propel,
> for its basis well under the skin has yet another
> lined in rubrics & this, then, is palpable
> & lends the eye whatever enchantment it wishes.

> it will enchant with the cool young shadows
> the sun, climbing vertically down windows,
> leaves behind. it will enchant in it repose
> by moving, shifting to the centre of its axiom,
> in its layering of reality & in imparting
> the sum of its being; every part, every space
> larger & more real than the entirety.
>
> (Space, p. 77)

The line wanders, the eye wonders, refusing to settle on any object as a focal point. The poem's linear trajectory and the shifting and layered perspective replicate an empirical seeing that resembles Klee's (1968) aesthetics: "The pictorial work was born of movement, is itself recorded movement, and is assimilated through movement (eye muscles)" (p. 185). Like "dramatis personae", the poem locates a liminal and contingent world, the "liquid graphics" tracing a world of shifting forms, "at the water's edge a library of margins" (*Space*, p. 78). In its "layering of reality" and seeing "every part, every space / larger & more real than the entirety" it adumbrates a theory and practice of seeing that is very close to the Cubist approach of French painter Robert Delaunay (1968):

> Seeing is in itself a movement. Vision is the true creative rhythm. Discerning the quality of rhythms is a movement, and the essential quality of painting is representation — the movement of vision which functions in objectivizing itself toward reality. That is the essential of art, and its greatest profoundness. (p. 317)

While Yap's work is largely muted in cadence, it enacts the experience of perception itself, the act of seeing and reading words and images, through syntactical and grammatical shifts, wordplay and the omission of punctuation, and through the lower-case line and sentence beginnings. All these combine to create a metonymic mode that generates a spatial poetics that in turn destabilizes perspective and image.

WINDOWS

While the linear motif in Yap's painting and poetry generates the binary distinction between the observer and observed, landscape and its representation, language and silence, the fluid and unpredictable trajectory of the line suggests that the boundary between these sets of binary terms is shifting and permeable. The line connects and conjugates images that are fragmented and seemingly unrelated, but at the same time it reveals disjunctive, ambivalent relationships in the field of objects. This results in a complex, almost Cubist process of seeing in which both the experience of perception and linear perspective itself is distorted and literally re-visioned. Running through Yap's poetry and art is a meditative play with perspective, a sustained meditation on the aesthetics of perception and poetics of composition. The line is often extended into the image of the window to frame the moment of perception, the moment when a composition of objects triggers a moment of aesthetic and poetic recognition.

Windows abound in Yap's art and poetry. As Brewster (1986) notes, "many of [Yap's] scenes are framed by a window" (p. xvi). Windows are conduits to the world outside; at the same time they reinforce the division between the observer and the observed, the poet and his subject, the painter and pictorial field. They contain moments of perception, providing a pictorial frame for both the interior objects and what is outside; they also refract the external image and light into a perceived image. In Yap's poem "precedence" the window refracts the outside image: "the sky will tremble with stored storms / that seen across the window will be / rain hanging over the road ..." (*Space*, p. 14). The window is a medium that translates looking into seeing. In "it rains today", the poet sits in his room while

> the trees in front of him
> exist for every rain
> and every rain
> outside my window
> comes before my gaze
> becomes this familiarity
> i always see.
> (*Space*, p. 15).

In "sunny day" "sunny day / comes through the window / and sits on the table" (*Space*, p. 5) while in "Sunday" the speaker watches "the day / with the morning / opening my window-sill" (*Space*, p. 20). In "june morning", the implied window acts as a compositional frame, a mediator between that which is outside and the artist-writer speaker who muses: "this scene is also very brittle, / copes with the problem of the accidental / to make it come more fully to life" and "it is you who structure this scenery" (*Space*, p. 37). The window in these poems foregrounds both conceptual and perceptual themes. It captures the moment of perception when the images resolve into a composition.

In "down the line" windows reflect rather than refract, performing an architectonic function: "the sun, climbing vertically down windows" outlines a shifting urban landscape "in its layering of reality & in imparting / the sum of its being" (*Space*, p. 77). Here, again, Paul Klee's aesthetics may have inspired Yap's use of the window as a thematic and structural motif. Klee, Kathryn Aichele (2006) tells us, was influenced by Robert Delaunay's *Window* series and his "multifaceted concept of simultaneity" (p. 101). In Klee's paintings, the window "functions as both an architectural motif and a pictorial metonym that signifies a new way of looking at the external world" (Aichele 2006, p. 101). In *View from a Window*, Klee subverts the traditional landscape painting by framing and refracting the exterior landscape and marking the window curtain with repeated weave patterns and window-like motifs, resulting in a conflation of "interior and exterior points of view" (Aichele, p. 102).

In *Commonplace*, Yap also deploys the window motif in a patterned repetition to connect the verbal and visual. It is a collection where Yap the painter and poet are reconciled, and where the relationship between painting and poetry is at its most reciprocal, not only through the inclusion of Yap's *black & white* paintings, but also through leitmotifs that unite both the poetry and art. Although Yap eschews any direct link between his poems and paintings in this collection, we should not construe this statement at face value as Yap takes pains to avoid a merely illustrative role for the paintings, which are connected to the poems at deeper structural and thematic levels. It is a multimedia practice that juxtaposes the visual and verbal in a rhythmic pattern, letting the common motifs resonate and bind the poems and paintings in a lyric sequence or suite.

The arrangement and typographical layout of the poems and paintings reveal a carefully considered compositional structure: the opening series of ten poems is succeeded by four paintings, followed by a block of fourteen poems and another group of four paintings, and then another suite of fourteen poems, with a last group of seven poems bringing up the rear. There is a meticulous internal logic to this numerical arrangement of poems and paintings: the four blocks of poetry and three suites of paintings add up to seven, which is the number of poems in the last group. This intricate numerical patterning contributes to the sense of patterned repetitions that inform the paintings and poems and weave them into a rhythmic whole, belying Yap's avowal that there is no link between them. Thematically, the first group of poems is playful, surreal, satiric, not grounded in identifiable locales. The second group, containing the central poems in the collection, is located in England, where Yap studied linguistics in 1975 at Leeds University. The third contingent returns to Singapore and offers the much-quoted poem "there is no future in nostalgia", while the last group takes up the playful and speculative note of the first group, albeit more grounded in identifiably Singaporean contexts.

At the heart of the patterned repetitions is the figurative motif of the window. "things", with its visual layout, comes close to being concrete poetry in half-mirroring the window frame:

> chair
> wall
> window
> desk
> bed
>
> chair makes us fat, upholstered in blubber.
> long shot: wall. no one has ever succeeded
> in being hung up like a portrait, truly dead.
> medium shot: window. open it.
> let the sun in, let suicide out.
> before hitting the ground, frame it in slow motion.
> reverse repeat, pan it back to window, its source.
>
> (*Commonplace*, p. 60)

The poem, in its minimalist way, captures the thingness of things. Concrete nouns are deployed to fill the textual space with images that compose an interior picture. Yap is imagistic in his practice here, heeding the injunction of the American modernist poet William Carlos Williams (1983) that there are "no ideas but in things" (p. 133). The four nouns, unadorned with adjectives and each comprising a monosyllabic line, are physical reference points for the pictorial frame, but what makes them cohere into a composition is the window, their "source". It is a medium that illuminates the interior space and turns it into a tableau. The shifting light ensures that the perspective is splintered, multilayered and fluid.

While the window in "things" contains and composes an interior pictorial space, the window in "absolute" mediates between outer and inner spaces:

> morning is already late
> in rounding the corner of living,
> windowpanes of tiny raindrops
> cling uncertainly, left from night rain.
>
> strange you are asleep,
> often waking so early
> to see the leaves weave
> skeins of cool air between trees
> at the corner of these buildings.
> i think I'll get this in a picture,
> hang it on a nail
> & set the sky within its frame.
>
> <div align="right">(<i>Commonplace</i>, p. 47)</div>

The window articulates a poetics of seeing; it creates a pictorial frame and also acts as a medium through which the image is refracted. It is the conduit between inner and outer spaces, between the observer and the scene. Spatiality, however, is unsettled here by the demonstrative pronoun "this", with its ambiguous antecedent. This poem may be read as a curious aubade — a poem in praise of dawn's arrival — that also converts time into spatial terms, slowing perception down to discrete units or frames of apprehension that capture the phenomenology of perception.

The most effective use of the window motif occurs in one of the poems based on Yap's Leeds sojourn. "north hill road, leeds" offers an oblique self-portraiture:

> i'm already in my room
> wallpapered with a few numbed thoughts;
> all the books piled high on the shelf
> make me think only of hot coffee.
> looking out of the window, i see myself
> walking up the road, down the steps:
>
> this image i seem to see continually
> as if it demands a profile
> now that i'm longer there.
>
> <div align="right">(<i>Commonplace</i>, p. 20)</div>

The detached observer is a recurrent figure in Yap's work. Travelling through foreign landscapes and cultures, the persona is insulated, withdrawn, inspecting the landscape without involvement. This alienation of observer from the observed continues in *Commonplace*, which introduces a few rare autobiographical moments in Leeds. It is a stark moment, when the sense of separation of the self from its context, of the self from itself is made visually palpable. The window frames not only the wintry landscape but the lonely figure of the poet at the window; the liminal moment divides the interior from outside, the observer from the observed, and self from other. It is a moment when the self is on the point of being erased even as it perceives its existential space.

This sense of existential disconnection and alienation is also tangible in "new year '75 leeds". After a meal with a "Vietnamese friend", and a flashback to an earlier moment when they "had been to the plaza where x-rated films / are lined up each week, cheek by jowl …" (*Commonplace*, p. 21), the poet again returns to his room, to a sense of loneliness and transience. Instead of the festive spirit and the celebratory meal with the friend, the poem gives a cursory tour of the Leeds cityscape; places are named without affection or attachment, reinforcing the liminal status of the poet-outsider:

> all somewhat remotely outlined in a thin swirling snow.
> his hostel first, half a mile more for me:
> everything behind were already soft-focal —
> snow, steaming noodles, celluloid close-ups,
> & night's myopia. next day. next year.
>
> (*Commonplace*, p. 21)

Again a sense of absence closes the poem, with the snow and the cinematic dissolve erasing the memory in the preceding lines. The "soft-focal images" echo the book's paintings, enhancing the mood of loneliness and the elements of ambiguity and ambivalence.

The same bleak isolation and absence is mirrored by a corresponding window motif of the *black & white* paintings that alternate with the poetic texts. The series is probably indebted to Rothko's black on gray painting of 1969. Rothko's last paintings are unrelentingly stark, stripped to the bone, using "a dialectical method" in imposing a dark panel over a lighter lower panel, placing "an enormous weight on the reduced means" to convey the sense of desolation and despair that culminated in Rothko's death in 1970 (Novak and O'Doherty 1998, pp. 280–81). Yap's series is nothing as bleak, but the black and white register and the gray gradations between mirror the loneliness and alienation Yap felt in Leeds: "It was winter and the scenery was very drab, yet somehow captivating. And that's when I sort of decided to experiment with these two colours" (*New Nation*, 6 December 1975). While Rothko has all but extinguished all colours and forms to just two empty panels of black over gray, Yap plays with the rhythmic repetition of shapes and contrasts hard lines and blurred shapes. There is also the window, if not clear outlined by distinctly painted borders, then implied by the vertical format and the views of the landscape framed.

The series yields predominantly bleak prospects, the moody and monotonous atmosphere reinforced by the duotones, the "soft-focal" wash, and repeated motifs and rhythms. In *No. 1* a strongly articulated white window is imposed on a landscape (see Plate 6). Resting on its side in the lower half of the window is what resembles a capital E. With its sharp black outlines the vertical columns and horizontal strip are foregrounded; they are suggestive of a cityscape. On the receding plane are blurred forms suggesting distant hills and open spaces while in the upper panel float grey clouds and a big white space containing three blurred triangles, whose shapes answer the hills at the bottom and whose number corresponds to that of the vertical urban columns. All the elements of structure and pattern are arranged and scaled to create a unitary image that is like a window into the psychic landscape darkened by the desolate Leeds winter. The painting could very well be a visual representation of "north hill road, leeds". The window frames the landscape outside as much as the lonely subject who recognizes his image in the same moment that it is being effaced. The motifs in *No. 1* are repeated in the series, most clearly in *No. 15*, where the E motif in the lower panel is duplicated on a smaller scale in the upper panel (see Plate 7). The repetition, in this and many of the others in the series, suggests a poetic rhythm and also underscores a self-reflexive instinct at work in both Yap's art and poetry, a postmodern double-take and bifocal vision, an awareness that our perceptions of the world and ourselves are at best tentative and contingent.

Yap is careful to avoid any obvious links between the paintings and window but *No. 12* seems to indicate otherwise (see Plate 8). With its patterned and varied repetition of what looks like Greek or Japanese Noh theatre masks, its placement next to the poem "another look" invites a comparative reading. The poem can be considered ekphrastic in an indirect and distant way. It carries an epigraph from perhaps the most famous ekphrastic poem of the twentieth-century, W.H. Auden's "Musée de Beaux Arts," inspired by Brueghel's *The Fall of Icarus, No. 12*, with its abstract faces, offers a range of human responses to the idea of suffering broached in Auden's and Yap's poems. The vertical rhythm of the painting, ordained by the two upright columns that split the painting into a triptych, is mirrored in the poem's "up and down" direction. Together the three panels form a visualization of the poem's "sectorial suffering":

> how an adaptation
> between canvas & the hand:
> an old masterly breath
> dispensed sectorial suffering.
> here, where it all is going on
> is not the locus; but further
> up or down are the spatial reactions
> for surprise or sadness.
>
> *(Commonplace*, p. 50)

The painting's palette of expressions embodies the poem's "spatial reactions" and underscores the fluidity and range of human emotions. With its "catalogue-listing" and "contemporaneous occurrence", mirrored in the painting by the rhythmic arrangement of the motifs, the poem pays homage to Auden and Brueghel; at the same time, it broaches the idea of simultaneity that informs Auden's poem and Brueghel's painting. The multiple images of *No. 12* point to a multifocal and multifaceted process of seeing and artistic vision that can take in a variety of impressions and experiences related to a single theme.

The patterned repetition also recalls Paul Klee's pictographic paintings. In examining how Klee sought to reconcile the pictorial and poetic through architectonic means, Aichele (2006) observes that Klee casts figurative motifs in linear patterns so that "the visual signs are repeated in structural rhythms that are not unlike the sound and metric patterns of poetry" (p. 125). Klee strove "to reconcile architectonic and poetic painting, or at least to establish a harmony between them" (p. 122). The architectonic and structural rhythms of the paintings make them poetic. Likewise, Yap's patterned repetitions in the *black & white* series approximate the lyric cadence of the poems. They are not there as illustrations, but comment on and interact with the poems in a heuristic and aesthetic exploration of the liminal zone between the verbal and visual, between the artistic process and lyrical perception.

ZEN AND THE ART OF THE COMMONPLACE

The opening poem of *Commonplace*, "black and white", announces the visual syntax and theme and is an exercise in defamiliarization, turning a road accident into an arresting tableau: "… black and white dissolve / into grey. traditional chinese painters adduce 7 greys, / 7 grey days a week. 7 dead zebras" (p. 1). The greys announce the visual chromatics of the collection, while the surreal juxtaposition of disparate objects unsettles our assumptions about everyday scenes and objects. Yap's poetry has been praised for the way it endows the everyday with artistic significance; housing estates, conversation between housewives, and various other bits and pieces of daily life are captured with wry humour. His is the art of the quotidian that captures the intractable reality of each object and phenomenon. The title poem of *Commonplace* is the closest Yap comes to announcing his artistic credo:

> & I should never whip the commonplace
> for the meaning of its opposite,
> especially at daybreak, with blue
> shadows to protract into a shadowless noon.
> 2 o'clock: 2 stained blobs on a clear canvas,
> 3 o'clock: 3 fingers tapping a tattoo on the table
> are 3 upwind gulls, sliding, side to side,
> wings hung out still.
>
> (p. 29)

Things are seen for what they are, in all their irreducible thingness, variety, and alterity. It is an art rooted in the quotidian, but there is also the proclivity to abstraction, as signalled by the "blue shadows" and "blobs on a clear canvas". Abstraction, in Yap's work, is not a diminishment or erasure of the particulars, but paradoxically heightens the materiality of experience and the complex substance of rationality and affect that makes up each object and mood. Rothko declares: "I adhere to the material reality of the world and the substance of the things" (López-Remiro 2006, p. 45). It is a credo that Yap endorses, who, like Rothko, sees continuum rather than opposition between the abstract and the representational styles of painting and poetry.

A certain number of Yap's poems fix their attention on the everyday and at the same time identify themselves in aesthetic terms, making overt links between Yap's visual art and poetry. These are the still-life poems that sit unnoticed in each collection like "almost still life" and "things" until they culminate in a salient sequence in *Man Snake Apple*. Yap never painted any still lifes but these verbal approximations of a visual genre come close to the proportions and conditions of a still life. In these poems Yap reinforces the analogy and connections between painting and poetry through the still life both as subject and metaphor. These poems are exercises in composition; they demonstrate the artistic eye at work, seeing and capturing a field of objects or human action and conveying them into a pictorial space. In miming the process of construction and presentation, the poems elide the distinction between the verbal and visual, poetry and painting, and reveal the artistic consciousness as much as the tableau. Wallace Stevens (1951) is again instructive here: "The selection of composition as a denominator of poetry and painting is the selection of a technical characteristic by a man whose center was painting, even granting that he was not a man whom one thinks of as a technician. Poetry and painting alike create through composition" (p. 163).

Yap's poetic rendering of the genre points to his affiliations with the Modernists. Paul Cézanne, Juan Gris, and Georges Braque all liberated the still life from its merely mimetic role and made "the genre so central in the development of modernism" (Bryson 1995, p. 81). Classical still life places seemingly trivial everyday objects at the centre of the painting. The tableau of objects is transfigured by artistic attention, each object captured in its arresting particularity and in its conjunctive arrangement with other objects. What Modernists, or more precisely the Cubists, have done is to destabilize the still-life cliché and introduce into its tableau fractured planes, dislodging the idea of stillness with movement of perception. Yap's still life, while obeying the strictures of a miniature, further subverts the convention. First, it is transposed from domestic interior to outdoor space. Traditional still life abolishes distance and the vanishing point and creates closeness and intimacy; in contrast, Yap, by displacing the still life from its interior anchor, restores the vanishing point. Furthermore, it is not inanimate objects that take centre stage in the poems but the human figure, which Yap keeps out of his paintings. In "still life: woman with birds at Richmond" the still life is wrenched from its interior space:

> no one could, of course, mistake her
> for a pigeon; the many flying about
> do not mistake her for a tree, a large tidbit:
> imperfect composition.

> she sits in full sunlit river breeze
> heavily sinking in her plastic bucket-chair,
> pigeons fly at the command of her hand
> -thrown bits of rock-buns the café sells
> & hardly anybody ever eats.
> whirr of wings, grey in harsh sunlight,
> dazzlingly white in postcards.
> the woman's stillness & toothy smile:
> one composition.
>
> (*Commonplace*, p. 19)

The *mise-en-scène* begins with an almost surreal image, evoking the compositional process, the artist's eye exploring Cubist perspectives. In describing Cezanne's still lifes, Norman Bryson (1995) observes how "[e]ach stroke is saturated with self-reflexive attention, so that what is presented in the end is not the objects but the consciousness that builds their (re)presentation" (p. 82). Here, in Yap's poem, each line offers a different possibility, an aesthetic option that could yield a different perspective and composition. For a still life, it is anything but still; however, the movement is captured and reconciled with stillness of the composition. In a typical metonymic operation, the composite figure of the woman in the chair is reduced to the fragments of the last four lines. The binaries of stillness and motion, lyric and narrative, human and non-human, are held in balance, in "one composition".

Still life is perhaps the most reticent of all painting genres and it is most congruent with Yap's temperament. Still life's deliberate arrangement of objects, its visual containment and miniature scale are of a piece with Yap's reticence and understatement, his predilection for what is small and overlooked. Yap's poems have always leaned towards the tableau or what Susan Stewart (1993) calls "the miniature" that "always tends towards the *tableau* rather than narrative, towards silence and spatial boundaries rather than towards expository closure" (p. 66, Stewart's italics). With its avoidance of the autobiographical and narrative, and its preference for the metonymic listing and the signature use of lower-case sentence beginnings, Yap's poems offer miniatures of stillness and silence abstracted from the grand narrative and muscular symbols of nationalist politics. Stillness and silence are the values that have informed Yap's work from the beginning; they are foregrounded in his last collection, *Man Snake Apple*, not just in the still-life series but also in the Japanese poems where Yap's art and poetry fuse. In these travel poems, inspired by a visit to Japan and his friendship with Miyuki Nagaoka, Yap's liminality and spirituality discover an aesthetic framework where the poet and painter become one.

The first poem in the still-life sequence, "still-life I", presents the possibilities of a human portrait and in so doing outlines an ontology or an explanation of the substance of the art of painting:

> if she sits out in the garden, she's a pile of leaves
> with a face. sunk in an armchair, it has an extra pair
> of arms, gaunt. day in, day out, she's an arrangement
> with different settings. a crab near the kitchen table,
> a photograph of a head above a brown dress.
>
> (*Man Snake Apple*, p. 3)

In *Man Snake Apple*, Yap is being a painter and poet at once, unravelling the twinned processes of painting and poetry, suggesting how the arrangement of the subject through word and image can result in a composition that stands outside of historical time:

> brooding silence filled with enigma & wonder;
> nothing to threaten her now, this pile of leaves.
> nothing to threaten now,
> nothing to threaten now.
>
> (p. 3)

The end of both poetry and painting is to arrive at this Zen-like stillness, a lyric calm freed from narrative tension. The last poem in the sequence reiterates and affirms this still point: "the rain the shower, the sun a hot towel. / the tiled pate on top knows all, holds all / to an entire point" (p. 9).

This point of stillness and calm is central to the collection and the Zen spirit that pervades it. From Yap's earliest poems, the Zen elements are discernible: the attentiveness to the mundane and "commonplace"; the sensory contemplation of things or objects; the haiku-like concentration of image; the motif of the line; the minimalist spareness, and the simplicity of form and diction; the restraint and understatement; and the liminal interplay between poetry and painting, the rational and the intuitive, time and space, and language and silence. The fundamental Zen concept of negation, emptiness, silence and stillness can be found in the poem "words" from *Commonplace*:

> words have sometimes a way of stilling themselves
> & then, no, we have a way of stilling words
> in a way to still ourselves:
> a choice of being still
> & quiet to be still.
>
> *(Space,* p. 92)

Within the Zen framework Yap's art of the commonplace arrives at its apotheosis. In his foreword to *Commonplace* Ee Thiang Hong comments on Yap's affinity with "the Chinese tradition":

> There the picture and the poem inscribed on it reinforce the mood of each other and both are integral to the total visual effect that at the most abstract level is to be seen in calligraphy. Within the poems themselves the posture is that of the traditional Chinese painter whose real concern is the essence of things manifest in mood and rhythm, not things themselves, which essence is to be abstracted through contemplation, "undisturbed analysis." (p. xi)

Ee's observation is accurate with respect to many of Yap's poems and is applicable also to his paintings. Indeed, the only truly ekphrastic poem in Yap's oeuvre, "a scroll painting", supports Ee's comment. It does not name its referent, which is the painting that inspired it, but reproduces the image with the economy of strokes that characterizes Chinese ink painting:

> the mountains are hazy with timeless passivity
> sprawling monotonously in the left-hand corner
> while clouds diffuse and fill the entire top half
> before bumping daintily into a bright red parakeet
> perched suicide-like on a beautifully gnarled branch
> arched by the weight of fruit and one ripe peach
> hung a motionless inch from the gaping beak
>
> here is transient beauty
> caught in permanence
> but of what avail is such perpetual unattainment?
>
> i know the stupid bird can never eat the stupid peach
>
> *(Space,* p. 21)

The reconciliation of motion and stasis, echoing John Keats's "Ode to a Grecian Urn", the telescoping of foreground and background, intimacy and distance, testify to the Taoist spirit that governs classical Chinese landscape painting. However, the last line, with its deconstructive and irreverent humour, is more Zen than Tao. Yap's restrained, ascetic, but playful imagination has more affinities with Zen than Chinese art, as the poems in *Man Snake Apple* reveal. Here Yap's focus falls on things themselves, rather than try to distill their essence. The collection is strewn with lists of things, objects named and collected like Cornell boxes, and imbued with a Zen spirit. There is a spiritualization of Yap's art of the quotidian here, his vision attaining a Zen-like concentration.

The poem "a list of things", recording a visit to the market at Ueno, gleans a long inventory of objects, from the "gesticulating fingers of lentil, unwriggly eels", "powdered kabuki faces of cake", "paragraphs of beancurd", and "alliterative clogs" to "sassy tomatoes" (*Man Snake Apple*, p. 39). This long noun-chain is followed by the predicate "are all there", the objects thus compressed and composed into a single moment of seeing. Yap's preference for lists is evident in previous collections; here it has found exuberant expression in a Zen milieu. Lists are static as they slow down time, and because of the "absence of any straightforward authorial presence" they are "at the same time the most actively constructing and passively recording of representations (Spufford 1989, p. 5). Yap's tableau in "a list of things" is unburdened by history and narrative, focussing on the here and now, evoking marvel in what seems insignificant. In his penetrating dissection of Juan Sánchez Cotán's still lifes Bryson (1995) observes:

> In much of still-life, the painter first arrays the objects into a satisfactory configuration, and then uses that arrangement as the basis for the composition. But to organise the world pictorially in this fashion is to impose upon it an order that is infinitely inferior to the order already revealed to the soul through the contemplation of geometric form: Cotán's renunciation of composition is a further, private act of self-negation. (p. 70)

Yap's objects, collected higgledy-piggledy in a paratactic relationship, subvert any idea of hierarchy and narrative. This renders it more like a found poem and also points to the vanishing self of the poet for whom art is a way of erasing the ego.

In "12-Times Table" Yap privileges the metonymic over the metaphoric. Things are seen for what they are, without "that depicting & that transmogrifying beyond":

> it was at gifu. it was at osaka.
> it was blue-&-white ceramics at gifu;
> it was amethyst ceramics at osaka.
> camellias, egg-plants, pines: designs of the fingers.
> gourds, other forms: shapes of the fingers.
> it was here. It was also here
>
> what took place was very possible
> without the restive rankle of grass, water, sky, hills.
> (*Man Snake Apple*, p. 34)

The tableau refuses the horizon, the deep perspective and vanishing point, opting for the flatness of the picture plane, advocating Mark Rothko's declaration: "We are for flat forms because they destroy illusion and reveal truth" (Gottlieb and Rothko 1968, p. 545).

The poem "paired stills" further enacts the Zen principle in garden and flower arrangement and also continues the interplay between poetry and painting that runs through Yap's work. Visually the haikus are arranged in pairs, each pair linked by repeated words, alliterative, assonantal as well as semantic echoes:

> at heian shrine   grass sprang from the hem
> a handpainted kimono   stopping short of the obi
> rustled like wild grass   & walked up those steps
> (*Man Snake Apple*, p. 40)

The haiku tableaux mime the Zen aesthetic, the spontaneous but calm arrangement of objects into a poetic composition reconciling stillness and motion, human and nonhuman, art and nature. The haikus themselves become objects, their collocation forming a collage that demonstrates simultaneity of seeing. This poetic technique can also be seen in the poem "the shisen-do", which describes a Zen garden in Kyoto; it is a composed field of images miming the aesthetic concept of a Zen garden:

> you can almost hear the sap raise newer leaves.
> past the simple rustic outside-gate,
> a slightly ascending passage with stepping-stones

> leads to the inside-, the garden front.
> the interior garden reveals shaped azalea bushes,
> sand combed into a pattern, a spent wisteria,
> little white daisies. a low waterfall,
> the clacking of the sōzu. not too many flowers,
> not too many lives.
>
> the woman bending over some plants
> thought they were a kind of chrysanthemum,
> her words never once staying her tending hands.
>
> no photographer to record the scene, to fail.
>
> a bowl of green tea, a biscuit on a paper square.
>
> always the same tableau, intrinsically still,
> the kindling of every sentience.
> it is always the same & one can see
> it had always been, will be.
> <div align="right">(<i>Man Snake Apple</i> p. 33)</div>

The Zen garden is "a living lesson in the Zen concept of nothingness and nonattachment" (Hoover 1978, p. 110). It is a poetic composition, with the objects such as rocks and gravel arranged to give "a symbolic experience of the world at large, distilled into a controlled space but suggesting the infinite" (p. 93). Yap's poem replicates the Zen juxtaposition of movement and stillness, space and infinity, time and timeless. The observer, be it the speaker or the reader present in the second-person pronoun, disappears in what is observed. Though there is a suggestion of movement in the "ascending" and "leads" and "bending", the stative and passive verbs cancel them out, and the last static image of the green tea and biscuit completes the tableau in a haiku-like concentration of restraint and tranquility.

Yap's art is an informing and inspirational presence in his poetry from the first collection, tilting the poems towards abstraction, ellipsis, understatement. The aesthetic concerns and values that underpin his painting are also operative in his poetry. The linear and window motifs pervade the poems and paintings, creating binaries of inside/outside, closeness/distance, observer/observed, self/other. The paintings' "soft-focal" shapes and the poems' resistance to closure create an ambiguity and liminality that shrug off the clutches of nationalist poetics and politics. In the liminal spaces between painting and poetry, Yap has found a voice and style that have made him one of the most complex and unique poet-painters of the world. Wallace Stevens (1951) says: "The poem must resist the intelligence / Almost successfully" (p. 281). Yap's poetry as well as his painting do just that, their abstraction implying that reality is untranslatable and what the poem or painting offers are subjunctive or conditional ways of seeing instead of declarative or denotative statements of meaning. His poetry and painting were twinned from the start, infusing each other, each a necessary presence in the other. It is no surprise that when Yap's poetry ceased and a decade-long silence ensued till his death, his painting also petered out.

References

Addiss, Stephen. *The Art of Zen: Paintings and Calligraphy by Japanese Monks 1600–1925*. New York: Abrams, 1989.

Aichele, K. Porter. *Paul Klee, Poet/Painter*. New York: Camden House, 2006.

Borchardt-Hume, Achim, ed. *Rothko: The Late Series*. London: Tate Publishing, 2008.

Breslin, James E.B. *Mark Rothko: A Biography*. Chicago: University of Chicago Press, 1993.

Brewster, Anne. "Arthur Yap — dramatic personae". In *Critical Engagements: Singapore Poems in Focus*, edited by Kirpal Singh. Singapore: Heinemann Asia, 1986.

———. "Foreword". In *The Space of City Trees: Selected Poems*, by Arthur Yap. London: Skoob Books, 2000.

———. "An Interview with Arthur Yap". *Asiatic* 2, no. 1 (2008): 3–12 <http://asiatic.iiu.edu.my/Archive/articles/ An%20Interview%20with%20Arthur%20Yap.pdf>.

Bryson, Norman. *Looking at the Overlooked: Four Essays on Still Life Painting*. London: Reaktion Books, 1995.

Delaunay, Robert. "Letter to August Macke". In *Theories of Modern Art: A Source Book by Artists and Critics*, compiled by Herschel B. Chipp. Berkeley: University of California Press, 1968.

Goh, Robbie B.H. "Imagining the Nation: The Role of Singapore Poetry in English in 'Emergent Nationalism' ". *Journal of Commonwealth Literature* 41, no. 2 (2006): 21–41.

Gottlieb, Adolph and Mark Rothko. "Statement". In *Theories of Modern Art: A Source Book by Artists and Critics*, compiled by Herschel B. Chipp. Berkeley: University of California Press, 1968.

Guilbaut, Serge. *How New York Stole the Idea of Modern Art from Paris: Abstract*

Expressionism, Freedom, and the Cold War, translated by Arthur Goldhammer. Chicago: University of Chicago Press, 1983.
Hoover, Thomas. *Zen Culture*. London: Routledge & Kegan Paul, 1978.
Klee, Paul. "Creative Credo". *Theories of Modern Art: A Source Book by Artists and Critics*, compiled by Herschel B. Chipp. Berkeley: University of California Press, 1968.
López-Remiro, Miguel, ed. *Writings on Art: Mark Rothko*. New Haven, CT: Yale University Press, 2006.
Mancusi-Ungaro, Carol. "Material and Immaterial Surface". In *Mark Rothko*, edited by Jeffrey Weiss et al. New Haven, CT: Yale University Press, 1998.
Novak, Barbara and Brian O'Doherty. "Rothko's Dark Paintings: Tragedy and Void". In *Mark Rothko*, edited by Jeffrey Weiss et al. New Haven, CT: Yale University Press, 1998.
Patke, Rajeev S. "Voice and Authority in English Poetry from Singapore". In *Interlogue: Essays on Singapore Literature in English: Vol. 2. Poetry*, edited by Kirpal Singh. Singapore: Ethos Books, 1999.
Rosenberg, Harold. "Introduction to Six American Artists". *Possibilities* 1 (Winter 1947–48): 75.
Spufford, Francis, ed. *The Chatto Book of Cabbages and Kings: Lists in Literature*. London: Chatto and Windus, 1989.
Stevens, Wallace. *The Necessary Angel: Essays on Reality and the Imagination*. London: Faber and Faber, 1951.
———. *Letters of Wallace Stevens*, edited by Holly Stevens. New York: Knopf, 1966.
———. *The Palm at the End of the Mind: Selected Poems and a Play*, edited by Holly Stevens. New York: Vintage, 1990.
Stewart, Susan. *On Longing: Narratives of the Miniature, the Gigantic, the Souvenir, the Collection*. Durham, NC: Duke University Press, 1993.
Sullivan, Kevin. "Achievement: The Poet with an Artist's Touch". *Southeast Asian Review of English* 8, no. 2 (1984): 3–20.
Yap, Arthur. *Only Lines*. Singapore: Federal, 1971.
———. *Commonplace*. Singapore: Heinemann, 1977.
———. *Down the Line*. Singapore: Heinemann, 1980.
———. *Man Snake Apple & Other Poems*. Singapore: Heinemann Asia, 1986.
———. *The Space of City Trees: Selected Poems*. London: Skoob Books, 2000.
Williams, Willam Carlos. *Selected Poems*, edited by C. Tomlinson. Harmondsworth: Penguin, 1983.

4

"GO TO BEDOK, YOU BODOH"
Arthur Yap's Mapping of Singaporean Space

Angus Whitehead

Especially during his later years, Arthur Yap was generally regarded as a private and reclusive figure who kept out of both the public eye and Singapore's literary scene. Indeed, criticism about Arthur Yap's poetry often contends that his poems are more concerned with a general human subjectivity existing in an anonymous, modern urban space rather than with specific particulars of Singaporean society or history. In contrast to this prevailing view of Yap's writing, this chapter focuses on his direct engagement with and literary explorations of Singaporean local spaces that show us an active and democratizing engagement with everyday life in Singapore. I argue that Yap frequently utilizes encounters with such spaces to map moments in Singapore's social and cultural history, and to explore a complex relationship with personal and national memory in ways markedly different from other local poets of his generation. Yap's allusions to local space are therefore of special significance, given that in much of his verse he pares poetry down to its bare essentials, favours understatement, and only makes rare but precise references to identifiable places in Singapore.

Much of my exploration of Yap's engagement with local space and time will be interdisciplinary. While drawing upon both art history and local topography, my investigation is also informed by a critical tradition hitherto rarely referred to in discussions of Yap's work: historicism. For reasons of perceived political and pedagogical expedience, Singaporean literary criticism has until recently remained highly influenced by the traditionally hermeneutic, textually focused critical schools of New Criticism and Formalism. As a consequence the idea of the poem as an autotelic or self-enclosed artwork prevails in Singapore. In his own country therefore Yap is predominantly characterized as an almost self-effacing poet who is constantly making large, generic, and universal points that transcend the specificities of local culture and society. Yet, at the same time, Yap's work is often characterized by its ambiguity and ambivalence. These qualities might suggest that we too, as reader-viewers of Yap's work, need to exercise caution and probe the ambivalence surrounding the poet's self-effacement of his biography and background. In a significant number of poems Yap offers tantalizing glimpses of concrete and specific geographical, historical, and cultural particulars that invite readers to reflect on the implications of these details. In this chapter I suggest that historicism, looking outwards at the socio-cultural and historical framework in which Yap wrote, can complement earlier inwardly focused hermeneutic readings of Yap's work and in so doing engage with Yap's strategic use of these details, thus opening up new possibilities in our reading of Yap's work and ultimately revealing a markedly different Singaporean poet, deeply concerned with the city state's rapidly evolving here and now.

John Barrell (1988) has defined historicism as a "[refusal] to consider the literary text in ... isolation from history" (p. 2). Indeed, for Barrell, a literary text is a time bound "discursive account of reality" that responds to and impacts upon past, contemporary and future accounts (p. 12). Highly influential globally since the 1990s yet somehow making little impact on Singapore studies until comparatively recently, New Historicism — pioneered by such scholars as Michel Foucault and Stephen Greenblatt — is an attempt to comprehend literary works through their historical contexts while at the same time attempting to understand intellectual history through literature. Particularly pertinent to my discussion of Yap's poetry in this chapter are two key tenets of historicism: first, that every expressive act is embedded in a network of cultural practices; second, that no discourse gives access to unchanging truths nor expresses unalterable human nature. Historicism, drawing attention to the peculiarity, the uniqueness of the specific moments and places in which Yap's works are both engaged with and created in, will help by throwing new light on those of Yap's poems discussed here. These writings are at first glance predominantly linguistic and therefore invite primarily hermeneutically based readings; however, historicism as an interpretive framework reveals that these seemingly self-contained poems are just as time bound and focused as any other texts. As Gui Weihsin notes in his introduction to this collection of essays, there is as yet no extended study of Yap's life and work (compared to Edwin Thumboo, Lee Tzu Pheng, or Robert Yeo). This present historicist reading of Yap's poetry is carried out in the spirit of attaining a more balanced, deeper understanding of both (1) Yap as a poet who is a pioneering figure in Singapore's literary and cultural history and space; and (2) how Yap's poems engage with this very specific (and unique) history and space.

Given the accelerated and continuing transformation of Singapore's material landscape since the 1960s, the nuances of moments and spaces explored by any Singaporean writer are increasingly in danger of becoming unintelligible to new (Singaporean as well as non-Singaporean) readers of their work. As Koh Tai Ann (1993) observes, "since the sixties there has been such a rapid, almost thoughtless demolition of much of old Singapore ... and its familiar landmarks. The demolition has been so extensive that the landscape of the older settled parts of Singapore is hardly recognizable from what it was" (p. 158). This chapter attempts to reclaim something of the social and historical context surrounding a number of Yap's poems that encounter particular Singaporean spaces and moments, many of which have since been erased, before exploring how such contexts help to illuminate those works. The specific focus is in the material places Arthur Yap alludes to and explores in several of his earlier poems, which were composed during the period 1962–77, when Yap often wrote topically satirical poems relating to the national milieu. I suggest that Yap's references to the past are not merely nostalgic, and to this end I situate individual poems either in the contexts of the social, cultural, and historical moments in which they were conceived, revised, and reworked, or within the framework of specific moments in Singapore's history that Yap refers to. The conclusion of this essay explores an atypically specific allusion made by Yap to Singapore's margins or "heartland", namely the southeastern pre-Raffles settlement of Bedok, which has since been transformed into what Singapore's urban development authorities call a "new town". Both the geographical and the cultural space of Bedok may be read as an articulation of continuing tensions between the heartland and the city, between the periphery and the core of the country. It is hoped that this historicist reading of a major Singaporean poet's locally topical and topographical allusions may open up further discussion of Yap's poems, and their exploration of different aspects of Singapore's past, ongoing changes, and apparent trajectory of progress.

ARTHUR YAP AND SINGAPOREAN SPACE

Earlier scholars have discussed briefly and generally how Singaporean poets writing in English (c.1960–85) have explored their local space. In their introduction to *Journeys, Words, Home and Nation*, the editors note many Singaporean poets' "attachment to a place ... mingled with a sense of its passing" as well as their "dwell[ing] on the memory of a place connected with childhood" (Thumboo et al. 1995, p. xxvi). Wei Wei Yeo (2004) also remarks that "locale appears in the work of earlier poets as reminiscence of particular places in Singapore" (p. 23). Robbie H. Goh (2004) points out that in those poets' work,

> there is a recognizable topography ... nature reserves, the unscenic topographies of mud flats and wild grass patches, pockets of undeveloped rural spaces and the like, become sites invested with a spiritual signification, a valorization or emphasis alternative to the codes of money, social status and power evident in the developed city. (p. 108)

Such places and a sense of their passing are clearly evident in poems by Singaporean poets such as Robert Yeo, Dudley de Souza, and Edwin Thumboo. But, even in those poems by Arthur Yap directly engaging with local spaces, few exhibit a sense of attachment to or an awareness of the transitory nature of such places. When Yap explores or alludes to specific local spaces it is rarely through memories of childhood. On the contrary, Yap generally appears to be engaging with and exploring critically places firmly located in the present of his creative activity. Lastly, the specifics of Yap's topography appear to be not "undeveloped rural spaces", but rather developed urban civic spaces such as an airport, a hotel, a restaurant, or imminently threatened urban spaces such as an old shophouse at the heart of late-pre-redevelopment Chinatown. Yap's cosmopolitanism (particularly in his earlier poems exploring aspects of first Malaysia, England, and Wales, and then in later poems exploring Australia, Indonesia, and Japan) and his more generalized exploration of the new HDB (Housing Development Board) (sub)urban environment in "there is no future in nostalgia" and "2 mothers in a HDB playground" in many ways prefigures the style and sensibility of later Singaporean poets such as Boey Kim Cheng, Paul Tan, and Alvin Pang who began publishing their work in the 1980s. Although Yap claimed in an interview that he did not write for a particular audience, and did not have a sense of whom that audience in fact was (Sullivan 1984, p. 12), one might argue that several poems address a very local readership at a specific historical moment. Shirley Lim (1986) has demonstrated that Yap's spare, difficult (but not elitist) poetry demands not only a critical reader but also one able to fill in much of the local and temporal context for themselves. A historicist reading may therefore assist in the recovery of something of the socio-biographical contexts of Yap's poems that are overtly bound to his representations of contemporary moment and place, and also offer new and rewarding insights into these poems.

POETIC MAPS AND LOCAL SPACES

The Singaporean street names that appear in Yap's poems are not merely decorative features, primarily utilized for linguistic patterning; rather, they carry significant cultural and social connotations specific to Singapore's history. As Victor Savage and Brenda Yeoh (2003) observe,

> street names ... contain a mélange of meanings, which, when properly read and understood, provide an interesting commentary of the social, cultural and policy developments in Singapore. Embedded in the everyday landscape, they provide an oft-encountered text which not only helps to map locations and directions, but also serves to remind Singaporeans today of the country's changing historical geography. (p. 23)

We can compare this geographical analysis of Singaporean street names to Yap's remarks in a 1984 interview with Kevin Sullivan (1984):

> I think some poets set out with a very noble idea, that, you know, they want to change the world. I don't, because I don't think I like the world that much. Nor, on the other hand, do I hate it so much that I want to say — just let things go. I'm rooted in a particular area and I try to reflect the life styles and the folk ways of a particular area and I think that is what I try to do in my poetry more than anything else. (p. 4)

Indeed, Yap's allusions to specific spaces in Singapore rarely stray further than "the life styles and the folk ways of a particular area", the local, traditionally ethnically Chinese areas of the urban centre of Singapore he was familiar with. These include his childhood home and neighbourhood in Kim Seng Road (1943–79), near the intersection with River Valley Road and north of the Singapore River as well as a number of references to streets in Chinatown. Yap's poems reflect his familiarity with this immediate neighbourhood which in the late 1940s–1970s was almost exclusively Chinese, with only one Indian family nearby. However, even within the precincts of old Singapore city, Yap appears to have enjoyed what he described as a kampong-style childhood which involved cycling, picking fruits from nearby trees for drinks, playing along the then marshy banks of the Singapore river, where he would have encountered squatters' attap huts near Kim Seng Bridge (Jenny Yap, personal interview).

LOCAL FOLKWAYS: KIM SENG BRIDGE AND CHINATOWN

Perhaps Yap's earliest engagement with a specific and recognizable Singaporean space occurs in "Beggars All", a poem that appeared in early 1962 in the University of Singapore's literary magazine, *Focus*, by the nineteen year-old Yap, then a first-year undergraduate. The poem appears to make references to the folkways of Yap's childhood milieu, describing a "[b]lack clothed figure with a mean shuffle" visiting the speaker's neighbourhood each Sunday. "'Rumour' has it that "he comes from one of those huts / Squatting around the Kim Seng Bridge" (Yap 1962, p. 2). Yap is almost certainly referring to the wood and attap houses in this area that he would have encountered there as a child roaming his neighbourhood. However, it turns out that the "beggar-m[a]n" is in fact the comparatively affluent "Owner of some Chulia Street hard-ware store" south of the Singapore river. One of the oldest streets in Singapore, Chulia Street was the home of Indian and Chinese moneylenders and metal workers until the early 1980s, when the area was redeveloped as part of the central business district. Yap's "fire off Kim Seng Bridge" (composed before 1974) also refers to the neighbourhood of his family home (Yap 1974, p. 52). Although numerous fires ignited in this area during the 1960s and early 1970s, the poem surely carries an implicit allusion to the Bukit Ho Swee fire of May 1961, one of the worst fires in Singapore's history, in which a squatters' settlement burnt down leaving about ten thousand people homeless. The area was promptly cleared and rebuilt as one of the first HDB estates, foreshadowing the mandatory migration of most of the Singaporean labouring population from city dwellings and kampongs to high-rise apartment blocks over the next two decades. Robbie Goh (2004) has recently suggested that in the poem "a recurrent event" (written in 1971) Yap is both reporting and providing some form of social commentary upon an element of contemporary Singapore: "the established rituals of ethnic groups in Singapore", and in the case of this poem, "traditional Chinese wake and mourning rituals" (p. 33). These Yap appears to describe as "the cruelest scenes". However, a reading informed by the poem's topographical-historical context complicates Goh's reading. "a recurrent event" is set "in sago lane", at the heart of Chinatown. As Savage and Yeoh (2003) inform us,

> From the late nineteenth century ... Sago Lane became known for its Chinese "death houses".... This was the place where people close to death were left to die, with the funeral parlour prepared below. All the Chinese paraphernalia (clothes, appliances, paper models) related to death rites were sold in shops in this lane. The Cantonese thus called Sago Lane "street of the dead". (p. 337)

In this light, Yap's poem touches upon not merely funeral but also pre-death traditions. And indeed the first stanza's references to "a dead relative [who] / rises from the bed to undie / another year" and "an aunt in shroud/ [who] wonders" are as likely to refer to the dying as the dead occupants of the Sago Lane death houses. Yap, who probably composed the poem during the 1960s, was hardly unique in associating the death houses' treatment of the still living with "the cruelest scenes". A letter to the *Straits Times* published on 25 July 1957 urged that, "On the eve of making Singapore known to other countries through the tourist trade I do hope that visits to the 'death houses' of Sago Lane will be stopped" (p. 6). Four years later, in 1961, the death houses were abolished. In publishing this poem in 1970, less than ten years later, at the time that much of the original Sago Lane was being demolished to make way for the Kreta Ayer complex, Yap appears to recall events out of Singapore's colonial past rather than its contemporary situation. However, given Yap's lengthy composition period for his poems, the poem may have its roots in an episode that occurred before 1961. During the 1940s at their residence at Kim Seng Road, the Yap family first employed a Chinese amah (servant) principally to look after the infant Arthur Yap. In the late 1950s, when she became terminally ill, despite invitations to remain with the family the

(Buddhist) amah insisted on leaving the (Christian) Yap residence and spending her last days attended by fellow servants on the first floor of one of the Sago Lane death houses. The teenage Yap together with his eldest sister visited their dying amah there on at least one occasion. Finding her unconscious and in neglected surroundings was a distressing experience (Jenny Yap, personal interview).

Yap's most sustained engagement with Chinatown is to be found in "old house at ang siang hill" from his first collection *Only Lines* (1971). Both national as well as the poet's personal contexts illuminate the poem. In 1996 Yap told Anne Brewster (2008):

> I'm not just interested in the past for its own sake. Nor am I interested in development for its own sake either. But certain aspects of the past ... I think it would be regrettable if these were to disappear totally ... you know, houses, certain traditions and so on. (p. 105)

Like Sago Lane, Ang Siang Hill is located off South Bridge Road at the centre of Chinatown. The speaker appears to address himself standing in the interior of a house formerly belonging to his grandfather. Yap's phrase "three storied gloom" suggests a large Chinatown dwelling. Koh Tai Ann (1993) has suggested that in this poem,

> [t]he lines of the first stanza mimic the hushed, respectful tones of filial piety or religious worship ("tread softly", "sit gently" and "speak quietly") elicited by the old house with its "straits-born furniture" (like its owners, originating "from China") which function as a reminder of ancestors, the traditional past or Chinese cultural heritage. (p. 157)

Although the contextual details of the poem discussed below substantiate elements of Koh's reading, they trouble others. It has previously been assumed that Yap composed "old house at ang siang hill" about 1980, during the "heyday of urban renewal" in Singapore (Lin 2005, p. 58). In fact the poem was written considerably earlier. It was included in Yap's first collection *Only Lines* (1971), but had previously appeared a year earlier in an anthology edited by Edwin Thumboo *The Flowering Tree: Selected Writings from Singapore/Malaysia*. Yap had therefore completed the poem by or before 1970. His telling use of contemporary government argot in the lines: "re-development / which will greatly change / this house-that-was" suggests Yap may have begun composing "old house at ang siang hill" as early as 1966, perhaps in response to recently published details of government initiatives to renew the older parts of the city. One such HDB publication, *50,000 Up: Homes for the People*, came out in 1966 and extolled the virtues of urban redevelopment in this manner:

> What is Urban Renewal and why the need for it in Singapore? In Singapore, Urban renewal means no less than the gradual demolition of virtually the whole 1,500 acres of the old city and its replacement by an integrated modern city centre worthy of Singapore's future role as the New York of Malaysia. (quoted in Kwek 2004, p. 114)

Thus, although the shophouses on Ann Siang Hill would not in fact be demolished until 1975, at least six years earlier the speaker in the poem seems aware of the ultimate and inevitable fate of the ancestral home. Yap's paternal grandfather, an emigrant from China, did own a three-storied house on Ann Siang Hill. However, the poet never knew his grandfather, who died several years before Yap was born. During the period Yap accompanied his family to his grandfather's former house (1943–75) on formal visits during festivals and other occasions, the house was occupied by a paternal aunt and her family. Yap therefore knew and was related to "contemporary occupants" of an old house closely resembling that mentioned in the poem. Those occupants and relatives are described as "not afraid of" the speaker and "waiting for you to go / before they dislocate your intentions". However, the house retained evidence of Yap's late grandfather's Buddhist Chinese past. As well as Peranakan style ("straits born") hard wooden furniture inlaid with mother of pearl, his grandfather's ancestral tablet and soul house or urn were still visibly present. While this seems a poignant detail, bearing in mind Yap's own Anglican rather than traditional Chinese upbringing, it also provides a context for the speaker's initial reverence and awe on entering the house and a reference to his grandfather's (now absent) ghost. Here, Yap is almost certainly making a reference to Chinese beliefs concerning death. The deceased is first a wandering ghost (threatening to other ancestors) before becoming an ancestor on the completion of a series of death rituals. A contented ancestor is welcomed back into the home, and if worshipped and appeased will care for his descendants. Presumably Yap's grandfather was perceived by his Buddhist descendants as having attained ancestor status. With his grandfather long dead there is a sense of the old house performing the function of a shrine to an ancestor born in the mother country. The Chinese tradition appears as a past that cannot speak: eyes not tradition "tell you" that after "redevelopment" "nothing much will be missed".

Details of Yap's life and heritage therefore throw some light on the poet's inspiration for "old house at ang siang hill". This is especially significant now that we have evidence of the poet drawing upon his personal folkways. The fact that Yap never knew his grandfather, who was therefore a remote absent former owner of a house the poet only visited (perhaps reluctantly?) on formal occasions suggests that the poem does not draw specifically upon Yap's childhood, or cherished nostalgia concerning past traditions, but rather more pedestrian present experience. The poem is not an elegy to his personal threatened past, because even before Yap's birth a dislocation between "the old house" and the poet's "family past" had occurred. Instead the poem seems to be a meditation on the future: imminent radical change engendered by "redevelopment". A close and informed reading of "old house at ang siang hill" demonstrates how real time and contemporary social events may have had an impact upon Yap's creation of this poem. Despite modern Singapore's relatively short history and the fact that the house at the time Yap wrote the poem was perhaps only seventy years old, the poem affords a real sense of future events obliterating traces of the poet's unexperienced past. The fact that the grandfather is for Yap long dead and not even a memory, and that redevelopment is to occur years in the future of a country which is officially only a few years old, has the simultaneous effect of extending both the remoteness of the house's past and its future. Such contexts give the poem a powerful sense of personal and national history and tradition under threat, in the context of a new country hastily dismantling an irreplaceable past in the name of future "development".

ELITE CIVIC AND CULTURAL PLACES

Several of Yap's poems appear to engage with recently constructed public spaces in the new republic. Shirley Lim has described "10th floor song" (1971) in the collection *Commonplace* along with "old house at ang siang hill" as containing "documentary details and social commentary", adding that "[t]he point of view is ... ironic and satirical, pointing to the presence of a private individual making moral judgments on public affairs" (Lim 1986, p. 153). The poem's reference to "cuscaden house at the corner" is an allusion to the Cuscaden House Hotel, a cultural space which in 1971 featured the Raya Art Gallery where Yap may have exhibited paintings as well as a live performance venue, restaurant, and club called "The Eye". The poem also refers to "raffles village pausing in time / before its evening historical pageant / seldom laid on for us." Raffles Village, at 3A Cuscaden Road, was an entertainment complex opened in August 1969 and claiming to offer a recreation of a Malay fishing village (of the kind in reality rapidly disappearing in Singapore), presumably for foreign tourists. As the *Straits Times* reported, "[n]ot far from bustling Orchard Road is a quaint little village which gives the impression that it has been forgotten by time. There are attap huts, a Malay palace, bullock carts, [and] rickshaws" (10 July 1969, p. 7). Yap's reference to "its evening historical pageant / seldom laid on for us" suggests an average Singaporean describing nearby Raffles Village's nightly tourist event called "Singapore Night". Newspaper advertisements of the time suggest that both Cuscaden House and Raffles Village were elite civic spaces for variously official meetings, educational talks, and casual gatherings. However, in "10th floor song" Yap uses these prominent spaces of "urban rehearsal" as mere backdrop to a less public narrative concerning a local woman's fatal fall from the speaker's high rise building, a narrative which was probably inspired by recurrent accounts of such incidents then reported in the *Straits Times*. Such a juxtaposition of tourist-friendly appearance and violent neighbourhood reality could be read as providing implicit commentary on domestic social concerns eclipsed by the new nation's anxieties to generate revenue and global prestige.

Indeed, not a few of Yap's poems specifically name or reference prominent buildings or landmarks in Singapore that serve as the focal point or backdrop for the action that unfolds in the poem itself. "mixed shots", one of Yap's poems published posthumously in 2008 in the *Quarterly Literary Review Singapore*, is set "in the energy of Orchard Road" and describes a tourist photographing "a sculpture fronting a mall". The sculpture can be identified as an abstract work, "Mother and Child" (1980), by fellow artist Singaporean Ng Eng Teng (who had previously exhibited his work together with Yap) outside the entrance to Far East Shopping Centre (see Plate 9). Interestingly, it appears to be the Singaporean host who deems the work a "silly statue", while a Taiwanese tourist is enthusiastic enough about the work to attempt to photograph it. Other poems appear to mark the transition from old colonial to independent, redeveloped Singapore city, a transformation punctuated by the erection of imposing high rise buildings in the centre of Singapore. In the 1977 collection *Commonplace*, "opening day" features the speaker's encounter with "a tall, slim hexagonal artifact [which] foregrounds a stretch of s'pore river" that can be identified as the first stage of the United Overseas Bank tower on the Singapore River, near Cavenagh Bridge which opened in mid-October 1974. But Yap's most detailed exploration of a modern civic building in Singapore occurs in "in passing", which was published in Yap's first collection *Only Lines* after first appearing in the anthology *The Flowering Tree* in the spring of 1970. The speaker in this poem addresses a New York visitor to Singapore. After excursions to "the seaside restaurant" and Chinatown, a group of Singaporean hosts, of which the poem's speaker is a member, return the guest to the airport. There they wait silently for the visitor "to comment / on the fine building, the mural assembling the sea- / front or, even, the air-conditioning." Yet, the mural, building, air-conditioning are unnoticed by the visitor, quite literally leaving him cold. Adrian Barlow has suggested that "in passing" portrays "[t]he restlessness of the modern world ... in the image of the international traveler" and that "Arthur Yap's poem ironically recalls the words of the welsh poet W.H. Davies: 'What is this life if, full of care, / We have no time to stand and stare?'" (Barlow 1993, p. 171). However, Yap's portrayal of the "restlessness of the modern world" can be identified not merely in the international traveller but also in the Singaporean hosts who attempt to frame and to regulate the visitor's first encounter with Singapore.

Barlow also suggests that in the phrase "the mural assembling the sea" the speaker is alluding to "a three-dimensional mural at Changi International Airport" (p. 171). However, as Yap wrote the poem in or before 1970, over a decade before the opening of Changi Airport, the speaker must be referring to Singapore's previous international airport at Paya Lebar. Built in 1955, the airport was a remnant of the last years of British rule in Singapore. However, in mid-1964, a year after independence from Britain and membership of the Federation of Malaysia, an impressive new passenger terminal was completed. The unique interior of Paya Lebar Airport provides context for the last section of "in passing". During the 1960s the terminal was comparatively rare in South East Asia and in Singapore as an example of superior modernist architecture functioning as a public space. The white, futuristic environment made a striking contrast with the rest of Singapore in the 1960s (the interior of the terminal building at Paya Lebar still exists in the present day, although it is currently not accessible to the general public). Daven Wu (2009) describes the new terminal as:

an aggressively sleek creature, all haughty in its low slung modernist right angles. The arrival hall, for instance, was a long box-shaped building with a relatively small entrance that, like the TARDIS, opened into a light-washed, double-volumed space where the high ceiling was held aloft by thick pillars sheathed with white-veined black marble and muted gold mosaic tiles. Floating dog-leg staircases on both ends of the hall led up to a viewing gallery dominated by a ravishing mosaic mural depicting the Singaporean waterfront at night."

This mural is referred to twice at the end of the poem "in passing". The speaker's pride in the new terminal suggests a date not long after its opening on 2 May 1964. The terminal featured three murals, the designs for which had won a national competition in March 1963 judged by the Malaysian film magnate Loke Wan Tho, who had taken a key interest in the development of air travel in Malaysia (Mundy, email to the author). Clearly the murals, projecting an image of Singapore internationally, were considered of national importance. In late July 1963 then Deputy Prime Minister Dr Toh Chin Chye awarded prizes to the two winning designers who were both employees of the local advertising firm Papineau Studios Advertising (*Straits Times*, 27 July 1963, p. 64). William P. Mundy won prizes for two designs, namely "Panoramic View of Singapore Skyline in the Evening" and "Malaysian Rural Scenes: Occupations, Pastimes, Conveyances.".[1] Yap, in describing Mundy's skyline mural as "assembling the sea front" appears to refer both to the content and media of the mural. Each mural was created in mosaic form from Venetian smalti glass, chosen for its durability (Mundy, email to the author). Mundy's colleague, Shamsuddin H. Akib, a future cartoonist for the *Straits Times*, also won a prize for his mural design "Cultural Dances of Malaysia" (see Plate 10). Mundy's Malaysian mural featured the four main races of Singapore — Chinese, Malay, Indian, and Eurasian — reflecting the People's Action Party's initial determination to forge the four main racial groups of Singapore into one body of people. Although Mundy recalls no topical guidelines for the competition, Akib remembers that the competition organizers had suggested the four races and nation building as a theme (interview with the author). Akib's mural also portrayed four races with one difference: instead of Eurasians, people from Sarawak, a fellow member of the Federation of Malaysia, were included. As Akib notes, the four dances featured in his mural are from the northeastern Malaysian state of Kelantan (thenconsidered the core of Malay culture), China (Chinese opera), Sarawak, and India (interview with the author).

What is important here is that the speaker in Yap's poem "in passing" only mentions the seafront mural, which may reflect the positioning of the murals at the terminal of Paya Lebar Airport. While Akib's and Mundy's Malaysian murals were both exhibited on the ground level, Mundy's "Singapore Skyline" mural was prominently placed on a second-floor viewing gallery overlooking the terminal. As Mundy recalls, "it was the first thing you saw as you entered the concourse" (email to the author). Alternatively, perhaps the two Malaysian-themed works featuring four nations, originally commissioned in early 1963, did not sufficiently reflect the Singapore government's international aspirations by mid-1964. This may explain the more prominent displaying of Mundy's Singaporean skyline mural, an image perhaps partially redolent of recent British colonial rule, but also asserting Singapore's emergence as an independent, commercial nation to international visitors. Such nationalist, representative, commercial art is unlikely to have reflected the tastes of an abstract painter like Yap.

In light of the opening of the new Paya Lebar International Airport and accompanying national anxieties concerning Singapore's international position, one might read "in passing" as a satirical poem. Whereas in "old house at ang siang hill" where Yap appears to be identifiable with the speaker, Yap cannot be comfortably identified with the culturally immature Singaporean persona of "in passing". Instead Yap simultaneously ventriloquizes and satirizes the speaker's bemused, even perplexed, reaction to the Western visitor's genuine, if uninformed fascination with shabby, pre-redevelopment, but "intriguing" and "so different" Chinatown and other areas of Singapore in a similar state. But at the same time, tellingly, the speaker seems shyly eager for praise concerning the new sophisticated, Western-looking airport.

BEDOK AND BODOH

In his poetry Yap rarely explores Singaporean spaces located beyond what might be described as his own familiar folkways, specifically his family neighbourhood surrounding Kim Seng Road, Chinatown, and several newly built central civic spaces reflecting Singapore's redevelopment. From the 1960s onwards, provincial Singapore with its kampongs or villages on the peripheries of the city state, was steadily replaced by HDB estates. These rural and peripheral spaces are only represented generally and explored obliquely, with the sole exception being Bedok, an area alluded to twice in Yap's 1977 collection *Commonplace*. In his notes to *The Space of City Trees* Yap merely describes Bedok as "a residential area in singapore" (p. 145). However, this southeastern locality is invested with rich social-historical significance. As Savage and Yeoh (2003) observe, "Bedok is one of the early native place-names in existence around the time of Raffles ... the Malay word *bedoh* [pronounced 'bedok'] refers to a large drum for calling people to a mosque for prayers" (p. 51). Yap would have been familiar with the southeast coast of the island from extended childhood summer vacations at his uncle's beach house at nearby Katong during the 1950s and early 1960s, and would almost certainly have been aware of Simpang Bedok and other nearby villages and their inhabitants (Jenny Yap, personal interview). The East Coast Reclamation Scheme, which took place from 1963 to 1986, extended Singapore's coastline from Bedok to Kallang by over a kilometre. In about 1970 this scheme necessitated the destruction of the villages at Bedok, some of the first of the 120 Singapore kampongs expunged between 1969 and 1989 (Savage and Yeoh 2003, p. 24). The building of Bedok New Town, the fifth new town to be built in Singapore, began in April 1973 and its three- to four-room HDB flats accommodated many low- and middle-income Singaporean families displaced by redevelopment initiatives throughout Singapore. In about 1978 redevelopment in the Kim Seng Road area of central Singapore also caused Yap to move with his parents and siblings, from a one-storey terrace in Kim Seng Road to a twentieth-floor private apartment. Their apartment building was constructed on the recently reclaimed land at Marine Parade near Bedok. Today Bedok is largely Chinese populated, reflecting national ethnographic statistics. However, at the time Yap wrote "group dynamics II" (c.1967–77), a decade or so before the introduction of Singapore's Ethnic Integration Policy to prevent the development of ethnic enclaves in any residential district, Bedok still retained much of its centuries old Malay-Muslim character and cultural features. Indeed, despite radical geographical and ethnographic change, something of the region's ethnic past lives on in both the name and the place "Bedok".

According to Ee Tiang Hong's preface to *Commonplace*, "Singapore's urban renewal programme, on a mammoth scale though it is, is mentioned [by Yap] only in connection with the tide at Bedok, the poet's interest being the shape and colour of the tide, and the personal meaning it evokes" (p. x). However, more recently, Dennis Haskell (1999) has argued that "& the tide" may have a more social agenda revealing "the city [as] a consciously made artifact" where even the tide is "being urban-renewed", suggesting "that curtailment of nature means curtailment of imagination also" (pp. 245–46). Like the majority of Singapore's population during this period, in adjusting to redevelopment Bedok's tide "must go on its own tidy ways / without too much of a fuss" (Yap, *The Space of City Trees*, 2000, hereafter *Space*, p. 58). A similar agenda informs Yap's second allusion to Bedok, and the poem "group dynamics II".

As Haskell (1999) observes, Yap is "a poet with a sharp eye and an ear for satire" (p. 25). Yap himself described the role of writers in society as "[o]bservers of a particular time, a particular context" (Brewster 2008, p. 103). These statements seem apposite in discussing "group dynamics II", a poem set in the late 1960s or early 1970s, in which the speech, thoughts and actions of a group of young Singaporeans predominate rather than the single narrative voice of a poetic speaker. Yet, earlier readings of this poem have focused on either the stylistic aspects of the work or its postcolonial implications. In the former sense, the poem is as an example of "[o]ne of Yap's main areas of development ... 'dramatic forms' in which Singaporean voices are played off, almost musically, against one another" (Bennett 1994, p. 1672), while Shirley Lim (1986) observes how Yap "turns to a different linguistic level used by Singaporean teenagers in order to dramatize aspects of that teenage world" (p. 146). Ismail Talib (1999) agrees with Lim and argues that "Yap is able to gauge the appropriate *level* of language use of the group of pre-university students he portrays in the poem", which is "the more elegant level of Singapore English" (p. 122, Ismail's italics). But, the context in which such "elegant" Singapore English is utilized in this instance has not been discussed. I will now explore that context, focusing on the phrase "go to bedok you bodoh".

In "group dynamics II" (*c.*1977), Reginald, Wingho, Benny ("both ... wong"), May-Lin and Julie ("also wong"), a group of predominantly or exclusively Chinese Singaporean pre-university students crash their speeding sports car. The poem's title, together with its companion poem "group dynamics I" (a meditation on "dead" empty and inflexible pieties imposed by the new nation's legislators) suggests the minor narrative and accident featured in "group dynamics II" may have wider, national significance. The poem is a critical representation of racism and bigotry in Chinese Singaporean youths, hence the title is "group dynamics II" as their behaviour seems to point towards a larger group attitude among young and affluent Singaporeans in the 1970s. Since the youths end up in a car crash due to their irresponsible actions and callous attitude, the poem can almost certainly be read as critical. But several specific details in the poem help bring such a reading into clearer focus. Reginald presumably owns the crashed Japanese Honda sports car. At the end of Yap's poem, post-crash, a chastened Reginald, Wingho, and Benny take two new girls, Susie and Bee Ngah, to the Troika, a trendy penthouse Russian restaurant of the period at Liat Towers, near Orchard Road. The Troika restaurant moved to Liat Towers in 1966 where it remained till the early 1980s. Popular with expatriates, the Troika was a fashionable restaurant for functions and, like Raffles Village and Cuscaden House, a privileged relatively elite Singaporean social space during the 1970s. Yap and other University of Singapore staff dined there regularly. The students' "pre-u.'s [are] real strong, you know" suggesting that May-Lin and several other members of this group are doing well academically and will take places at the (then) locally prestigious University of Singapore, though "never mind what faculty". The sports car, elite restaurant, and assured future attendance at university in the context of the 1960s–1970s therefore suggests that the protagonists are the well-educated but (initially) complacent children of postcolonial Singapore's affluent and successful. On a night preceding the crash, the teenagers overtake and taunt older, slower drivers on the highway:

> let's chase them. reginald sped. stupid nut
> may-lin said. stupid nut wingho said
> to any driver Reginald had overtaken.
> to bedok Julie said. go to bedok you bodoh
> wingho said. we'll send you a postcard, Julie
> indicated, forming an oblong with her fingers.
> swiftly passed-by drivers registered no surprise.
> (*Commonplace*, p. 65).

At first glance, Wingho's "go to bedok you bodoh" might be dismissed as a throwaway line of an excited teenager chasing and overtaking other drivers. Hermeneutically inclined critics might merely discuss the playfulness of Yap's sense of the possibilities that lay within such colloquialisms. But reading such a sparsely worded poem by Yap so superficially we give Yap little credit. While one might question whether a Singaporean then or now might use a phrase like "go to bedok you bodoh", the Malay word "bodoh" remains a widely used Singaporean term denoting "idiot". In everyday parlance far easterly "Bedok" still carries connotations of provincialism and lack of sophistication ("such a bodoh; must be from Bedok, what?").

An astute reader with an historicist eye might therefore be tempted to ask: why, during the late 1960s–early 1970s, should a group of Chinese and upper-middle-class teenagers, the up-and-coming social intellectual elite of Singapore, deem Bedok a Singaporean "outer depth" in which to cast the addressee? What does Bedok signify for Wingho and his friends speeding in the imported sports car?

Significantly, the abusive phrases that Julie and then Wingho hurl from Reginald's sports car at passing drivers, "go to bedok" and "go to bedok you bodoh" respectively, feature two of the four Malay words Yap uses in his poetry. In his notes at the end of *The Space of City Trees*, Yap simply glosses *bodoh* as "idiot". However, the word also carries other connotations of dull, simple, naïve, and silly. When used domestically, "bodoh" can also carry connotations of affection. Yap capitalizes effectively upon the similar sounding words "Bedok" and "bodoh". If he had substituted the name of another provincial HDB new town of the period such as Bishan, Hougang or Tiong Bahru, the linguistic effect would have obviously been far weaker. However, as Yap was surely aware, "Bedok" carries connotative significance far beyond mere wordplay. In Yap's poem, Chinese Singaporean youths express themselves in Malay, the mother tongue of the indigenous minority. Initially this detail might suggest a healthy sense of cross-fertilization between the two cultures, circa 1970. However, the pairing of Bedok/bodoh is strongly connotative of the "Malayness", the perceived indigenous nature of Bedok, as well as a simple and — from the perspective of the pragmatic Singaporean social policies of the 1960s and 1970s — a slow and therefore impractically obsolete way of life. Another wider context, albeit one rarely publicly discussed in Singapore, might also inform the racial and group dynamics in the poem: the recent violent racial riots between members of the Chinese and Malay communities in Malaysia and Singapore during July and September 1964 and May 1969. In his poem "1-2 MIN. POEM", published in 1970, Yap appears to make an implicit reference to recent unrest as student motorcyclists at a red light on Malaysia's Merdeka highway discuss "this racial 'thing' ... a real bother", and that "the carnival that has ended / Becomes a real farce, though damn well attended / The organizers should be shot" (Thumboo 1970, p. 71).

In both "1-2 MIN. POEM" and "group dynamics II" Yap appears to touch upon the continuing (if unarticulated) fragility of racial relations between indigenous and exogamous communities in Singapore during the 1970s. It seems significant that Yap makes "group dynamics II" the last piece, and therefore in a sense the last word, in his 1977 collection

Commonplace. It might also be argued that in this poem Yap also offers a critical investigation of relations between his own familiar folkways (the Chinese Singaporean majority) and one of Singapore's other racial communities. Here it might be argued that Yap's more nuanced attitude was influenced by his own middle class, kampong-style childhood as well as his experience of life beyond the majority-Chinese society of Singapore. By the time he completed this poem Yap had not only travelled extensively in Malaysia but had also spent a year studying in the north of England. However, by the time "group dynamics II" was published in 1977, Bedok's transformation from a largely Malay-populated pre-industrial settlement to an urban industrial multi-ethnic new town for workers on the outer edges of an increasingly prosperous city state was well under way. By the mid-1970s, therefore, the phrase "go to bedok", might refer to the incomplete new town and its inhabitants and coastal extension projects, and therefore to reflect ongoing social as well as racial tensions between the heartlands and the city, the peripheral and the core.

Indeed there are two ways in which we can understand this line, spoken by Wingho, who is echoing Julie's earlier "to bedok" (the three boys' telling pursuance and aping of the two girls through the poem foreshadows the ultimate separation of genders through accident and later through the military draft or "national service"). First, the phrase "go to bedok" could be meant as an insult to the other drivers the youths are overtaking on the road. In this case, the other drivers seem absolutely indifferent to the youths' taunts: "swiftly passed-by drivers register no surprise". If "go to bedok you bodoh" is indeed a racially tinged taunt, this indifference seems remarkable, in the light of the history of racial violence a decade prior to the poem's publication just discussed. While one might argue that Wingho's insult cannot be heard or understood by other drivers as the car speeds past them, the fact that no one cares about Bedok, or has forgotten what it signifies, might suggest that by the 1970s Bedok is indeed already losing its rich Malay cultural character and becoming much more urbanized and industrialized. In this reading race and history are effaced in the name of progress — and it is only the privileged Chinese Singaporean youths speeding along in their modern sports car who feel entitled to make Bedok a pejorative term on social as opposed to racial grounds.

In a second, alternative reading, Wingho may be directing "go to bedok you bodoh" to someone in the car — perhaps Reginald, the driver. Since the stanza begins with Reginald or one of the passengers saying "let's chase them", Julie's "to bedok' could be understood as "let's chase them [the other drivers] to Bedok", and therefore Wingho's "go to bedok you bodoh" is poking fun at Reginald to get him to hurry up and drive faster, implying that Reginald is just as idiotic as the slow drivers the youths want to chase to the outer eastern limits of Singapore's circumscribed space, Bedok. Soon after the speeding teenagers end up crashing their car. Is Yap here commenting on the possible consequences of social and racial arrogance expressed by young, affluent Singaporeans? It is unclear whether the teenagers ever reach Bedok, and as we have seen the other drivers seem indifferent to their antics. At the close of the poem Reginald, Wingho and Benny, post-crash, suspended, waiting alike for transport and national service call up and left behind by university-bound May-lin and Julie, end up taking two new girls to the Troika restaurant, a more attractively cosmopolitan and elite locale than the Bedok neighbourhood. Read in this light, Bedok is gestured towards in a pejorative manner but quickly forgotten in favour of the Troika and all the modernity and cosmpolitanism it represents. Race and history are again passed over in favour of social class and mobility, if tempered by the democratization of the national service, bus and taxi the boys are now waiting for after the crash.

CONCLUSION

The topical and topographical poems discussed in this chapter question the idea of Yap's poetry during the 1970s and 1980s as partaking in any notion of Singaporean nation building. Indeed this chapter might be said to substantiate Rajeev Patke and Philip Holden's recent portrayal of Yap as a poet with a "deliberate habit of seeming to go against the stream in the genteel and well-heeled conformism and docility of contemporary Singapore" (Patke and Holden 2009, p. 118). Yap does not indulge overtly in pronouncements concerning Singapore's progress but rather critically explores the human condition, often through familiar folkways, namely his own neighbourhood, and a specifically Chinese Singaporean experience. As the poems discussed here appear to suggest, Yap's overt and specific engagements with Singaporean spaces have a distinctly Chinese flavour. Anne Brewster (2008) has discussed Yap's "[r]ewriting of official discussions of nationalism by drawing on a vernacular and informal sense of history and the singularity of everyday life" (p. 25). Yap appears to have mediated his engagements with wider issues concerning Singapore's material and cultural progress during the

1960s onwards through those familiar folkways. From such a position he appears to have been able to speak carefully and truthfully, with integrity and authority. Such quotidian folkways might be deemed Yap's strategy for dealing obliquely but tellingly through print media with problematic Singaporean issues, such as race relations and the effects and trauma of redevelopment upon Singapore's working class majority. For the vigilant reader a poem such as "group dynamics II" begs important questions regarding Singapore's inner and outer development as a nation state. Today, more than thirty years after Yap wrote his most important poetry, much of the work of those of Yap's literary contemporaries who largely allied their work with Singapore's nation-building project has already become of historical rather than literary interest. In contrast, Yap's crafted, critical and demanding responses to contemporary Singapore are likely to enjoy an enduring appeal in contemporary Singapore, as "the gap separating political independence from cultural maturity" (Patke 2006, p. 75) gradually narrows and the nation's population becomes increasingly autonomous, sophisticated, and interrogative.

Note

1. The mural features Singaporean and Malaysian monuments and places of religious worship. The images of the buildings portrayed in the mural probably derived from photographs in the Papineau guides for Singapore and Malaysia (Mundy, email to the author). The mural features such details as from left a prominent mosque in Malaysia (as yet unidentified), Silat (Malay martial arts), a Hindu temple (as yet unidentified), an Indian snake charmer, one of the politically symbolic lions formerly placed at the entrance to Singapore's Merdeka Bridge over the Kallang river (added 1956, removed before 1979), a rubber tree, a satay seller with stove, a Chinese temple at Penang, a man painting a chinese lantern, and the Catholic cathedral of the Good Shepherd, Bras Basah Road, Singapore (my thanks to Shamsuddin H. Akib for assistance with these identifications).

References

Barlow, Adrian. *The Calling of Kindred: Poems from the English Speaking World*. Cambridge: Cambridge University Press, 1993.

Barrell, John. *Poetry, Language and Politics*. Manchester: Manchester University Press, 1988.

Bennett, Bruce. "Arthur Yap". In *Routledge Encyclopedia of Post-Colonial Literatures in English, Volume 2*, edited by Eugene Benson and E.W. Connolly. London: Routledge, 1994.

Brewster, Anne. *Literary Formations: Post-colonialism, Nationalism, Globalism*. Melbourne: Melbourne University Press, 1995.

———. "An Interview with Arthur Yap". *Asiatic* 2, no. 1 (June 2008): 97–108.

Ee, Tiang Hiong. "Foreword". In *Commonplace*, by Arthur Yap. Singapore: Heinemann Educational Books, 1977.

Goh, Robbie B.H. "Evangelical Economies and Abjected Spaces: Cultural Territorialisation in Singapore". In *Beyond Decription: Singapore Space Historicity*, edited by Ryan Bishop, John Phillips, and Wei-Wei Yeo. London: Routledge, 2004.

———. "Imagining the Nation: The Role of Singapore Poetry in English in 'Emergent Nationalism'". *Journal of Commonwealth Literature* 41, no. 2 (2006): 21–41.

Haskell, Dennis. "'Authority' in Modern Singaporean Poetry". In *Interlogue: Studies in Singapore Literature, Volume 2: Poetry*, edited by Kirpal Singh. Singapore: Ethos Books, 1999.

———. "'People, Traffic and Concrete': Perceptions of the City in Modern Singaporean Poetry". In *Perceiving Other Worlds*, edited by Edwin Thumboo and Thiru Kandiah. Singapore: Marshall Cavendish, 2005.

Koh, Tai Ann. "Literature in English by Chinese in Malaya/Malaysia and Singapore: Its Origins and Development". In *Chinese Adaptation and Diversity: Essays on Society and Literature in Indonesia, Malaysia and Singapore*, edited by Leo Suryadinata. Singapore: National University of Singapore Press, 1993.

Kwek, Mean Luck. "Singapore: A Skyline of Pragmatism". In *Beyond Decription: Singapore Space Historicity*, edited by Ryan Bishop, John Phillips, and Wei-Wei Yeo. London: Routledge, 2004.

Lim, Shirley. "Arthur Yap — 2 Mothers in a HDB Playground". In *Critical Engagements: Singapore Poems in Focus*, edited by Kirpal Singh. Singapore: Heinemann Asia, 1986.

———. *Nationalism and Literature: English Language Writing from the Philippines and Singapore*. Manila: New Day, 1993.

Lin, Benedict. "Old Houses, Linguistics, and the Relevance of Literature in Singapore: The Stylistic Analysis of One Poem". *NUCB JLCC* (2005): 53–71.

Patke, Rajeev S. *Postcolonial Poetry in English*. Oxford: Oxford University Press, 2006.

Patke, Rajeev S. and Philip Holden. *Southeast Asian Writing in English*. London: Routledge, 2009.

Savage, Victor R. and Brenda S.A. Yeoh. *Toponymics: A Study of Singapore Street Names*. Singapore: Eastern Universities Press, 2003.

Sullivan, Kevin. "Achievement: The Poet with an Artist's Touch...: Arthur Yap Talks to Kevin Sullivan". *Southeast Asian Review of English* 8 (1984): 3–20.

Talib, Ismail. "The Language of Singapore Poetry". *Interlogue: Studies in Singapore Literature, Volume 2: Poetry*, edited by Kirpal Singh. Singapore: Ethos Books, 1999.

Thumboo, Edwin, ed. *The Flowering Tree; Selected Writings from Singapore/Malaysia*. Singapore: Educational Publications Bureau, 1970.

Thumboo, Edwin et al. "General Introduction". In *Journeys, Words, Home and Nation: Anthology of Singapore Poetry (1984–1995)*. Singapore: Unipress, 1995.

Wu, Daven. "Paya Lebar airport, Singapore", 14 June 2009 <http://www.wallpaper.com/architecture/paya-lebar-airport-singapore/3341>.

Yap, Arthur. "Beggars All". *Focus* 2, no. 1 (1962): 2.

———. *Commonplace*. Singapore: Heinemann, 1977.

———. "fire off kim seng bridge". In *Five Takes: Poems*, edited by Yee Chong Chung. Singapore: University of Singapore Society, 1974.

———. *Down the Line*. Singapore: Heinemann, 1980.

———. "mixed shots". *Quarterly Literary Review Singapore* 7, no. 1 (2008) <http://www.qlrs.com/poem.asp?id=588>.

———. *Only Lines*. Singapore: Federal Publications, 1971.

———. *The Space of City Trees: Selected Poems*. London: Skoob Books, 2000.

Yeo, Wei-Wei. "Of Trees and the Heartland: Singapore's Narratives". In *Beyond Decription: Singapore Space Historicity*, edited by Ryan Bishop, John Phillips, and Wei-Wei Yeo. London: Routledge, 2004.

5

ON PLACES AND SPACES
The Possibilities of Teaching Arthur Yap

Eddie Tay

The personae in Arthur Yap's poetry are often standing still, immobilized and yet moved to contemplation. The often-unnamed settings in his poems frequently receive a second or third mental visitation, as if inviting us to explore the treatment of the spaces and places of his poetry. This essay takes up Yap's poetic invitation while at the same time approaching Yap's poetry from a critical as well as pedagogical perspective. The first part of the essay deals with the initial frustrations and difficulties of reading Yap's poems, which are often solipsistic and reflexive, as if refusing to engage with social reality and hence not always amenable to a reading that probes for their engagement with social and cultural issues. As a reader, writer, and teacher of poetry and literary criticism, I draw on my personal encounters with Yap's writing in order to illustrate the uniqueness of his style and illuminate the nuances of his verse. The second part of the essay draws on basic concepts of urban and cultural geography to enable an examination of spaces and places in Yap's poetry. The last part of this essay looks at Yap's poetry through general insights offered by Henri

Lefebvre in his book *The Production of Space* and more recent and specific scholarship on the relationship between space and history in Singapore. These provide a useful starting point for understanding how Yap maps a variety of spaces and critiques spatial practices in Singapore.

ENCOUNTERING YAP'S SOLIPSISM AND REFLEXIVITY

I first encountered Arthur Yap's poetry alongside those of Edwin Thumboo and Lee Tzu Pheng as an undergraduate at the National University of Singapore. Unsurprisingly, I was frustrated by Yap's poems; unlike other poems such as Thumboo's "Ulysses by the Merlion" that cements the relationship between poetry and nation building and Lee's "My Country and My People" that is wary of being co-opted by patriotic discourse, Yap's verse seems hesitant about saying anything in this regard. Yap's poems read frequently like arrested departures; they are often negations of the past without any promise of a movement into the present or future. Many of his poems are solipsistic and express a profound sense of resignation from everyday reality, not unlike the Zen garden celebrated in his poem "The Shisen-Do":

> always the same tableau, intrinsically still,
> the kindling of every sentience,
> it is always the same & one can see
> it has always been, will be.
> (*Man Snake Apple*, 1986, p. 33)

Rightly or wrongly, Yap's poetry left this dominant and persisting impression on me.

At the University of Hong Kong and at the Chinese University of Hong Kong, I teach at various times the poems of Thumboo, Lee, and Alfian bin Sa'at in an undergraduate introductory course on poetry that culminates in a reading of the urban anglophone poetry of contemporary Singapore, Hong Kong, and Malaysia. I include Alfian's poems in the course because his voice represents a development in Singaporean poetry that is publicly and explicitly anti-establishment. His scathing and unruly voice is especially significant since Singapore's development as a nation has been premised on state control with the acquiescence of its citizens. However, I consciously avoided teaching Yap's poems, for they seem reticent about offering commentary on Singapore's society and culture. For what is one to do with poems such as "paired stills" in *Man Snake Apple*, a poem that celebrates the way language is able to present a series of tableaux unadorned with any social or cultural commentary whatsoever?

To appreciate Yap's poems in order to teach them in a way that explores the various aspects of Singapore society, we must contend with two important but also frustrating features of his poetry. First, solipsism is the main characteristic and theme of Yap's poetry. In poems such as "street scene II", we are witness to a "solipsist's nightmare" in which the external world diminishes the self, to the point where the self is annihilated and becomes "a big foeval eye" (*Man Snake Apple*, p. 24). Second, the poems tend to revel in wordplay and keep external reality at bay. Prominent examples include "the grammar of a dinner" and "a lesson on the definite article" in *Down the Line* (1980). To give another example: in "paraphrase", a journey is contained within language, to the extent that "the word swallows the world / [and] the word comes close to carrying its own ontology" (*Man Snake Apple*, p. 31). The poems appear to refrain from engaging with the world at large and developing a common view of society in favour of a purely literary and metaphysical perspective on reality. These features of Yap's poems bemuse readers to such an extent that, as critic Rajeev Patke (1999) observes, they seem to possess "the riddling solipsism of one who would rather talk to himself" (p. 94).

One way of making sense of Yap's poems is to read them alongside those of the nineteenth-century French poet Charles Baudelaire, as their poems present "the gaze of the alienated man" (Benjamin 2006, p. 40). Baudelaire's poetic speakers adopt the role of the *flâneur*, a disinterested observer of urban life who watches and describes events taking place on the city streets. Yap's personae, in contrast, are often immobilized by street scenes in Singapore. Time and again, in poems such as "late-night bonus" in *Down the Line* as well as "street scene I" in *Man Snake Apple*, Yap's speakers withdraw from engagement with what they see or hear; they meticulously observe but resolutely shun human contact. Walter Benjamin (2006) points out that Baudelaire "placed shock experience ... at the very center of his art" (p. 178). In contrast, Yap's poetry is the very inverse of Baudelaire's as it recedes into language and away from sense impressions, such that the shock of reality is withheld and deferred for as long as possible. If an engagement with the external world is presented as a nightmarish proposition for the solipsist (as in the case of "street scene II"), and if Yap's poetry wishes for language to carry its own ontology such that it cannot bear the weight of a reality that is external to language (as evidenced by "paraphrase"), then to what extent can one say that Yap's poetry is actually offering some commentary about Singaporean culture and society?

To answer this question we must consider the relationship between literature and the Singaporean nation-state and its society. Rajeev Patke (1999) argues that, given Singapore's rapid development from colony to modern nation-state, "the poet in Singapore bears an over-determined relation to the development of the state into nation, especially during the first few decades of the history of poetry in Singapore" (p. 90). As Patke points out, the voices of poets in Singapore have been arbitrarily split into the private and the public, and both sides of this dichotomy rely on the fossilized relationships between poets, the authoritarian state, and national culture and society that have been taken for granted in the writing of poetry (p. 96). This critical approach to literature that traces the relationship between state and society, and the development of state power into the national body, creates a pedagogical situation in which the poems of Alfian, Thumboo, and Lee are most explicable and accessible, because they can be easily read in terms of their relationship to the state and to the nation-building project. Alfian's poems can be read as having a public voice that resists the intrusion of the state; Thumboo's verse expresses a public voice aligned with the project of building a nation; Lee's writing articulates a private voice that is wary about making public pronouncements about state power and the creation of a nation.

Arthur Yap's poems, on the other hand, often forestall this arbitrary dichotomy between the public and the private because they are so reflexive. The poem "in the quiet of the night", in the collection *Man Snake Apple,* is about the act of reading poetry; it situates the act of reading as switching back and forth between the public and the private and between contrastive states of understanding and ignorance (p. 17). The poem is content to move back and forth between opposing states, forestalling attempts at meaning-making and signification. Furthermore, many of Yap's poems are often meta-poetic: they draw attention to themselves as linguistic artifices before entering into the process of signification that allows us to read and find meaning in the poem's words. Consider the following from "still-life II", which is a comment on the act of writing:

> i think everything's comical,
> as comical as anything that isn't
> in this arrangement:

> this rite of writing
> which doesn't provide an option
> to any other kind of mindedness.
>
> it is very clear
> this scribble has no ambiguity
> because you haven't.
> <div align="right">(<i>Man Snake Apple</i>, p. 4)</div>

To the solipsist, everything external to the poem is comical; eventually, so is everything within the poem. The poem demonstrates the signifying process by which a poem, as an artifice crafted out of language, begins to establish or point towards meaning through a combination of individual words. It acknowledges that we, as readers, are meaning-making beings who cannot tolerate ambiguity. Even as the poem seeks to establish a linguistic enclosure with its own ontology or substance, it fails to do so. The solipsism is dismantled. The poem *must* have a speaking persona, an "I" for other people, and it *must* mean something for others. The poem lacks ambiguity because it has a reader who refuses to grant ambiguity to the poem. In "still life II" the reader encounters echoes of the final moment in Samuel Beckett's novel, *The Unnamable*, where there is a struggle both against and for meaning: "in the silence you don't know, you must go on, I can't go on, I'll go on" (1997, p. 476).

I have devoted some time to draw attention to the solipsistic nature of Yap's poetry, to its reflexivity and its preoccupation with linguistic play, because these are the aspects and thematic concerns of his poetry that we must acknowledge and work through before we can read and understand the poems' engagement with social reality. The "poetics of the nation" in Yap's poetry, as examined by Robbie B.H. Goh (2006), is first and foremost a poetics that is reflexive and conscious of itself as a linguistic artefact (p. 26). Yap reminds us again and again that poetry is, first and foremost, artifice forged out of language. Against the socially and politically charged backdrop formed by the relationship between literature, society, and the nation-state in contemporary Singapore, Yap's linguistically reflexive poetry asks us to consider the twists and turns of of language itself, and illuminate the complex rhetorics of cultural and social discourse, thus opening up a space for dialogue that is not already determined by the split between public and private poetic voices.

However, the spatial metaphors I have used to describe the nuances of Yap's self-reflexive writing suggest that we can trace a path out of the solipsism of Yap's poetry. His poems often leave an opening out of this solipsism, as indicated in the poem "paraphrase", in which the speaker acknowledges that "the word comes close to carrying its own ontology" (*Man Snake Apple*, p. 31). Language is *almost* granted its own ontology, its own substantive existence, but not completely. If language's "scribble has no ambiguity" (*Man Snake Apple*, p. 4), it is by virtue of the fact that we as teachers and readers have to work through ambiguity in order to arrive at the meaningfulness of ambiguity itself. Ambiguity does not denote an absence of meaning, but the presence of two or more possible meanings that coexist or are in tension or dialogue with one another. We have to be stubborn readers who read against the grain, who refuse to settle for "the rite of writing" that "doesn't provide an option / to any other kind of mindedness" (*Man Snake Apple*, p. 4) and consider the potential meanings that await us in the seemingly frustrating ambiguity of the poem's text.

Michel de Certeau's (1984) playful characterization of reading may be instructive here, as de Certeau suggests that the text is a site for "advances and retreats, tactics and games" (p. 175), and that these reading practices are performed by a *bricoleur*, or improvising amateur, as opposed to a dedicated specialist. A teacher and a reader of poetry may be thought of as an artless *bricoleur* who improvises and makes do with "the materials at hand", in this case words and language that were originally fashioned for other uses in other contexts (de Certeau 1984, p. 174). To understand the treatment of spaces and places within Yap's poetry, we need to follow the path out of poetic solipsism that Yap gestures towards and think about some concepts in cultural geography as well as ecocriticism, and explore how these concepts pertain to Yap's poetic representation of spaces and places in Singapore.

SPACES AND PLACES IN YAP'S POETRY

Cultural geography, broadly speaking, is the study of the relationships between cultural processes/conventions/commodities and spaces/places, and there is an aspect of geography that pertains to the study of literature. As Alison Blunt (2009) points out, "[g]eographers have increasingly turned their attention not only to 'writing' and the 'world' being written about, but also to the wider politics and poetics of representation" (p. 68). As she observes, "[o]ne key theme has been an attempt to explore geographies of writing in both imaginative and material contexts and in the very form of writing itself" (p. 70). Drawing on Blunt's observations, it is useful to direct undergraduates to concepts such as place, space, public space, public housing, and so on, as a way of entering into an exploration of Yap's poems as geographies of writing.

Space is the most accessible, and therefore arguably the first, concept to introduce to students of Yap's poetry. As Nigel Thrift (2009) notes, geographers have "abandon[ed] the idea of any pre-existing space in which things are passively embedded ... for an idea of space as [that which is] undergoing continual construction as a result of the agency of things encountering each other in more or less organized circulations" (p. 86). As such, space is not viewed simply as a vacuum which people and objects inhabit, but rather as a dynamic construct transformed by its negotiation with people as well as social and cultural processes, norms, and objects. Closely related to the notion of space is that of *place*, which "consists of particular rhythms of being that confirm and naturalize the existence of certain spaces" (p. 92). A place is a space that is internalized in the minds of people so as to possess certain meanings and purposes. Place "is involved with embodiment", and this means that a place has an effect on the behaviour of those within it (p. 92). One would behave differently in a wet market as opposed to in a public library, partly because these different places have different functions and possess different codes of behaviour. Looking at Yap's poetry with these concepts in mind, we realize that many of his poems map out for us micro-processes whereby space and places influence the behaviour and norms of the people who inhabit and move through them.

A critical approach to Yap's poetics of emplacement may begin with the treatment of public space in his poetry. The word "space" in the phrase "public space" has more than one meaning. On the one hand, it may refer to the "space used in common by the public", such as parks and playgrounds; on the other hand, it may "refer to the spaces that are owned and controlled by the state", such as government and parliamentary offices (Latham et al. 2009, p. 177). In view of this, on the one hand, the term "public" may simply mean a collection of private individuals; on the other hand, it may imply "a notion of the public as being conceptually homologous with the state and its citizens", hence drawing attention to the contract between the state and its people (p. 177). It is important to highlight the fact that Singapore is an island-nation-state, and much of its spaces are compressed within a relatively small land area. Hence, there is a need for efficient management and regulation of land so as to meet the demands of economic growth without compromising the standard of living of its inhabitants. In Yap's poems, we find an articulation of this condition to the extent that, rather than society's needs determining the allocation and use of public spaces, it is the public spaces that are portrayed as organizing and regulating the behaviour and norms of society.

Social behaviour and norms in a public space are critiqued in the poem "dramatis personae". The flowers in a park are not meant to be picked, because "they are for the public", whereas "we in public are private figures" (*Down the Line*, 1980, p. 6). As the poem demonstrates, the notion of the public that operates within a public space such as the park is a disciplinary logic that regulates the private individual. The poem draws attention to the notion that it is space that regulates us, or, to put it in another way, we are circumscribed by our spaces, for "we would never have been / more than all these things we have seen" (*Down the Line*, p. 7). This poem gestures towards but does not fully articulate a form of ecocriticism, as there is a suggestion that the polluted beach portrayed in this tableau, created by human neglect, in turn circumscribes our vision of who we are.

If public spaces operate with a disciplinary logic, then what about *public* housing? In Singapore, approximately eighty-five per cent of the land allocated for residential purposes is developed by the state and provided for as public housing by the Housing and Development Board (HDB), Singapore's public housing authority. Public housing, especially within the context of Singapore, represents the ambivalent nature of what constitutes public and private space. On the one hand, they are private spaces as they are familial and personal sites; on the other hand, they represent contracts on the part of citizens with the state. That these HDB flats are sold on a ninety-nine-year leasehold basis further complicates the notion of ownership and hence complicates the dichotomy between what is public and private, and between what is public and private ownership.

The ubiquitous nature of HDB public housing in Singapore's physical landscape is testimony to the extent to which the state is able to intervene in the everyday lives of Singaporeans. Sociologist Chua Beng Huat (2000) observes that in the 1960s, the public housing programme "was initially met with resistance from residents affected by resettlement"; however, "by the mid-1970s, such resistance had dissipated" and the "successful provision of public housing and concomitant improvement of the material conditions of Singaporeans have paid great political dividend" in terms of securing the allegiance of Singaporeans to the state (pp. 47–48). Hence, HDB flats are a testimony to the legitimacy of the state; they also signify the state's power in fostering a culture concerned with upward social mobility that is aligned with capitalist values.

Yap's poems demonstrate this collusion between the space of public housing and material acquisition, competition and education, which is seen as a guarantor of upward social mobility. "2 mothers in a HDB playground" in *Down the Line* presents two mothers engaged in verbal one-upmanship, each extolling the academic abilities of their children as well as their material extravagance (pp. 54–55). In "i think (a book of changes)", the story of Singapore's economic development is told from the point of view of someone who considers moving into a high-rise flat as a sign of financial and material attainment (*Down the Line*, p. 53). In "samson & delilah", other parents are portrayed as being concerned over the image of their neighbourhood as a result of a boy's unkempt appearance and preoccupation with rock music (*Down the Line*, p. 20). While "samson & delilah" may not explicitly set its narrative within a HDB flat, the prevailing sense of claustrophobia, social intimacy, as well as the concern over how one is perceived by one's neighbours and friends suggest a community of high-rise dwellers. Given that Yap's *Down the Line* was published in 1980, his poems may be said to anticipate the work of Alfian bin Sa'at, whose poems "Void Deck" and "Jobweek 1992" in his 1998 collection *One Fierce Hour* further develop the critique of everyday life in HDB flats.

This critique of city life also occurs in other poems, where Yap maps out in minutiae the consequences of living and working within urban space. Built-up areas of high human density are regularly portrayed as sites of disenchantment and apathy. As Yap puts it in the poem "down the line", there is "a habit by which the world moves, [whereby] people will not / look at the centre of things" (*Down the Line*, p. 10). In more than one poem, Yap demonstrates a preoccupation with suicide and society's apathy towards such incidents. Hence, in the poem "statement", a person's declared intention of suicide is regarded with indifference in the office: "so if you say: please may I jump / off the ledge? & go on to add / this work is really killing, / you will be told: start jumping" (*Down the Line*, p. 5). Likewise, in "down the line":

> we say that a person who had stabbed himself
> 19 times & then thrown his own body over
> the balcony is unbelievable reportage.
> if you tell me times enough, tired, i will believe

> or, at least, agree. & if you tell me
> times more, angered, i will throw
> the narrated body back at you
>
> (*Down the Line*, p. 9)

Again, in "10th floor Song:"

> no need to bring the ambulance
> to the porch
> (whoever she was)
> left leg over first floor ledge
> was quite dead.
>
> (*Only Lines*, p. 25)

Insofar as balconies and ledges form the backdrop to actions and intentions, the logic of urban space is a logic that is inhuman, "for its basis well under the skin has yet another / lined in rubrics" (*Down the Line*, p. 9). Urban space is presented in Yap's poems as a totality that consumes its inhabitants, to the point that any articulation of the human is futile: "if tomorrow someone sings a confessional / of some 'ism or other, the refrain sinks in / as only a totality & any event, being given, / predetermined, is at the onset already silent" (*Down the Line*, p. 9). Likewise, in "topnote", urban space is presented as a "superordinate thing", to the extent that it subordinates and overrides human agency (*Down the Line*, p. 25). Given the pessimism of Yap's poetry, it is easy to see why his poems refuse to form explicit connections with reality and tend to remain within language, as in the case of the poem "paraphrase" mentioned earlier.

If the logic of urban space is such that it absorbs human impulses into its own totality, then it is no wonder that Yap's poems portray the development of urban space with some measure of anxiety and resignation. The poem "old house at ang siang hill", which is Yap's most frequently anthologized and studied work, is a good example — we are told that the addressee's personal past in the house is "superannuated grime" (*Only Lines*, p. 21). The house may have been an "unusual house" because it holds special memories for certain individuals or perhaps because it represents "straits-born" (Peranakan) tastes and culture in terms of its furnishings. Yet this does not prevent the house from being demolished (*Only Lines*, p. 21). The persona in the poem is articulating the urban logic to which the eradication of "this house-that-was" is necessary in the name of progress. In the end, there will be no sign that the house and the culture it represents once existed as "nothing much will be missed". Yap's other frequently-discussed poem "there is no future in nostalgia" likewise displays a measure of resignation, pertaining less to the loss of cultural memory but more to the loss of human presence. The "corner cigarette-seller" is "replaced by a stamp-machine", "the old cook by a pressure-cooker" and "the old trishaw-rider's stand by a fire hydrant" (*Commonplace*, p. 39). What is particularly disturbing, of course, is that human roles are replaced with utilitarian material objects, and this is an inevitable replacement that occurs in the name of modernization and progress.

It is clear that much of Yap's poetry has to do with dwelling or its absence. Dwelling, a concept drawn from the field of ecocriticism, has to do with "practical existence as an immediate reality", "a relation of duty and responsibility" as well as "the long-term imbrication of humans in a landscape of memory, ancestry and death, of ritual, life and work" (Garrard 2004, p. 108). In much of Yap's poetry, and as already anticipated by the earlier discussion of "old house at ang siang hill", we are witnesses to the failure of dwelling. In "late-night bonus", the unruly behaviour of teenagers at night is something "every street has known" (*Down the Line*, p. 43), just as in "sights", urban spaces are arranged and packaged for tourists rather than for its inhabitants: "the sights are like every city's offerings. / the difference is that, here, it is possible / to combine country & sea, a lovely / bilocation for the economy tourist" (*Down the Line*, p. 46). The poems may be suggesting that much of this failure of dwelling has to do with the pathological relationship of inhabitants towards their environment. In "nature study", nature is presented as subject to instrumentalization: "the tree moaned in a series of multiple snaps", and a tree trunk is now ironically a wooden "frame around the picture / of trees & idyllic nature" (*Down the Line*, p. 41). In "old tricks for new houses", Yap offers a sardonic comment on the process of land reclamation to build residential areas: "your neighbours will hang crabshells / on their pomegranate plants as saline testimony" (*Down the Line*, p. 26), indicating the kind of one-sided relationship that exists between the environment and its unmindful inhabitants. There is a clear and troubling split between the realm of the human and the environment, with the latter depicted as something inert, to be acted upon, shaped and manipulated. While it cannot be said that Yap's poems constitute an explicit and elaborate ecocritical agency, nonetheless it cannot be denied that there is an ecocritical aspect to his poetics.

From our reading of the various poems, a portrait of the relationship between space and human agency begins to emerge. On the one hand, urban space connotes economic and material advancement; on the other hand, the price of these is the rapid alienation of people from the environment and from themselves. There is, as demonstrated in the poems "old house at ang siang hill" and "there is no future in nostalgia", the loss and eradication of memory, meaning, and culture even as urban spaces are being developed and redeveloped in the name of social and economic progress. The promise of material and economic advancement is negated by scenes of stasis, immobility, and alienation. In poem after poem we witness organized spaces and places that are inhospitable to human agency. There is an irony at the heart of Yap's poetry in that socio-economic progress as permeated through physical space results in the loss of the social and personal aspects of modern life.

DWELLING

In this respect, the writings of French social theorist and urban studies critic Henri Lefebvre are helpful in directing us towards the critical possibilities of Yap's poetry through the notion of space. Three concepts pertaining to space, or what Lefebvre (1991) calls "the triad of the perceived, the conceived, and the lived", form the underlying structure to Lefebvre's study of *The Production of Space* (p. 39). Perceived space leads to the creation of "spatial practice", which has to do with people's understanding of physical and concrete places (p. 38). Spatial practices structure a person's behaviour and routines which in turn engender the wholeness and durability of a society. Conceived space, or "representations of space", is "conceptualized space, the space of scientists, planners, urbanists, technocratic subdividers and social engineers ... all of whom identify what is lived and what is perceived with what is conceived" (p. 38). In other words, conceived space is the product of mental abstraction, of the political and rational-instrumental impulse. It is executed through state-planning, blueprints, and technology. Lived spaces, that which is experienced in our everyday lives, are "representational spaces" (p. 39). They evoke collective or personal emotional associations and are invested with meanings. They are the space of social relations, of recognition and action. A church, a post office and a house are examples of lived spaces. Lefebvre's *The Production of Space*, as Stuart Elden (2004) reminds us, "should be read between Marx and Heidegger" (p. 189). Marx, because Lefebvre is interested in critiquing space as a function of capitalism, arguing that we are alienated from ourselves because of the conceived spaces we are used to inhabiting. Heidegger, because spaces and places, insofar as they are something felt, lived, and experienced, come under the rubric of phenomenology. What emerges from Lefebvre's book is the insight that, given a state-driven capitalist mode of production, conceived space — the space which is the product of mental abstraction — colonizes lived and perceived space.

Yap's poetry converges with Lefebvre's insights as it presents us with spaces and places that are overwritten with state power. We see in Yap's poetry the product of conceived space, the space of technocrats, politicians, and urban planners. The ending of "old house at ang siang hill", for instance, testifies to the eradication of lived places by conceived places: "nothing much will be missed / eyes not tradition tell you this" (*Only Lines*, p. 21). In the end, one's memory of lived spaces is overwritten by the materiality of conceived spaces. As Lefebvre (1991) argues, the "modern state promotes and imposes itself as the stable centre", and this is manifested in its administration of space (p. 23). Urban spaces, as portrayed in Yap's writings, are revealed to be conceptualized around a rational-instrumentalist logic such that it has "rearranged / the calefaction of the thermometer / we regulate by" (*Down the Line*, p. 11).

Often, the tone of Yap's poetry takes on a tinge of disaffection and cynicism. The voice is often sardonic, as in the case of "down the line", a poem that speaks of disenchantment with conceived space which is the space of management, regulation and control: "the wind that weaves across buildings / carries the calculus the city is reckoned on" (*Down the Line*, p. 9). What is conspicuous in the poem "down the line" is the absence of life, of dwelling, of the human; it is a poem portraying a dystopia, a community of automatons: "what everyone will tell you is what everyone / wants to hear, has been told" (*Down the Line*, p. 11). As such, a reading of Yap's poetry would quickly reveal that the poems are testimony to the exhaustion of the psyche and imagination. Many of Yap's poems speak of exhaustion and disappointment. In "still-life V", a persona speaks of the gap that exists between the self and one's environment, be it a library or park: "where does rigour end & rigor mortis begin? / so slender is the distinction, & practice / ensures the perfection of numbing the sensibilities" (*Man Snake Apple*, p. 7). There is a suggestion here that, despite the technical mastery over one's environment, there is a sensitive gap between the external landscape and the human cultural world.

Such conceived spaces are accompanied by diminished social life. Lefebvre (1991) argues that "[i]f reality is taken in the sense of materiality, social reality no longer *has* reality, nor *is* it reality", as everything has to be placed within a circuit of "money, commodities, and the exchange of material goods", to the extent that one person's interest in another does not exist outside of this circuit (p. 81, Lefebvre's italics). Yap's poetry articulates this insight as in the case of "street-scene I", wherein an encounter between two strangers demonstrates the loneliness of urban experience:

> i think he didn't want to ask anything
> except: why am i so lonely & have to stop you?
> i felt the same then, as he walked on,
> he seemed to grow larger & larger,
> ignoring the laws of perspective.
> <div align="right">(<i>Man Snake Apple</i>, p. 23)</div>

If the physical enlargement of the figure of loneliness is depicted here as a conceit against the laws of perspective, it is because the loss of the social cannot be adequately expressed in the material world. This loss of the social is presented even more poignantly in "still-life IV", a poem about a gathering of friends. In the poem, the gathering of friends is presented as a non-event, to the effect that even their children are immobilized, knowingly impassive and insensible: "they have no demands / to make of anyone. they have nothing to remember / or to forget. they know exactly what is, isn't, / going to happen next" (*Man Snake Apple*, p. 6). The conversation is of no consequence, and material objects such as cups, plates, and the table form the centre of the scene, implying that only the material objects are of consequence. Yap's poetry overlays a disquieting poetic and emotional geography over the material space of Singapore. Hence, it is not surprising that the emotional quality of many of the poems is that of resignation.

This resignation, along with Yap's preoccupation with solipsism, suggests that material urban space and the objects in it are inadequate to a poetics that seeks to engage with social reality. In this respect, Yap engages with the very same concerns Martin Heidegger explores in his essay "Building Dwelling Thinking", which takes up the issue of dwelling and its relationship with physical buildings. For Heidegger (1975), dwelling is not the same as residing within a building or house: "today's houses may even be well planned, easy to keep, attractively cheap, open to air, light, and sun, but — do the houses in themselves hold any guarantee that *dwelling* occurs in them?" (p. 146, Heidegger's italics). Rather, dwelling has to do with one's sense of self and one's place in the world. Yap's "still-life VII" may be regarded as a rejoinder to Heidegger's question:

> a house, i know, is but a temporary abode
> but how satisfying to find one which harmonizes:
> curtain ears close to the ground,
> the forehead slopes towards glasspanes
> & holds up a nose, a plant in a beige pot
> spreading little moist sibilances in the rain.
>
> two big arms run a path in the garden,
> draw up sparrows, dun squirrels, still as stone
> near columns of grass, green as spring tea.
> (*Man Snake Apple*, p. 9)

The poem portrays the house as an embodiment of the self: it is "habitual" in the Heideggerian sense that one is able to inhabit a building or home (1975, p. 147). What Heidegger calls dwelling is presented as harmony in Yap's poetry, whereby one's abode is symmetrical to the self. This poem serves as a reminder of what has been lost to Singapore's urban landscape, as portrayed in many of Yap's other poems: our capacity to dwell.

Our conventional thinking about dwelling, as Heidegger informs us, is analogous to our conventional thinking about language: "Man acts as though *he* were the shaper and master of language, while in fact *language* remains the master of man" (p. 146, Heidegger's italics). Language exists before we were born, and our acquisition of language is akin to finding a place within the symbolic domain already in existence. Likewise, to dwell is to recognize one's place within a pre-existing space. But if this pre-existing space is a conceived space in the way Lefebvre discusses it, in the sense that it has already been overwritten by technocrats, politicians, and urban planners, then the notion of dwelling has to be revised. For if we continue with the analogy of space with language, then that which is homologous to Lefebvre's notion of conceived space is something like Newspeak in George Orwell's dystopian novel *1984*. This explains why so many of Yap's poems we have seen are testimonies to failure of dwelling. The home is often the space of intrusion, as in the case of "old house at ang siang hill", in which we see the eradication of a much-cherished and personal interiority in the name of progress.

If Yap's poetry is preoccupied with solipsism, it is because for the solipsist, urban space is a space that is already compromised. Dwelling for the solipsist is possible only when interiority is reduced to the self. That is why Yap's poetics are so different to those of Thumboo's and Alfian's. Thumboo's often-discussed "Ulysses by the Merlion" addresses itself mostly to conceived spaces of national commemoration. Its attempt at conferring a mythic status on to the Merlion is compromised right from the beginning by the Merlion's ubiquity as a commodified tourist icon and gift shop souvenir. Alfian's (1998) poems, in contrast, are able to present conceived spaces as imbued with "[a] sense of things reduced" and hence as "place[s] to be avoided", even though they do not comment on the impossibility of avoiding conceived spaces ("Void Deck", p. 4). Furthermore, in articulating this notion of self and space, Yap prefigures the arguments made by Ryan Bishop, John Phillips, and Yeo Wei Wei (2004) in their discussion of space and historicity in Singapore: "[as] an exemplar of a certain kind of technological rationality, Singapore produces its self-identification in ways that often conflict with its actual conditions", because Singapore's "history involves extended, strategic engagement with the twin enterprises of postcolonialism and globalization, as well as with colonialism" (p. 2). This engagement hinges upon a simultaneous hollowing and filling out of Singapore's historical self, because "Singapore flaunts its colonial past and postcolonial/global present through the historical maintenance" of buildings from the British colonial era, and "the act of renovation preserves the colonial shell of the building while reworking the buildings from the foundation up to better suit contemporary use", resulting in "a continuation, perpetuations, and multiplication of colonial richness into the present global order" (Bishop et al. 2004, p. 2). In other words, Singapore's urban space is a medium in which the nation-state's colonial past is retained but resignified for use in its global present through an apparently seamless act of renovation. In this light, Yap's poetry and its characteristic resignation should not be read as an expression of futility, because his poetic resignation marks the tensions and paradoxes inherent in the economic resignification of space. As Bishop et al. remind us, "[a]rchitecture does not simply *enclose* but rather it *produces* space. The question of architectural constraints and enclosures forces the space of thinking to interact with the space of dwelling" (p. 5, italics in the original). Yap's poems may be read as such a productive architecture set in language that, through a solipsism which draws attention to its own verbal and cognitive artifice, performs and invites an interaction between thinking and dwelling. They ask us to consider the distinction between Singapore as a living space and a space for making a living.

This essay began by acknowledging in the first part the difficulties of reading Yap's poetry. Very often, the poems tend to fold into themselves and elude attempts at meaning-making. The second section of this essay drew on basic concepts in geography to explore Yap's poetry within a pedagogical setting. The final part combined the insights of Lefebvre and scholars who specifically analyze Singapore's space and history into our reading of Yap's poetry. What gradually emerges from our reading of Yap's poetry is an urban poetics that seeks refuge in solipsism because urban space has been overwritten by the state. What is a poet to do in response to the state dominance of urban space? For Yap, the answer is to be "a big foeval eye", to fold into the self and be constantly vigilant, always looking outwards (*Man Snake Apple*, p. 24).

References

Alfian Sa'at. *One Fierce Hour*. Singapore: Landmark Books, 1998.
Beckett, Samuel. *Molloy; Mallone Dies; The Unnamable*. New York: Knopf, 1997.
Benjamin, Walter. *The Writer of Modern Life: Essays on Charles Baudelaire*, edited by Michael W. Jennings, translated by Howard Eiland, Edmund Jephcott, Rodney Livingstone and Harry Zohn. Cambridge, MA: Belknap Press of Harvard University Press, 2006.
Bishop, Ryan, John Phillips, and Wei-Wei Yeo, eds. *Beyond Description: Singapore Space Historicity*. London: Routledge, 2004.
Blunt, Alison. "Geography and the Humanities Tradition". In *Key Concepts in Geography*, 2nd ed., edited by Nicholas J. Clifford, Sarah L. Holloway, Stephen P. Rice and Gill Valentine. London: Sage, 2009.
Chua, Beng Huat. "Public Housing Residents as Clients of the State". *Housing Studies* 15, no. 1 (2000): 45–60.
De Certeau, Michel. *The Practice of Everyday Life*, translated by Steven Randall. Berkeley: University of California Press, 1984.
Elden, Stuart. *Understanding Henri Lefebvre: Theory and the Possible*. London: Continuum, 2004.
Garrard, Greg. *Ecocriticism*. London: Routledge, 2004.
Goh, Robbie B.H. "Imagining the Nation: The Role of Singapore Poetry in English in 'Emergent Nationalism'". *Journal of Commonwealth Literature* 41, no. 2 (2006): 21–41.
Heidegger, Martin. *Poetry, Language, Thought*, translated by Albert Hofstadter. New York: Harper and Row, 1975.
Latham, Alan, Derek McCormack, Kim McNamara and Donald McNeill. *Key Concepts in Urban Geography*. London: Sage, 2009.
Lee Tzu Pheng. "My Country and My People". *Tides of Memories and Other Singapore Poems*. Singapore: AsiaPac Books, 2002.

Lefebvre, Henri. *The Production of Space*, translated by Donald Nicholson-Smith. Oxford: Blackwell, 1991.
Lévi-Strauss, Claude. *The Savage Mind*. London: Weidenfeld and Nicolson, 1966.
Orwell, George. *Nineteen Eighty-Four*. New York: Harcourt, Brace 1949.
Patke, Rajeev. "Voice and Authority in English Poetry from Singapore". *Interlogue: Studies in Singapore Literature, Volume 2: Poetry*, edited by Kirpal Singh. Singapore: Ethos Books, 1999.
Thrift, Nigel. "Space: The Fundamental Stuff of Geography". *Key Concepts in Geography*, 2nd ed., edited by Nicholas J. Clifford, Sarah L. Holloway, Stephen P. Rice and Gill Valentine. London: Sage, 2009.
Thumboo, Edwin. "Ulysses by the Merlion". *A Third Map: New and Selected Poems*. Singapore: UniPress, 1993.
Yap, Arthur. *Commonplace*. Singapore: Heinemann Educational Books (Asia), 1977.
———. *Down the Line*. Singapore: Heinemann Educational Books, 1980.
———. *Man Snake Apple & Other Poems*. Singapore: Heinemann Asia, 1986.
———. *Only Lines*. Singapore: Federal Publications, 1971.

6

ARTHUR YAP'S ECOLOGICAL POETICS OF THE DAILY

Zhou Xiaojing

Arthur Yap's poems which portray the human condition and the environment through everyday scenes in public spaces demand an interpretation that radically challenges the anthropocentrism and nature-vs.-culture dualism of Western classical humanism. Nature is a prominent presence in some of Yap's poems, and conspicuously absent in others. Both its presence and absence are intertwined with the human sociocultural environment shaped by historical forces. Underlying this relationship is an ecological perspective that informs the subject matter and poetics of Yap's poetry, which can be considered "ecopoetry" to a certain extent. Although Yap's work shares ecopoetry's ecological awareness and concern with environmental issues, it refuses to be confined to any narrow definition of ecopoetry as "a new brand of nature poetry" (Bryson 2002, p. 3). This is the case partly because of its subversive postcolonial mimicry of Eurocentric perspectives on the human/nature relationship, and partly because of its central concern with daily urban life. While the characteristics of ecopoetry as described by American and British critics can shed some light on Yap's poems and poetics, they are inadequate for a fuller understanding of Yap's thematic concerns with the relationship between nature and culture, which are significantly different from those of the British and American nature poets whose work some critics consider early ecopoetry.

In his definition of "ecopoetry", J. Scott Bryson traces "the history of nature poetry ... back to the roots" of the English language, from *Beowulf* to Blake, to English Romantic poetry, and eventually to "a new form of nature poetry" produced by "antiromantics" such as Robert Frost, Robinson Jeffers, and Wallace Stevens, among others (2002, p. 2). Bryson's definition of "ecopoetry" draws on Robert Langbaum's discussion of a paradigm shift in twentieth-century poetry from traditional "nature poetry" largely as a result of scientific discoveries such as those in evolution and geology (p. 2). According to Langbaum, "the best twentieth-century nature poetry 'defines itself precisely by opposing, or seeming to oppose, the pathetic fallacy ...' which characterizes overly romantic nature poetry" (quoted in Bryson 2002, pp. 2–3). In the poems of twentieth-century antiromantics, Langbaum maintains, one feels "in nature an unalterably alien, even an unfeeling, existence", thus carrying "empathy several steps farther than did the nineteenth-century poets who felt in nature a life different from but compatible with ours" (quoted in Bryson, p. 3).

Expanding on Langbaum's study of nineteenth- and twentieth-century nature poetry by British and American poets, Bryson considers "ecopoetry" a "newer brand of nature poetry" which grew out of an awareness of and concern about environmental issues shared by poets and the general public (2002, p. 3). For Bryson, ecopoetry is a "a subset of nature poetry that, while adhering to certain conventions of romanticism, also advances beyond that tradition and takes on distinctly contemporary problems and issues" (p. 5). He singles out three primary characteristics of ecopoetry, which include (1) "an emphasis on maintaining an ecocentric perspective that recognizes the interdependent nature of the world"; (2) "an imperative toward humility in relationships with both human and nonhuman nature"; and (3) "an intense skepticism concerning hyperrationality, skepticism that usually leads to an indictment of an overtechnologized modern world and a warning concerning the very real potential for ecological catastrophe" (pp. 5–6).

Even though Yap's poems contain these three characteristics of ecopoetry, they refuse to be completely identified with the cultural and poetic "roots" of British and American nature poetry. Nature in Yap's poems does not assume either a "compatible" or an "unalterably alien", "unfeeling" attribute; rather nature, culture, and humans are fused into an infinite process of evolution. In fact, many of Yap's poems undermine the Eurocentric view of humans' relationship to nature through a strategy similar to what Homi Bhabha (1994) calls "mimicry". Bhabha argues that a subversive postcolonial mimicry works "through the repetition of *partial presence*" of the normative colonial discourse; it "articulates those disturbances of cultural, racial and historical difference that menace the narcissistic demand of colonial authority" (p. 88). Yap's poems, such as "man snake apple" and "tropical paradise" collected in *Man Snake Apple* (1986), are characterized by a postcolonial mimicry that counters normalized Eurocentric knowledge and hegemonic culture. From this perspective, Yap's poetry can be identified in part with what Shirley Geoklin Lim (1994) calls a "counter tradition" in Singapore English-language writing, which demonstrates some shared attributes of a "certain colonial and/or cosmopolitan mentality not always conscious with nationalistic or indigenous identity and values" (pp. 120, 124). Nevertheless, Yap's poetry and poetics resist being defined within a national literary tradition, or being placed in a particular school of poetry. This uncontainable attribute of Yap's work opens up more possibilities for interpretation from multiple and contrasting perspectives.

I contend that Yap's poetry proposes a re-conceptualization of the relationships among nature, culture, and human beings, and demonstrates an ecological poetics that breaks away from the anthropocentric traditions of British and American lyric poetry in which the lyric "I/eye" operates as the organizing principle of the poem. Yap's poem "man snake apple" provides a useful framework through which both the subject matters and forms of many of Yap's other poems, as well as their ecological poetics of the daily can be fruitfully interpreted. As the title indicates, this poem evokes the creation story in the Book of Genesis. But instead of a creation story, Yap's poem presents an evolutionary process of three elements in the world — man snake apple — and their interrelationship of autonomous yet intertwining coexistence. Alluding to the Genesis narrative that God creates the world and all things in it in six days and rests on the seventh day, Yap uses seven days to structure the development of the poem "man snake apple". Yet God and Eve are absent from the poem, as are the Genesis concepts of good and evil, sin and shame embedded in the relationship between God and humanity as embodied by Adam and Eve. Also absent in Yap's poem evocative of the Garden of Eden is the perilous relationship between human beings and nature embodied by the seductive snake and the tree of the knowledge of good and evil. Moreover, in Yap's poem time is cyclical rather than linear, suggesting that death is part of the cycle of life and renewal, rather than the consequence of humans' original sin. Hence the poem begins not with the creation of the world but with a stage in the cycle of life on earth:

> "man snake apple"
>
> ages the apple slept on the tree
> dreaming of stars & storing the distillation
> of a thousand storms, outlasted cheiroterous ravages
> & survived more golden-red if the moons also blessed.
> the snake jounced up & down the tree,
> investigated the apple from all round angles,
> a circumoral need. but it had no need to feed.
>   (Yap, *The Space of City Trees*, 2000, hereafter *Space*, p. 113)

At once alluding to and departing from the narrative of Genesis about omnipotent divine power, the knowledge of good and evil in the forbidden fruit, the danger of the serpent, and human vulnerability, capacity and responsibility, Yap strips the apple, snake, and man of their biblical meanings, and alters the perilous relationship among them. As the speaker emphasizes: "the apple had no meaning. man was trying out / & being tried out by his circumstance. / apple snake man were one, two, three" (*Space*, p. 113). In Yap's poem the apple exists for its own sake without God's design, serving no function in determining the fate of human mortality. The snake, too, coexists with the apple and man as part of the environment, posing no threat to man. Its investigation of the meaningless apple encompasses only "a circumoral need" (p. 113). But this separate coexistence of the three — man snake apple — is not constant; it is only one stage in a process of change without beginning or end: "this was day one, / the first day from anytime" (p. 113). Yap's representation of the intertwining of human beings and nature disrupts the linearity of time that structures the Christian biblical creation narrative, and dismantles the hierarchical order of beings, a hierarchy that privileges the mind over the body, and underlies colonialist domination over the colonized "savages" of the tropics.

As the poem moves from day one to day five, each of the three — man snake apple — undergoes significant transformations. On day one, "the snake could rise & walk over man, the apple / of the circumbient eye.

Man could walk / slither-poised, hang on branches like a growth." But this status of the man seems to be a metamorphosis from the angel, or rather from a creature with wings: "he could no longer fly; his wings were lain still" (p. 113). Moreover, while the young "lie of the land / produced prodigiously, floriferously", man assumes no knowledge of, and shows no desire for anything in "dazzling" nature; he "looked at everything / with the calm of unknowing eyes & did not want", with the apple lying "absolute on the tree, the snake near" (p. 113). Here, man is neither outside of nature, nor above it, but rather is part of the living environment or of "the world community", to borrow Bryson's (2002) phrase for defining the relationship between human beings and nature in contemporary "ecopoetry" (p. 3). Thus, there is no intimate relationship with the "natural world" for the "human self" to have lost, to be breached, or to "heal" in facing environmental crises, as Bryson says of a "historical phenomenon" that in part at least gave rise to ecopoetry (p. 3). Even before the advent of contemporary ecopoetry, Yap's ecopoetic re-representation of the world not only breaks away from the cultural and poetic "roots" of conventional British and American nature poetry in which nature is "compatible" or "unalterably alien", "unfeeling"; it undermines the Western anthropocentric conceptualization of the world as embedded in the creation myth of Genesis. However, man's indifference to his surroundings, including the apple and the snake, does not last, since nothing remains the same in the ecological community of "man snake apple":

> this day,
> day two
>
> of whatever calendar wasn't.
> butterflies flew with the snake that changed
> more swiftly than a spectrum of rainbows on short-loan
> & the apple effloresced into protoneons; red, gold,
> purple, a runnel of liquids & fugitives, visions.
> man looked & felt the first flash of the pain of beauty.
> the apple stirred in his heart, its stalk a tuning fork
> regulating the earth, orchestrating symphonies of mountains,
> suzerain dragons that immolated in hauteur.
>
> *(Space,* pp. 113–14)

Distinctive changes are taking place in each of the three — the snake, the apple, and man — without divine design or intervention. Yet, transformation in one affects that in another. Man loses his indifferent calm as he watches butterflies (an image of metamorphosis) fly "with the snake that changed / more swiftly than a spectrum of rainbows on short-loan / & the apple effloresced into protoneons; red, gold, / purple, a runnel of liquids & fugitives, visions" (pp. 113–14). Seeing these, man begins to feel "the first flash of the pain of beauty" and "the apple stirred in his heart". It is worth noting that Yap employs complex syntax and arranges line breaks in such a way as to foreground the interconnections among the snake, apple, and man who are transformed by their environment which they themselves in part constitute. Yap's ecopoetics then is more than part of a postcolonial "counter tradition"; it offers an alternative episteme that refuses to be categorized under any national or ethnic tradition.

In breaking away from the seven-day sequence of events as told in Genesis, and eliminating the biblical meanings embedded in apple, snake, and man, while still using seven days to structure the narrative of his poem, Yap creates anticipation, uncertainty, suspense, and surprise. At the same time, he enhances this structurally produced unsettling aesthetic, ideological, and epistemological effect by sustaining a subversive resonance, one that simultaneously evokes and departs from the biblical text. More important, Yap's poem does not simply reject or subvert the normalized knowledge about the world or the relationship between nature and human beings as inscribed in the Bible. It offers an ecological perspective on life and death, nature and culture embedded in the interlinking changes throughout the seven days that make up the poem.

As the poem unfolds, "man snake apple" changes drastically after the uneventful third and fourth days. So too, does the apparently harmless relationship among them. They "disappeared on day five / because day five was day five / & all prior pluses & minuses / were not cued this day, / not gathered, not resown, not wanted" (p. 114). Rather than bringing the completion of God's creation of the world as described in Genesis, day six is a transitional day in Yap's poem: "from morning to noon, from noon to dusk, / storing upon itself, conserving to have itself reborn" (p. 115). Even though everything appears to be still — "the finagling snake / quiet as coiled repose" seemed to be in a "comatose inertia", "the voluptuous apple slept on, / heavy as a stone", and "ruminative man, poised as his own shily shadow" — a profound change is taking place in the status of their coexistence: the apple is in man's head slowly rattling, and "the snake in his heart undulating in lazy loops" (p. 115). The penetration of apple and snake into man's mind and body leads to further unexpected changes:

> day six died.
> the world grew young & day seven happened;
> a minimum of event, fanfare, cheer-leading.
> sun, moon, stars were freshly reordered.
> man snake apple multiplied; in endless succession,
> the progeny, men killed snakes, ate apples.
> apples, detached from trees, dropped on men
> & germinated ideas, created patents,
> became the targets of crossbows.
> snakes bit into serum & have carried it ever since;
> popped out of watering holes, appeared in circuses,
> slid over tarmac lanes, were run over by cars.
>
> *(Space, p. 114)*

The apparently harmless renewal, reproduction, and mutation resulting from the cycle of life and death actually have unexpected disturbing results when men become dominant over other species ("men killed snakes, ate apples") and modern technology is introduced into the environment and subsequently destroys the natural habitat for snakes, which "were run over by cars". This phenomenon anticipates current environmental degradation and ecological catastrophe underlying the thematic concerns of ecopoetry.

The ending of Yap's poem highlights the intertwining of nature and culture with humans (who are part of both), and points out the transformation of the world in which human civilization dominates the landscape where butterflies used to fly with the snake, while the apple was ripening on the tree, and man "looked & felt the first flash of the pain of beauty". But now, the peaceful coexistence of man snake apple is replaced by a transformative fusion which is itself a result of metamorphosis:

> man snake apple were no longer one, two, three.
> a fused combination, the progeny in infinite permutations.
> mensnakesapples built cities, flew as they once did,
> fought wars, archiving them as later documentaries,
> invented organized leisure, civilized swindle,
> top-ten everything, mass trances, pop-whatever.
>
> it was forever & forever & forever
>
> & a day,
> today, it begins again today.
>
> *(Space, p. 115)*

Yap strategically employs repetition with variation in structuring the development of the poem with the three major life forms — man snake apple — human beings, animals, and plants, whose altered relationship in their coexistence is mirrored in the collapse of the three words into one — "mensnakesapples". This change is accompanied by the transformation of the environment shaped almost entirely by human agency in which nature (snakes and apples) is subsumed into culture. However, there is no celebration of the achievements of mensnakesapples. In fact, the speaker indirectly asserts a social critique of mass culture and corruption through irony: mensnakesapples "invented organized leisure, civilized swindle, / top-ten everything, mass trances, pop-whatever". Significantly, Yap's portrayal of the ecological transpositions of man snake apple goes beyond undermining normalized Eurocentric knowledge to offer an alternative view on the human conditions and a world in which nature and culture are mutually constituent and transformative. The ecological view of the world articulated in this poem, and the "infinite permutations" of the interpenetration of nature and culture — "a fused combination" of "mensnakesapples" — and of the resulting impact on the environment recur in Yap's other poems.

Embedded in Yap's ecological poetics is a subversive strategy of "repetition of *partial presence*" (Bhabha 1994, p. 88), which undermines normative colonial discourse by at once evoking and breaking away from the images and narrative of the Garden of Eden. For instance, like "man snake apple", the poem "tropical paradise" simultaneously evokes and contrasts the biblical paradise in Heaven, but with a focus on change and decay as a necessary condition for the vitality of life. In this earthly paradise, the presence of human beings claims no domination over fauna and flora; it is merely part of the diverse vibrancy of life. Countering timeless, stagnant eternal life in Heaven, life in the tropical paradise is in constant motion and change. The poem begins with the sensual "feel of things. textures. the elastic skin, / gently pliant tote touch. the old metallic shock / of water in a shaded pool, galvanizing all the pores;" (*Space*, p. 107). There is no shame, no sin, no violation of divine rules attached to sensuality. In fact, the reproductive organs of the flowers (as of humans) are part of the intricate ecosystem of decay and renewal:

paradise:

staminate & prisillate, they all dance to the thrall of
primeval rhythms. things, things growing so fast; feel the

> heat of their regeneration. the friction of leaf against leaf,
> bud & bee, pod to pod. among the green mysteries of
> certainty, they consume the decay of aged life:
>
> paradise:
>
> at sunrise, a stone falling endlessly
> & in it the silence of before & after.
> in the silence of before & after, a new stone
> falls endlessly &, before it is done,
>
> a head falling.
> o lord, it is to you it falls.
>
> jungle, a tall tree falling eternally.
> ...
> in the timelessness before & after, a new tree
> falls within the fallen. being done,
>
> a limb falling.
> a lord, it is to you it dies.
>
> (*Space*, p. 107)

The falling of the stone, the tree, and the head of a person calls to mind, yet counters, the biblical narrative of the Fall of humanity from innocence and paradise in Heaven. These falls in this earthly tropical paradise are part of the inevitable cycle of life and death ("a new tree / falls within the fallen"). The last line of the poem highlights this perspective by evoking the Christian God, yet addressing a god in a different light — as a figurative beginning of life that follows death, death that gives way to new life: "o lord, it is to you it dies" (p. 107).

In other poems such as "seasonal" Yap further undermines the anthropocentric view of the world by suggesting that the natural world existed before human beings, who are merely part of the aftermath of the motion and forces of nature. This perspective is embedded in the structure, imagery, and development of the poem which begins with the motion of wind in tree leaves:

> soft-pawing the sky
> are splayed leaves,
> otherwise they're falling down:
>
> ancient wind

> swells this garden like a balloon
> every minute blown larger
> until it's about to burst:
>
> ...
>
> every casualty is happy
> mindless in an abstract way
> tracing where the wind ends
> and it is right here
> (we're the aftermath next month).
> where it began, we were there:
> ancient monsoon.
>
> (*Space*, p. 24)

Not only does nature exist independent of God's creation or human consciousness, it brings humans into being. Yap enhances the decentred presence of human beings in the poem by foregrounding the activity in nature, and inserting human presence as a reference note in parenthesis — "(we're the aftermath next month)". But significantly the poem emphasizes the inseparable connection between nature and humans in the cycle of seasons: "where it began, we were there: / ancient monsoon" (p. 24).

Departing further from the concepts underlying the Garden of Eden, and from the sublime landscape in British and American nature poetry, Yap often depicts public spaces, including gardens, markets, and parks, which are examples of the "infinite permutations" of the "progeny" — "a fused combination" of "mensnakesapples" in the world. Several of his poems, such as "the shisen-do: A ZEN GARDEN IN KYOTO", "at nagoya", and "a peony display, ueno park", portray everyday experience in public gardens in Japan. While the location of these poems may indicate Yap's cosmopolitanism, the meticulously cultivated Japanese gardens seem to provide an appropriate place for Yap to portray one of the variations of "infinite permutations" of an ecological fusion of nature, culture, and humans. In "the shisen-do: A ZEN GARDEN IN KYOTO", for instance, nature, though cultivated, is not reduced to merely the object of human pleasure. Rather, nature shapes human culture and enriches human experience even as human beings shape and cultivate nature. Together, they constitute an aesthetic environment that heightens the values of all sentient beings.

> the interior garden reveals shaped azalea bushes,
> sand combed into a pattern, a spent wisteria,
> little white daisies, a low waterfall,
> ...
>
> the woman bending over some plants
> thought they were a kind of chrysanthemum,
> her words never once staying her tending hands.
>
> no photographer to record the scene, to fail.
>
> a bowl of green tea, a biscuit on a paper square.
>
> always the same tableau, intrinsically still,
> the kindling of every sentience.
> it is always the same & one can see
> it had always been, will be.
>
> <div align="right">(<i>Space</i>, p. 131)</div>

Yap sets off the line, "a bowl of green tea, a biscuit on a paper square", in the midst of the garden scene to spotlight a phenomenon of culture (which is already a transmutation of the fusion of nature and culture) as part of the "tableau" of the total environment of the Zen garden, which includes the woman tending the plants. Here the coexistence of nature and culture entails human appreciation of, responsibility for, and labour in attending nature, while human beings themselves are nurtured by nature in return. This cultivated, aestheticized environment asserts no hierarchical or binary relationship between nature and human culture; it is "the kindling of every sentience". It is worth noting, moreover, that rather than attributing this intricate tableau of nature, culture, and human beings to the uniqueness of a Japanese Zen garden, Yap emphasizes that this relationship and the environment it constitutes "had always been, will be", suggesting an ecological world view.

This world view challenges Yap to explore various ways for portraying a non-hierarchical relationship among all things in the world through different poetic forms. In "a list of things: A MARKET AT UENO", for instance, Yap dismantles the centrality of human presence, and unsettles the binarized relationship between nature and culture, thorough collage or an apparently random list of heterogeneous things:

> gesticulating fingers of lentil, unwriggly eels,
> spearheads of bamboo shoot, soothing water chestnusts,
> green snakes of cucumber, jetsams of seaweed,
> wrinkled-nose pickles, earspans of brown mushroom,
> calm persimmons, outlandish roly-poly apples,
> air-licking clams, dry earth-crusts of fish,
> icy-eyed bream, powdered kabuki faces of cake,
> paragraphs of beancurd, exhaling piles of garlic,
> enpurpled piccolo noses of aubergine, lazy grapes,
> no-nonsense tangerines, arms-folded-over squid,
> shrine-pillars of celery, bullets of green chillie,
> hibernating squares of hardkerchief, fat tabi,
> expandable sweaters, ventilated t-shirts, healthy cod,
> ...
>
> are all there.
>
> (*Space*, p. 137)

Despite the radical difference of its form, this poem, like "the shisendo: A ZEN GARDEN IN KYOTO", suggests another variation of the "infinite permutations" of the "progeny" of "a fused combination" of "mensnakesapples" in the world. Unlike the Anti-Romantics, Yap unabashedly employs "pathetic fallacy" to anthropomorphize almost all the things on display at the market without assuming anthropocentricism. His strategy of nondiscriminatory listing renders it impossible to impose a hierarchy or a binary of sentient and non-sentient things. While "exhaling piles of garlic", "lazy grapes", and "no-nonsense tangerines" have taken on individual characteristics respectively, "grumpy red mullet, macho beef, sassy tomatoes" seem to be much more interesting than human products of "expandable sweaters, vertilated t-shirts", and "brisk aprons" (*Space*, p. 137). Yap's virtuoso manipulation of syntax and diction makes it extremely hard, if not entirely impossible, to separate things from "nature" from things of culture. After all, the public market itself is already an integral part of the blending of nature and culture in people's everyday life in the city, where there is no sublime wilderness or landscape to claim its alienness from or indifference to humans.

The juxtaposition or fusion of all things in the world in Yap's poems, however, is not always harmless or harmonious. As he continues to explore the infinite permutations of the "fused combination" of "mensnakesapples" in the world, Yap reveals disturbing, destructive impacts of modern technology and civilization on nature, as anticipated in "man snake apple" with its reference to the building of cities, the waging of wars, and the invention of "organized leisure" and "civilized swindle". Signs of the damage done by modern technology and urban development are discernable in poems such as "dramatis personae", in which the unsettling mingling of nature and culture suggests pollution of the natural environment. Just as "the sharp smell" of petroleum is mixed with "the warm scent of dirty sand" (*Space*, p. 27), the landcrabs have evolved according to their changed habitat altered by sewers and cement. Yet, here by the seaside, humans have no dominion over nature:

> (can you see?)
> here is the sea.
> sand and sea are less today
> as there is more of life.
>
> webbed up here by the sewer
> sewn to the hardness of cement
> trapped by piss-moss, little landcrabs
> are more crust than crab and salt.
> and caught here, we would never have been
> more than all these things we have seen.
> that cemented here, as we are not,
> we run away before the waves arrive
> with a little last fresh collapse
>
> (*Space*, p. 28)

Yap suggests that human beings cannot assume superiority over "all these things" on the beach, including the landcrabs; while humans "run away before the waves arrive" collapsing into the shore, other creatures are "cemented here".

Yap's other poems of urban scenes, particularly those set in the streets of the city, reveal that human beings are trapped in the unpleasant, even harmful environment they themselves have created. Yap alludes to the impact of urban renewal and urban sprawl in a place where "there is no future in nostalgia", and suggests that the transformation of the urban environment is related to the development of modern technology, which results from the process of "various variations & permutations" (p. 59). Instead of things from nature, or sentient beings, modern appliances and technology dominate the landscape:

Arthur Yap's Ecological Poetics of the Daily

> & certainly no nostalgia in the future of the past.
> now, the corner cigarette-seller is gone, is perhaps dead.
> no, definitely dead, he would not otherwise have gone.
> he is replaced by a stamp-machine,
> the old cook by a pressure-cooker,
> the old trishaw-rider's stand by a fire hydrant,
> the washer-woman by a spin-dryer
>
> & it goes on
> in various variations & permutations.
> there is no future in nostalgia.
>
> (Space, p. 59)

Yap critiques the apparent advantage of modern convenience through the speaker's indirect expression of nostalgia for familiar sights of people who have been replaced by machines. If this kind of change "goes on / in various variations & permutations", as the speaker states, its impact will have more profound results than merely prompting nostalgia.

In poems such as "commonplace", "street scene I", "street scene II", and "traffic", Yap portrays a modern urban environment which has not only severed humans from nature, but also reshaped their way of life and even their sense of self. He employs a flat tone, drab diction, and repetition to enhance the monotony of modern city life in "commonplace":

> daybreak, arms & legs.
> breakfast. day lengthens: commonplace
> situations & people. you say:
> let's meet for lunch.
>
> afternoon's 2nd movement, andante,
> as if groaning a bit.
> everything has happened before
> but there is nothing to compare it
> each time, with each time that it recurs;
> ...
> 2 o'clock: 2 stained blobs on a clear canvas,
> 3 o'clock: 3 fingers tapping a tattoo on the table
> are 3 upwind gulls, sliding, side to side,
> ...
> 4 o'clock: like yesterday's glance,
> still holds true, this morning's streets

are already rattling cars & buses back
into younger & less immediate parts of the city.
commonplace evening, the place is the same.
when night comes, it will come in neonlights.
when the night comes, will it come in darkness
or will it bring its own light to a well-scrubbed day?
will there be doubt that commonplace is?

(*Space*, p. 57)

Daybreak begins with no sense of freshness or excitement, nor scenes of nature, but "commonplace / situations & people" who are faceless "arms and legs", and whose routine amounts to nothing more than breakfast followed by lunch. As morning gives way to noon, the day simply lengthens with the same rhythm without variations of activities: "everything has happened before / but there is nothing to compare it / each time, with each time that it recurs". But while the day drones on as predictably as the movement of clock time, something extraordinary is taking place: "this morning's streets / are already rattling cars & buses back / into younger & less immediate parts of the city" (p. 57). The rapid speed of urban sprawl has transformed the normality of the everyday environment and experience. Stars have disappeared from the sky; "when night comes, it will come in neonlights." Modernity has not only changed the nature of night in the city, it has altered the day — our living environment and its meanings. As the speaker asks: "when the night comes, will it come in darkness / or will it bring its own light to a well-scrubbed day? / will there be doubt that commonplace is?" (p. 57).

The change of living environment in the city, Yap further suggests, has a profound impact on people's relationships with one another, and on their sense of self. In "street scene I", for instance, the lonely man who asks strangers in the street about "the hours for reduced rates" is trying desperately to interact with others. His situation is not unique, as the speaker says of the man and himself: "why am i so lonely & have to stop you? / i felt the same then" (p. 121). Although "street scene I" offers no explanation for people's isolation and loneliness in the city, "street scene II" seems to shed some light. The first three lines of the poem suggest a connection between the speaker's implied loneliness and the modern urban environment:

> there can never be too many people in the street.
> immediate evening, the afterimage is a bitter glow
> of neon moons creating their own sky.
>
> the street is neither too long nor too short
> for the night, too, is neither.
>
> & by losing oneself, the solipsist's nightmare
> in which everything exists but oneself:
> a big foeval eye.
>
> (Space, p. 122)

The opening statement indicates that the speaker likes to have people around, and the only way to be with many people is to be in the street. Yet, by formulating the sentence in the negative — "there can never be too many people in the street" — Yap, suggests that no matter how many people are in the street, they will never alleviate the speaker's sense of isolation resulting from the alienating artificial light of "neon moons" that create "their own sky". There is no waxing or waning moon, nor any Milky Way in the sky to create a sense of wonder or a sense of belonging to an infinite shared universe. The following lines further accentuate that modern technology and the constructed urban environment have altered the natural world — "the street is neither too long nor too short / for the night, too, is neither." Night has become as banal and meaningless as the length of the street. Night has lost its starry sky and its darkness because of the "neon moons" that create "their own sky", and with it, the loss of all sense and meanings of the mysterious, the extraordinary, and the unfathomable. Hence, the speaker in "commonplace" asks: "when the night comes, will it come in darkness / or will it bring its own light to a well-scrubbed day? / will there be doubt that commonplace is?" (*Space*, p. 57). Moreover, the mundane, alienating urban environment seems to have led to the loss of the self. As the speaker says with self-mockery: "& by losing oneself, the solipsist's nightmare / in which everything exists but oneself: / a big foeval eye" (p. 122).

Yap reveals other aspects of the changed urban environment which can further illuminate the feelings of banality, isolation, loneliness, and alienation in the city. In the poem, "traffic", Yap portrays an everyday experience in the city where pedestrians seem to feel out of place, where daily activities and sights are disconcerting, and where nature is no where to be seen:

> asked the way to park street
> the old man drew himself up,
> ...
>
> like any big city, this city
> offers her people a variety of ways
> in which moments of unhurry
> may be used. the old man knew
> roads never look like themselves,
> edging sideways from the curb,
> pushing over zebra zips. nevertheless...
>
> (*Space*, p. 96)

In contrast to the title of the poem, "traffic", the speaker and the old man are on foot in the city, where roads "never look like themselves", and walking seems to be faster than driving in arriving at a particular destination ("rounding a corner a little quicker / than cars"). Yet, there is no pleasure in being a pedestrian in a city of cars and imported cultures. Yap employs collage to assemble and juxtapose a jumble of incongruous activities, words, and images to foreground everyday experience in an urban environment without nature:

> & done. rounding a corner a little quicker
> than cars, one's eyes read the restaurant's menu
> for 'long soup' & 'short soup'.
> feet, hesitating speculatively,
> are like the feet on the cinema poster,
> 'porcelain anniversary', a French
> concoction of limbs. Simulated coitus,
> long soup, streaking cars
> blue to the gills, brick-clogged pores:
> a connection of many things
> that cannot undergo any physical editing.
>
> (*Space*, p. 96)

The speaker's statement that this unlikely assemblage demonstrates "a connection of many things / that cannot undergo any physical editing" suggests that the intricate connections among many things makes it impossible to change anything like "the feet on the cinema poster" and "brick-clogged pores". These phenomena are part of the various "infinite permutations" of "a fused combination" of "mensnakesapples".

Just as the permutations of the fusion of fauna, flora, and humans ("mensnakesapples") have led to unpredictable and uncontainable situations regarding the status of all sentient beings and their surroundings, Yap's ecological view of the world has generated a wide range of poems which resist being categorized within a single poetic genre or tradition. In her insightful Introduction to a collection of selected poems by Yap, *The Space of City Trees* (2000), Anne Brewster points out the characteristics of Yap's poetry, noting that "Yap is a poet of the mundane, the banal and the small familiar details of everyday life, and that the mundane and the familiar are made fresh and new in the poetry." However, Brewster adds, "This is not to say that they are translated into the realm of the mythic or symbolic. They remain firmly anchored in the realm of the quotidian, that is, of repetition and mundanity.... Everyday life is not contemptible or boring, according to Yap; it is the means by which we know ourselves in the world" (p. xii). This is true, but only partly. For Yap's poems of the daily are concerned with more than the meanings of the quotidian; everyday life in Yap's poems is a means by which we know not just ourselves, but also the world which we have shaped and in which we are trapped. In his book, *Writing for an Endangered World: Literature, Culture, and Environment in the U.S. and Beyond* (2001), Lawrence Buell calls critical attention to the inadequacy of traditional "nature writing" and "pastoral poetry" as environmental literature. He argues that a "complex understanding of what counts as environment" must take into account the fusion of "landscape of wilderness and technology into one like-it-or-not environmental web" (p. 8). And "It is on the basis of this complex understanding of what counts as environment, environmentalism, and environmental writing", Buell emphasizes, "that literature and environmental studies must make their case for the indispensableness of physical environment as a shaping force in human art and experience, and how such an aesthetic works" (pp. 8–9). The forms, aesthetics, and thematic concerns of Yap's poems demonstrate precisely the indispensableness of physical environment as a shaping force in human art and experience" entangled in the fragile, protean "environmental web." Enacting a keen awareness of the interpenetration between nature and culture, and the subsequent transformations of life and the environment, Yap's ecopoetics places him among the forerunners of ecopoetry.

Nonetheless, the ecological concerns and poetics of Arthur Yap's poetry require that it be read not only with but also against the grain of canonical British and American nature poetry and ecopoetry. Even though Yap's poems share similar concerns with those of ecopoetry which Bryson has identified, their conceptual and aesthetic characteristics in portraying the environment as constituted by the coexistence of and mutual transformations of animate and inanimate things refuse to be traced to the Eurocentric roots of either the "English Romantic poetry" or "a new form of nature poetry" produced by "antiromantics" discussed by Bryson. Yap's poetics challenge readers and scholars to broaden established definitions of poetic traditions, and urges us towards investigations beyond the commonplace into the remarkable or disastrous unexpected permutations of the fusions of nature, technology, heterogeneous cultures, histories, and literary tradition in both his poems and the world.

References

Bhabha, Homi K. *The Location of Culture*. London: Routlege, 1994.
Brewster, Anne. Introduction. In *The Space of City Trees: Selected Poems*, by Arthur Yap. London: Skoob Books, 2000.
Bryson, J. Scott. Introduction. *Ecopoetry: A Critical Introduction*, edited by J. Scott Bryson. Salt Lake City: University of Utah Press, 2002.
Buell, Lawrence. *Writing for an Endangered World: Literature, Culture, and Environment in the U.S. and Beyond*. Cambridge, MA: Belknap Press of Harvard University Press, 2001.
Fletcher, Angus. *A New Theory for American Poetry: Democracy, the Environment, and the Future of Imagination*. Cambridge: Harvard University Press, 2004.
Langbaum, Robert. "The New Nature Poetry". In *The Modern Spirit: Essays on the Continuity of Nineteenth- and Twentieth-Century Literature*. New York: Oxford, 1970.
Lim, Shirley Geok-lin. *Writing S.E. Asia in English: Against the Grain, Focus on Asian English-language Literature*. London: Skoob Books, 1994.
Yap, Arthur. *The Space of City Trees: Selected Poems*. London: Skoob Books, 2000.

7

"EXCEPT FOR A WORD"
Arthur Yap's Unspoken Homoeroticism

Cyril Wong

Arthur Yap was predisposed to silences. I had only ever spoken to him twice in my life, but we had been writing letters back and forth until a year before he passed away on 19 June 2006 of nasopharyngeal carcinoma. Standing before his coffin at his funeral, I could not believe that the poet who had befriended me and encouraged me to keep publishing my own poems was really gone. Gentle and soft-spoken in real life, his reticence had not been a consequence of indifference. I always believed that his silences stemmed from a desire to reserve quick judgment, an inclination that informs his poetry as well. I have tended to equate his general sense of restraint with kindness. In his poems, this quality of restraint opens up a spectrum of conflicting interpretations; the poet is like a quiet but generous host who has invited a whole range of readers to wander and settle comfortably inside the spacious house of his poetry.

Kindness was probably not what literary commentators had in mind when they underscored Yap's "private sensibility" (Singh 1999, p. 15) and his refusal to engage with nation-building discourses in outrightly opinionated and political ways in the poems. During an interview, Yap had once answered "no" to a question about whether he was in sympathy with the opinion of Edwin Thumboo, a poet regularly regarded as a literary pioneer in Singapore, that "the writer must explain his society, bring into focus the forces, whether healthy or pernicious, which move society" (quoted in Wong 2009). Yap seemed to express views that emanated from a temperament that was clearly not comfortable or convinced by the call for poets to take a public role on issues such as the formation of a national identity. In an earlier essay of mine, I made a case for the claim that the great majority of poems in Yap's oeuvre confront social discourses through an unwavering position of uncertainty and scepticism, in which contradictory attitudes are often juxtaposed and left without one winning out over the other. Hovering between a conscious and an involuntary response across a range of implied or explicit attitudes ranging from uncertainty, through ambivalence and ambiguity, Yap's sense of a Keatsian negative capability is bounded to a position of liminality that runs counter to any straightforward critique or analysis of socio-political concerns. As Boey Kim Cheng (2009) has pointed out, "liminality is central to the work of Arthur Yap, opening his work to a broad range of interpretative possibilities and making him the most elusive of the Singapore poets" (p. 22). Boey also suggests that Yap's poems "reveal a poet who gave himself to his art so fully that he and the poetry are one: tentative, restrained, and self-effacing" (p. 34).

To me, notions of elusiveness, self-restraint and liminality tend to conflate into a general impression of generosity and kindness. As Boey has already suggested, the art and the artist become, especially in Yap's case, inseparable. With a few poems in particular, gay readers of Singaporean literature like Alex Au, a political activist and commentator behind the widely read online site, *Yawning Bread*,[1] have found in Yap a kindred spirit, perhaps even a fellow queer. In his online article, "Homosexuality and the Problem of Scale", Au criticized the local media for refusing to even discuss the possibility that Yap was gay during their announcements of his passing. Au alluded to Ong Sor Fern's tribute article in the *Straits Times — Life!*, "A Man of Few Words" on 21 June 2006, in which, according to Au, the reporter had merely "alluded to his sexual orientation when she wrote about how after Yap's 'friend' Keith Watson passed away, Yap used to put a memorial notice in the *Straits Times* every year on the anniversary" (Au 2006). Au was affronted by the lack of consideration for this dimension of Yap's life: "Why such elliptical language? If the love of Yap's life had been a woman, would the *Straits Times* have been more forthright about the importance of the partner in his life?" (Au 2006). Au is also adamant that Yap had never tried to hide his relationship, even though the latter had never actually come out to declare his sexuality either. Nonetheless, Au's opinion is one that I share, and I would add that Yap's elusiveness about his private self is probably an extension of the deliberate, even playful, sense of ambivalence evinced in his poetry. To prove his point, Au points out that Yap dedicated both *Commonplace* (1977) and *The Space of City Trees: Selected Poems* (2000) to Watson, as well as this poem in *Man Snake Apple and Other Poems* (1986):

your goodness
for Keith

your goodness, i sometimes light
my anger with, is what you have. no one
can burn it away; it is not for my discussion.
i know, near you, i myself feel good.
& this is enough for me, my friend.

this is a life-time friendship; the poem
is short, inadequate &, except for a word,
totally redundant.

(*Man Snake Apple*, p. 14)

The unambiguous sentiment in the above poem sets it apart from most of Yap's poetry that is more well-known for its "vivid local observations, and indeterminate yet resonant and provocative timbre" (Holden, Poon and Lim 2009, p. 176). Ambiguity gathers around "life-time friendship" after that reference to "a word" that turns a knob in the poem, opening a door for gay readers to cross that threshold and enter its meaning. For me, reading this poem for the first time was like passing another gay man in the corridor of a busy mall or a darkened alleyway — the almost insignificant meeting of eyes during which a swift and tacit understanding is reached, a mutually empowering acknowledgement that I-know-that-you-know-that-I-know which is born out of an unspoken ethos of complicity between gay men. The thrill for gay readers in reading this poem remains in knowing that the unspoken has been referred to, but the deliberate guise of ambiguity around the "word" shields the poet in the same way as closet doors protect the vulnerable homosexual from social victimization. Alex Au, however, takes a more unequivocal view on the meaning of of that "word", asserting that it points to Yap's sexuality without a doubt, a fact that he insists is crucial for any reader to understand when reading the poem: "Why is it important to know he was gay? Well, the above poem gives you the answer. You cannot understand it unless you know the relationship between the poet and the 'you' — Keith Watson" (Au 2006).

Au's stance is understandable. Yap's poetic ambiguity creates for a multiplicity of readings that the poem is generously equipped to absorb. Not exactly disagreeing with Au that knowing the poet's sexuality provides important significance to that connection between Yap and Watson, I nonetheless prefer to think that the "word" can *also* refer to Keith's "goodness", as well as the "goodness" of their relationship. I have always found the poet too accustomed to semantic playfulness to allow for just one reading. The strategy of not openly declaring one's homosexuality turns the reader's attention away from the possible discussion of immorality and the repercussions of homophobia that might detract from the celebrated "goodness" of this "life-time friendship". The poem could be urging us to perceive this relationship in the same way that Yap has probably chosen to remember it — in terms of a final sense of affection and commemoration, without attaching that baggage of a history of prejudice or persecution that has dogged homosexuals since time immemorial. At the same time, if we do insist on reading the poem as pointing to that word, "gay" (which begins tellingly with the same letter as "goodness"), it is with an implied nod, a knowing wink and warm embrace that Yap welcomes our differing interpretations, or the variety of ways we may choose to understand and empower ourselves through his poetic tribute.

For a gay reader like myself (whose opinions on Yap's queerness usually never make it to the public sphere), Yap's frequent engagement with a politics of doubt and ambivalence may be interpreted as a politics of the closet, a way of negotiating with the potential consequences of censorship and homophobia that could have even influenced the poet's overall elliptical style. From just a handful of discrete homosexual-themed poems that I am engaging with here, it is clear I have no grounds in presenting an unbroken gay cosmology in Yap's work. But homoerotic elements and concerns do present themselves in ways that suggest the poet's implicit struggle or half-willingness to express homosexual feelings and desires. Engaging with this aspect of Yap's poems, I would argue, has the capacity to enrich and enliven our aesthetic appreciation of not only his oeuvre in general, but it could even deepen our sympathies for the psychology presented in a few revealing works, particularly when a sense of internal conflict becomes evident. Of course, the inevitable consequence of any gay reading of a work is that many readers would object that either such a reading is morally insensitive to the writer, especially one who kept his sexuality hidden from the public eye (an objection that barely veils a prejudiced view about the validity of being gay), or that any interpretation of queer desire is ultimately of little consequence, since homosexual desire can be dismissed as "simply another form of desire (read, heterosexual)" (Vincent 2002, p. 30). John Emil Vincent points out that any discussion of homosexual desire in poetry in the latter way "will be fundamentally flawed, if not also in the service of a homophobic fantasy of a world without gay people in it" (p. 30). Although Vincent wrote this with John Ashbery's poetics in mind, his point about the positive dimensions of a gay reading is worth noting here, when he writes that for gay to non-homophobic poets and readers of poetry, elements of homosexuality in a work can "vivify or deflate general effects" (p. 32). In other words, homosexuality shakes up our possible complacency not only with regard to the presence of different and marginalized sexual identities within society, but also to our more intimate connections to such identities.

A gay to anti-homophobic reading of literature can generate aesthetic, sociological and empathetic insights that are surprising and rewarding. For example, the critic Eve Sedgwick broke new ground when, drawing on feminist scholarship and the cultural criticism of Michel Foucault, she drew attention to covert socio-sexual subplots in the works of writers like Charles Dickens and Henry James. Sedgwick (2008) argues that any understanding of modern Western culture and literature would be incomplete or "damaged in its central substance to the degree that it does not incorporate a critical analysis of modern homo/heterosexual definition" (p. 1). As a leading queer theorist, Sedgwick focuses on discovering and exposing underlying meanings, distinctions, and relations of power in larger culture that others oversimplify. Similarly, with regard to Yap's poems and their sociocultural context, it would be a shame to disregard interpretive possibilities that allude to a private negotiation with sexuality and their implications for homo/heterosexual discourses in Singapore. Sexual identities exist on a continuum and do not remain in the neat labels we create to contain them. Sedgwick interprets texts in a way that deflate rigid heteronormative assumptions about sexual identities. In Henry James' prose, for instance, she observes that "words and concepts such as 'fond', 'foundation', 'issue', 'assist', 'fragrant', 'flagrant', 'glove', 'gage', 'centre', 'circumference', 'aspect', 'medal' and words containing the phoneme 'rect'… may all have 'anal-erotic associations'" (Edwards 2009, p. 59). Such associations serve not just to enrich our understanding of Henry James' literary technique and aesthetic, but just as importantly, an appreciation of these associations also challenges homophobic or prejudiced assumptions that might undergird our readings of a given text.

Sedgwick was, of course, drawing from the work of French historian and cultural critic Michel Foucault and how, as he tried to show, a multiplicity of sexological taxonomies "facilitated the modern freighting of sexual definition with epistemological and power relations" (Sedgwick 2008, p. 9). Foucault (1980) pointed out that sexual categories and identities were socially engineered and codified in order to energize and entrench power-relations as well as promote new extensions of erotic pleasure. For him, the homosexual only became "a species" (p. 43) in the nineteenth century and such a species was compared to, while serving to defend and cement, the heterosexual norm, and thus rendered as deviant, perverse, and negatively pathological. Although Foucault points out that homosexuals also used their newfound categorical identification in a rallying, self-empowering way (by way of fomenting an alternative community), it is worth emphasizing that homosexuals everywhere continue to find themselves hugely oppressed by societies that regard heterosexuality as not only dominant but also normal and natural, despite the critical effort of theorists like Foucault and Sedgwick to undo or interrogate the binary opposition of divided gender and sexual categories. Faced by such oppression, many homosexuals are forced into the metaphorical closet, negotiating with and expressing their sexualities in sublimated ways. The "closet", to draw from Sedgwick's framework, includes the processes of repression and prohibition, as well as the struggle to resolve tensions between "the explicit and the inexplicit around homo/heterosexual definition" (Sedgwick 2008, p. 3). For Foucault, prohibition works not only to contain that which it outlaws but it also cultivates its sanctioned objects in a new mode. The sexual repression of the Victorians, for example, did not so much eliminate an interest in sex in Britain during the nineteenth century as "produced new ways of representing and thinking about the sexual" (Michie 2006, p. 109), permitting the extension of erotic pleasures into the domain of language, making speech itself a site of excitement.

Camp, in this way, when it manifests in language, becomes a way by which homoerotic excitement, which has been repressed elsewhere, finds a release. This is a point I will return to later in my essay in relation to Arthur Yap's poem, "a list of things", in which a homosexual sensibility, expressed through flamboyance and sexual imagery, presents itself. Camp is often associated with homosexual culture, or at least "with a self-conscious eroticism that throws into question the naturalisation of desire" (Bergman 1993, p. 5), and it is arguably tied to and generated by Yap's inevitable need to keep his own sexuality hidden from view. As a gay reader or "a person who can recognise camp...[who stands] outside the cultural mainstream" (Bergman 1993, p. 5), I am in an empathetic position to appreciate not only the qualities of camp within Yap's poetry but also the internal tensions and contradictions that might have been the cause. A less sublimated expression of homosexual desires comes through in a later poem, "gaudy turnout", in which a (homo)erotics of space in Singapore that contextualizes a direct negotiation with difficult emotions becomes evident. Oppressed, repressed, and marginalized, homosexuals, especially in countries like Singapore, continue to operate outside of the system through their use of "public spaces as private spaces" (Russell 2006, p. 19), subverting such sites in a manner not envisaged by urban planners. As I try to show, this sense of a public space becoming a private space for queer desires is presented poignantly in "gaudy turnout", a poem that stands as a moving, early example of Singaporean literature that dared to document the problems homosexuals faced in negotiating with the public sphere from within the closet.

Gay people will always find ways to be simultaneously visible and hidden within any complex cityscape through "a world of space bodies in the formation of the gay ghetto" (Bronski 2000, p. 184) and Yap points implicitly to the presence of such ghettos in Singapore during his lifetime. The emergence of such eroticized spaces continues to be important because it encourages the continued formation of an alternative community that has been forced to survive underground. The fact that Singapore is an anti-homosexual nation is one that remains today, in spite of its self-perpetuated reputation as a progressive global city. Joseph Lo (2003), the founder of People Like Us (PLU), a gay equality lobby group, in discussing the troubles his group faced throughout the nineties in registering under the country's Registrar of Companies, has pointed out that Singapore continues to possess a worldwide "reputation of being rigid, unbending and ... oppressive" (p. 129). Even today, a colonial-era ban on same-sex relations has yet to be lifted. There are two clauses in Singapore's penal code that deal with homosexual sex and these are Section 377: "Whosoever voluntarily has carnal intercourse against the order of nature with any man, woman or animal, shall be punished with imprisonment for life, or with imprisonment for a term which may extend to two years, and shall also be liable to a fine"; and Section 377(a): "Any male person who, in public or private, commits or abets the commission of or procures the commission by any male person of, any act of gross indecency with another male person, shall be punished with imprisonment for a term which may extend to two years."

It was only as recent as the late nineties that the country's first Prime Minister (and present Minister Mentor), Lee Kuan Yew, famously announced that "what we are doing as a government is to leave people to live their own lives so long as they don't impinge on other people"; this was in answer to a question about the future for gay people in Singapore that was broadcast worldwide on CNN in December 1998 (Peterson 2001, p. 129). Since then, as Steve Frankham (2008) points out, in Singapore, "despite the law and the city's surface conservatism, the government appears to be actively courting the pink dollar. This is based on the theory that encouraging a more cultured and creative environment that is tolerant of homosexuality will improve a city's economy" (p. 546). Although it is debatable whether this sense of broad-mindedness brought about by pragmatic desires to bolster a growing economy is really the status quo of Singaporean society even today, it was surely not the prevalent paradigm of the time that Yap was publishing his poetry. In a relatively young nation-state where homoerotic writings continue to be few and undiscussed in the public and academic spheres, a poem like "your goodness" stands in poignant contrast to a predominant movement of poetry started since the seventies that remains caught up in "social reference" (Bennett 1978, p. 240) and a perpetual "re-examination of ourselves as Singaporeans" (Singh 1999, p. 15). Yap's poem is also a rare, early example of cultural resistance against hegemonic, socio-political discourses that have remained wary about the right of homosexuals to productive self-expression. Yap's manner of resistance is arguably passive-aggressive, couched in the politics of the unsaid and the mode of aesthetic ambiguity.

In the same collection as "your goodness", another poem evinces resistance through a different poetic strategy, one of flamboyance and excess through which a queer sensibility may express itself while still remaining sufficiently hidden:

A List of Things
A Market At Ueno

gesticulating fingers of lentil, unwiggly eels,
spearheads of bamboo shoot, soothing water chestnuts,
green snakes of cucumber, jetsams of seaweed...
no-nonsense tangerines, arms-folded-over squid...
alliterative clogs, knobbly topshell, discusses of sole...
brisk aprons, tough-guy pork, sectional ropes of radish...
humpy peanuts, leathery heels of abalone,
aerial spring onion, hour-glass pears, rotund avocados,
rib-caged pumpkins, chlorophyllic piles of iparella,
grumpy red mullet, macho beef, sassy tomatoes

are all there.

(*Man Snake Apple*, p. 39).

The poem's unguarded flair, with its lively, seemingly free-associative re-imaginings of banal, edible and non-edible items at a market, is ripe with an undeniable sense of descriptive camp. As a style of humour, camp is constantly caught up in its own playfulness, frivolity, and an ironic display of excess. Susan Sontag (1995) has pointed out that there is a "peculiar relation" between camp and homosexuality: "While it's not true that camp taste *is* homosexual taste, there is no doubt a peculiar affinity and overlap.... homosexuals, by and large, constitute the vanguard — and the most articulate audience — of Camp" (p. 108). Camp forms an "aesthetic sense" that homosexuals use to facilitate their integration into society, since it "neutralises moral indignation, sponsors playfulness" (Sontag 1995, p. 108). Deliciously indulgent, Yap's poem is full of leery gestures, phallic symbolisms and lusty vivaciousness, from the "gesticulating fingers", "green snakes of cucumbers" to the "humpy peanuts" and "rotund avocados". The "no-nonsense tangerines" and the "arms-folded-over squid" possess a daring effeminacy that stands out in contrast to the calculated ordinariness of "rib-caged pumpkins" and "chlorophyllic piles of iparella" and the performed masculinity (or "macho-mary-ness") of "tough-guy pork" and "macho beef".

After such an inventory of objects made evocative by the addition of bewildering adjectives, the poem takes a dramatic breath before ending with a humble flourish — "are all there" — like the understated tilt of a top hat at the end of an accomplished cabaret performance. Under the poet's scrutiny, food items and trinkets can be said to have given up their hidden personalities and suppressed emotions. To see it another way, the poet could also be encouraging us to recognize ourselves in these diverse items; the poem becomes a comedic way of alluding to and delighting in the superficial constructions of our identities. It can be enjoyed as a celebration of social diversity, or of the differences in our formations of selfhood. The present-tense mode of the final line hints that such a multiplicity of differences has always existed, regardless of unremitting pressures to conform to limited modes of behaviour, or to repress oneself for the sake of social acceptance and political mobility. By inscribing the characteristics of human behaviour on to commonplace objects, the poem also implies that if we strip away our restrictive essentialisms about how we perceive ourselves and each other, the bodies upon which we mark our identities are not so different from unspectacular slabs of meat or fruits and vegetables. This has implications for the trajectories of prejudice — from racism to sexism and homophobia — that limit our minds and dictate the way we treat one another. This poem is also Yap at his most zany and fun. Its light-hearted campiness does not feature in a majority of his poems; the latter tend to possess inherent critiques or ambivalent observations about urban society, the price paid for progress as it "lives on in the memory of its citizens", full of a persistent sense of "resignation, acceptance and endurance" (Brewster 1995, p. 110).

Whether it is to pay an intensely personal tribute to a lifelong love or to indulge in a recognizably queer aesthetic, the works discussed here thus far continue to dance like most of his other poems along the parameters of ambiguity; they remain focused on self-conscious modes of uncertainty. Yet the two poems also possess enough clues for gay readers like Alex Au and myself to relate with their creator as a fellow queer. Any controversy that arises from this perception of Yap would likely stem from the belief that to call the poet queer is to necessarily malign him (a belief that is itself inherently offensive to homosexuals who have come to terms with their sexuality — and who have no problem expressing their sexuality in public — as well as to anyone else who supports the right and freedom to be gay). Regardless of the possibility that Yap might have himself been uncomfortable with being perceived in this way, I would maintain that the poems continue to hold an affinity with queer readers who relate to the emotional content and aesthetic sensibilities of the works as though they have been composed by a writer who was gay. Unlike commentators like Au, however, I wish to draw attention to a lesser known poem by Yap (taken from *Commonplace*) that no one has analysed for its unspoken homoeroticism. It is even possible that this early work is the most homoerotic poem of them all:

gaudy turnout

if i were you, i would walk the dark night
into some brightness, a lamp-post or lit shop-front,
& stop at the door, adjusting shoelace or smile
i wish i could find the doorsteps of the cellar-club,

the quick of your heart. how i wish i could
know for sure about tomorrow's party:
how many, who, won't be there, sensitive is the ear
of night & hears a loneliness for miles.

will there be dancing cheek-to-cheek? will someone
be recounting minutely his peculiar operation?
& is someone keeping score? will you
shut the door? why do you groan & groan?

if i were you, a gaudy boy afflicted with joy:
sensitive is the eye of day & sees a leer for miles
                                        (*Commonplace*, p. 30).

What we can all agree on with regard to "gaudy turnout" is that the poem is haunted by loneliness and desire. But whose loneliness? Whose desire? And what is the nature of this desire?

The darkened urban setting in which the speaker eyeballs another male on a street (outside a certain "cellar-club") recalls a hundred other urban spaces energized by covert meetings between gay men. The anonymity of the men in such spaces is usually ensured by their nondescript behaviour, appearances and the use of discreet, non-verbal signs: "Eye contact, body language, and physical actions are the keys to communication" (Russell 2006, p. 27) when these men attempt to meet one another for an intimate encounter without being discovered by law-enforcement officers or unsuspecting heterosexuals who stumble upon the same spaces by accident. Gay cruising has long been a way by which homosexuals have erotically inhabited and reimagined city spaces, particularly before the advent of Internet chatrooms and indoor saunas or clubs, in which gays are more able to meet without apprehension. The title of Yap's poem brings to mind the gaudiness of such clandestine proceedings, as these encounters often consist of lingering looks and signalling gestures that might be deemed as lewd and distasteful. Given the limited options that gays have to meet one another in homophobic societies, the atmosphere of such spaces, electrified by unspoken exchanges and the possibilities of intimate relations, is also weighed down by an undercurrent of loneliness and quiet desperation. As the American psychiatrist, Martin Kantor (1999), has argued, "sexual preoccupation accompanied by an incessant cruising for sex that amounts to promiscuity is a typical gay behaviour" (p. 57), one which contributes to emotional disorders in homosexual men. And cruising areas are spaces where gays have been forced to occupy in order to fulfil their specific desires. Such spaces create a psychologically detrimental environment in which gays use sex to numb themselves from feelings of frustration and alienation caused by their marginalized status within the larger society. Gay promiscuity becomes "a way to create the illusion that relationships exist, and to express the hope that something will work out by chance alone if they meet enough people along the way" (Kantor 1999, p. 61). Long-term gay relationships are typically made difficult by the fear of societal stigma, a continual wrestling with issues of self-acceptance, and an inevitable addiction to the promiscuous lifestyle.

The speaker of "gaudy turnout" has found someone — maybe an acquaintance, but most likely a stranger — who has captured his desires. Just like in the tentative dance that gay men enact when cruising, an initial distance is established between them, one projected from the poetic spectator's position of solitude and a fear of rejection; the forestalling of a desired meeting in which the viewer pretends to hesitate, "adjusting shoelace or smile", in order to safely analyse his target from across a gulf of longing. If Freud is right, "the homosexual choice of object is originally more closely related to narcissism than the heterosexual" (quoted in Lewes 1988, p. 301). Narcissism is exemplified in the way the focalizer's lust includes an implicit wish to become the "you" in the poem; "if i were you" is repeated twice, and there is a double-take on a cliché about winning another person's feelings when the speaker longs to *possess* the "quick" of his object's "heart". The desire to *be* and the desire to be *with* conflates within the gay cruiser's "leer" which threatens to be exposed by the "eye of day". Daylight becomes connected to the dangers of exposure, the indictment that will follow when one's sexuality is revealed, or the embarrassment of being seen to be enslaved by one's desires. But at the start, the cruiser longed for his object to enter into "some brightness", which suggested not just the ability to better see his target, but also the possibility of happiness that a moment of intimacy would bring. Such a meeting also hints at a more metaphorical union of souls; or simply the desire to be overtaken by another, preferably someone "afflicted with joy", since joy has been denied the cruising persona. The notion of joy as something that "afflicts" suggests a bitterness projected by the observer on to his object of attraction; negativity that stems from a general sense of self-hatred which homosexuals have experienced as a result of disenfranchisement and the difficulties of accepting themselves as homosexuals and in securing meaningful relationships.

Painted in strokes of shadows, the "dark night" of the scene in the poem is not compensated by the promise of "tomorrow's party". It is probably the same "party" the cruiser and his desired object are planning to attend. At first the speaker refers to "dancing cheek-to-cheek", the success of others who have discovered intimacy, inspiring jealousy; then he remembers the repetition of someone always "recounting minutely his peculiar operation" or "keeping score", occurrences that keep happening at such a gathering. These recollected details emphasize the speaker's particular alienation, the repetitions that make up the potentially depressing life of a gay cruiser; repetitions that the benumbed homosexual nonetheless returns to out of loneliness. The nature of this "peculiar operation", the allusion to "keeping score" and the pornographic groans in the poem suggest that the party is, in fact, a space for erotic to sexual conquests, maybe even group encounters. The queerness of this eroticized space is further heightened by the fact that the club in which the party occurs is tucked away underground, by the shutting of its door to keep its premises from public or homophobic scrutiny. It is not really a party in any positive sense, considering that the speaker understands it as providing the conditions for long-term promiscuity and a continued emotional disaffection with oneself. To be "afflicted with joy" also sounds like an aggrieved re-explanation of the word "gay", an ironic play of layered meanings that confirms once and for all that the poem is, without any doubt, about the psychological pain and longing of a homosexual speaker yearning for "a gaudy boy".

To be "afflicted with joy" presents homosexuality as a burden, that is, if one were only capable of understanding the gay lifestyle in terms of promiscuity and a tragic inability to attain long-lasting love. A "leer for miles" stresses not just the lustiness of the speaker's stare, but also the interminable ache of longing that only drives the homosexual into a dark corner of physical addiction and mounting self-hatred. Compared to "your goodness", "gaudy turnout" turns out to be a tawdry and desolate affair. Its depiction of homosexual desire is miles away from Yap's later testament to the goodness of same-sex relations. In "gaudy turnout", the satirical and cynical refrain from Gershwin's song about romance and the poem's pornographic allusions to sex without love point to the poetic speaker's internal conflicts and ambivalence about being homosexual — full of yearning, but also full of contempt for the nature of that yearning. Given Yap's preference for ellipsis and doublespeak, the poem could also be interpreted as a reproachful reflection on homosexual desire articulated from within the confines of the closet.

Nowhere before "gaudy turnout" is its sense of reproach and self-loathing anticipated in the same collection. The poem is so different in mood and tone from the others that it is no wonder that it was not chosen to be included in the eventual compilation of selected poems published in 2000. Just one page before this poem in Yap's 1977 collection, the titular poem "commonplace" (p. 29) stands in particularly stark contrast to "gaudy turnout". "commonplace" is a more familiar sort of poem by Yap, one that persuades readers to re-look at the repetitive ordinariness of everyday urban life; it starts like clockwork from daybreak and ends at night:

> daybreak, arms & legs.
> breakfast. day lengthens: commonplace
> situations & people…
>
> everything has happened before…
> & i should never whip the commonplace
> for the meaning of its opposite…
>
> when night comes, will it come in darkness
> or will it bring its own light to a well-scrubbed day?
> will there be doubt that commonplace is?

Anne Brewster (1995) perhaps overstates the case when she describes "commonplace" as "a celebration of the everyday … dramatised through a series of defamiliarised images which mark the passing of the hours" (p. xv) in her introduction to *The Space of City Trees*. She is right, however, about how Yap constantly offers "a means of apprehending reality differently" (p. xv) and would "never whip the commonplace / for the meaning of its opposite"; poems like "commonplace" are not caught up in romantic lyricism or projecting the commonplace on to the mythic realm, but in doing a modest double take on what is precisely quotidian about contemporary life. The poem ends in "darkness" that nonetheless shines "its own light" upon a day that the poet describes as "well-scrubbed", implying that urban existence possesses a sanitized banality that we should not take for granted. The night can offer a new way of looking, and it is in the context of night's surprising "light" that we are encouraged to "doubt that commonplace is". There is nothing commonplace about the commonplace if we would only bother to take a second look, even as a fresh glance might not necessarily yield an overtly positive difference — the poem is obsessed with difference, a trick of perception as an end in itself. Yet in the larger context of the collection with its subsequent insertion of "gaudy turnout", I cannot help but perceive such an end as really a tipping point between poems. From "commonplace" to "gaudy turnout", I suspect that something repressed is waiting to kick to the surface.

What links the poems is the inexorable logic of time; in time, what has been hidden accumulates, only to burst its parameters. After ending in the night, "gaudy turnout" takes over to further investigate what the night has to offer, stepping out from "the dark night / into some brightness". It is a terrible brightness that flips the ambivalent impressions of a city over to expose a startling and disturbing underside, a suppressed geography thrumming with unspoken, unspeakable desires. What Yap has been silent about so far in the book, a silence upheld through a sustained position of doubt and ambiguity about the state of the commonplace, collapses as if under an internal pressure when the poet confesses uncharacteristically to both "a loneliness" and "a leer for miles". The trope of distance that began from the lengthening of day at the start of "commonplace" finishes with an unequivocal sense of professed longing and statement about an aspect of existential emptiness at the heart of a city. The distance is closed in "gaudy turnout", after which the poet returns to an earlier stance of detachment and intellectual play, choosing to further develop the latter instead. Another Singaporean poet, Robert Yeo (1999), has written about how *Commonplace* presages the later volumes, *Down the Line* and later *Man Snake Apple*, in terms of its "brilliant managing of some cohesive and other linguistic devices", containing the "beginnings" of Yap's "new mode" of language play (p. 138). A poem like "gaudy turnout", or one that engages with the psychological complexities of same-sex desires, never occurs again in the subsequent books. It makes me wonder if Yap's preoccupation with language play in the later volumes was a shift influenced, in part, by a private decision to recede further into the closet, considering Yap's early and unambiguous evaluation of the impasse of homosexual desires in "gaudy turnout".

But this is probably speculation, at best. We will never know the private details of what actually happened between "gaudy turnout" and "your goodness" that made Yap finally change his mind about same-sex relationships (we can only guess that the entrance of Keith Watson into his life had something to do with it). However, what is *not* speculation is how the poems discussed here provide enough evidence for gay readers to connect with their unspoken homoeroticism. No one else other than Alex Au and a few brave students in the literature departments of universities in and out of Singapore have taken the time to respond to the homoeroticism in Yap's work. The absence of published critical material on the subject is glaring; critics have continued to focus only on Yap's innovative linguistic play, his poeticizing of urban spaces and embedded commentaries on the price of progress within Singaporean society. Granted that the homoerotic poems are few, they still deserve attention for providing some insight into an aspect of the poet's life that must have inevitably shaped the tenor and concerns of his work, even to the point that "he and the poetry are one" (Boey 2009, p. 34). The best poems, irrespective of how mysterious or confessional we claim them to be, will always reflect a dimension of the poet's temperament and personality. The author might be dead, but the poems remain a memorialized extension of his thoughts on art and life. So far, we have tended to read Arthur Yap in relation to his language and society. Perhaps we should also remember (as I have tried to do here) those moments in his poetry when he had also expressed something about his perspectives on love and his sexuality.

Note

1. On 12 May 2006, in the aftermath analysis of the Singapore General Elections focussing on the novel role of the Internet in fostering political discussion and independent news coverage, the *Yawning Bread* website was called the top "blog" for providing non-official commentary, an emergent phenomenon made possible by technology and described as "citizen journalism".

References

Au Waipang, Alex. "Homosexuality and the Problem of Scale". Yawning Bread, June 2006 <http://www.yawningbread.org/arch_2006/yax-618.htm> (accessed 1 December 2009).

Bennett, Bruce. "The Subdued Ego: Poetry from Malaysia and Singapore". *Meanjin* 37, no. 2 (July 1978): 240–46.
Bergman, David. "Introduction". In *Camp Grounds: Style and Homosexuality*. Amherst: University of Massachusetts Press, 1993.
Boey Kim Cheng. "From the Tentative to the Conditional: Detachment and Liminality in the Poetry of Arthur Yap". In *Sharing Borders: Studies in Contemporary Singaporean-Malaysian Literature II*, edited by Gwee Li Sui. Singapore: National Library Board, 2009.
Brewster, Anne. "Arthur Yap and Philip Jeyaretnam". In *Literary Transformations: Post-colonialism, Nationalism, Globalism*. Melbourne: Melbourne University Press, 1995.
―――. "Introduction". In *The Space of City Trees: Selected Poems*, by Arthur Yap. London: Skoob Books, 2000.
Bronski, Michael. "The Gay Ghetto and the Creation of Culture". In *The Pleasure Principle: Sex, Backlash, and the Struggle for Gay Freedom*. New York: Stonewall Inn, 2000.
Edwards, Jason. *Eve Kosofsky Sedgwick: Routledge Critical Thinkers*. New York: Taylor & Francis, 2009.
Foucault, Michel. *The History of Sexuality. Vol. 1: An Introduction*, translated by Robert Hurley. New York: Vintage Books, 1980.
Frankham, Steve. "Gay and Lesbian Travellers". In *Malaysia and Singapore*. Bath: Footprint Travel Guides, 2008.
Holden, Philip, Angelia Poon and Shirley Geok-lin Lim, eds. "Section 2 (1965–1990): Introduction". In *Writing Singapore: An Historical Anthology of Singapore Literature*. Singapore: NUS Press/NAC, 2009.
Kantor, Martin. *Treating Emotional Disorder in Gay Men*. Westport, CT: Greenwood, 1999.
Lewes, Kenneth. *The Psychoanalytic Theory of Male Homosexuality*. New York: Simon and Schuster, 1988.
Lo, Joseph. "How PLU Can Act Smarter to Speak Louder". In *People Like Us: Sexual Minorities in Singapore*. Singapore: Select, 2003.
Michie, Helena. "Carnal Knowledges". In *Victorian Honeymoons: Journeys to the Conjugal*. Cambridge: Cambridge University Press, 2006.
Ong Sor Fern. "A Man of Few Words". *Straits Times*, Life! 21 June 2006.
Peterson, William. "Queering the Stage". In *Theatre and the Politics of Culture in Contemporary Singapore*. Middletown, CT: Wesleyan University Press, 2001.
Russell, Lynette. "From Beats to Cybersex". In *Boundary Writing: An Exploration of Race, Culture, and Gender Binaries in Contemporary Australia*. Honolulu: University of Hawai'i Press, 2006.
Sedgwick, Eve Kosofsky. "Introduction: Axiomatic". In *Epistemology of the Closet*. Berkeley, CA: University of California Press, 2008.
Singh, Kirpal. "Introduction". In *Interlogue: Studies in Singapore Literature. Vol. 2: Poetry*, edited by Kirpal Singh. Singapore: Ethos Books, 1999.

Sontag, Susan. "Notes on Camp". In *Art Theory and Criticism: An Anthology of Formalist, Avant-Garde, Contextualist, and Post Modernist Thought*, edited by Sally Everett. Jefferson, NC: McFarland, 1995.

Sullivan, Kevin. "Achievement: The Poet With An Artist's Touch". *Southeast Asian Review of English* 8 (June 1984): 3–21.

Wong, Cyril. "Uncertainty and Scepticism in Arthur Yap". *Quarterly Literary Review Singapore* 1, no. 4 (2002) <http://www.qlrs.com/essay.asp?id=212> (accessed 23 November 2009).

Vincent, John Emil. "Reports of Looting and Insane Buggery behind Altars: John Ashbery's Queer Poetics". In *Queer Lyrics: Difficulty and Closure in American Poetry*. New York: Palgrave Macmillan, 2002.

Yap, Arthur. *Commonplace*. Singapore: Educational Books (Asia), 1977.

———. *Man Snake Apple and Other Poems*. Singapore: Heinemann Asia, 1986.

———. *The Space of City Trees: Selected Poems*. London: Skoob Books, 2000.

Yeo, Robert. "Parts of Speech: A Speculative Note on Arthur Yap's *Commonplace*". In *Interlogue: Studies in Singapore Literature. Vol. 2: Poetry*, edited by Kirpal Singh. Singapore: Ethos Books, 1999.

8

"A LONG WAY FROM WHAT?" Folkways and Social Commentary in Arthur Yap's Short Stories

Angus Whitehead and Joel Gwynne

INTRODUCTION: THE EARLY STORIES (1962–64)

In this chapter we analyse Arthur Yap's short stories in two distinct segments: his early prose fiction written and published between 1962 and 1964, and his later stories from the period 1969–82. At first glance Yap's stories may appear slight, even undynamic. However, as careful readings of his sparse, understated poetry and visual art reveal, in Yap's works things are rarely as they initially appear. Through close readings of his short stories — so short we suspect almost every word takes on the metaphorical pressure per square inch we might expect in a poem — we demonstrate how these works repay closer scrutiny and merit a more prominent place in Yap's collected works. In many of his poems performative wordplay is overt; while in his short, often sparse, poems there is little room to subtly embed such performances, Yap's comparatively longer prose fiction provides scope for significantly more subtle and ambiguous linguistic performances. Beneath their quotidian surface, Yap's beguiling short stories are as rich and as enigmatic as his poems.

Yap's poetry is more representational than his painting and his stories appear at first glance even more representational than his poetry. On a cursory reading there appears to be little of the explicit absence of conventional grammar or overt linguistic exhibitionism we encounter in his poems. Yet those same spare, crafted poems engaging with the everyday may prepare readers to be wary of what might initially appear to be a slight, "commonplace" quality to the stories, where little seems to happen. The near absence of event draws Yap's readers' attention to other elements: specifically a subtly knowing deployment of language (notably in grammatical trickery and the use of telling vocabulary and phrases) contributing to the stories' ambiguous and, with successive readings, increasingly perplexing nature. As we demonstrate, Yap's stories benefit from wary, active, linguistically and historically sensitive readings. Yap is already recognized as a poet whose voice tentatively locates, satirizes, and subverts an emerging sense of Singaporean nationhood. We explore how the aesthetic and ideological trajectories of Yap's prose in many ways resemble those encountered in his poetry. While providing an initial overview and exploration of Yap's short stories, the essay initiates critical discussion of a neglected facet of his opus, hopefully prompting further exploration of these stories and their place in both Yap's and the wider Singaporean canon.

Even though Yap is seldom associated with the short story form, between 1962 and 1993 he published eight short fictions. Three of those publications, "Noon at Five O'clock" (1962), "A 5-Year Plan" (1962), and "A Silly Little Story" (1964) were published, while Yap was still an undergraduate, in the University of Singapore's literary magazine, *Focus*. The stories were written in the socio-political context of Singapore's transition from colonial rule to self rule (1959) and thence to independence and membership of the newly formed Federation of Malaya (1963). In his 1996 interview with Anne Brewster, Yap exhibits an artistic orientation that is both divisive and complex. Even though he is often identified as a non-representational painter and poet, Yap has asserted that "in order to arrive at anything that is abstract I think you need a basis that is representational" (Brewster 2008, p. 99). In his early short stories the reader often travels from the recognizably mundane to defamiliarizing linguistic and representational ambiguities. However, Yap has also stated that "abstraction is simply the paring away of things that are not essential" (Brewster 2008, p. 99). Here the artist appears to be suggesting that, paradoxically, representation — understood as a depiction of society and the world around us in ways that seem consistent with our everyday sense of reality or realism — is a fundamental basis of his non-representational style. His outlook seems borne out by (on the one hand) the economy and spare quality of his often "very short short-stories" (Patke and Holden 2010, p. 58) and (on the other) a representational style that on closer inspection is often troublingly non-representational. We might say that Yap refuses to recognize a dichotomy, created in the early twentieth century by European writers and literary critics, between an avant-garde, modernist vision of defamiliarizing style and a social realist vision of detailed representation. Yap's artistic principles go beyond the modernist-realist binary, as he avers that his subject is "[s]omething about the human condition, and more specifically about the community that I live in" (Sullivan 1984, p. 10). As Yap contends: "I don't think that is a contradiction ... since I live in a community I cannot help but reflect aspects of that community" (Sullivan 1984, p. 10). Thus, for Yap, an intensely inward, personal vision does not preclude more extensive social representation. If this apparent contradiction makes it difficult for us to position Yap's aesthetic sensibility in the milieu of modernism or social realism, then it is important to read his words carefully; his comment that he "cannot help but reflect" aspects of his community suggests that any nationalistic drives are an incidental consequence, rather than a deliberate aim of his fictional enterprise. Yap remains a writer who attempts to "pare down the descriptive bits", articulating himself "in as few words as possible" with the ultimate aim of representing the physical environment "sufficiently to give the reader a sense of what one feels, but not at the same time overwhelm the reader in any way" (Brewster 2008, p. 99). Again, Yap espouses a tentative position between realism and non-realism, humanism and anti-humanism: the paring down of description, in conjunction with a desire to inscribe feeling, appears to imply a modernist and impressionist sensibility concerned with the non-representational. Yet, his position is complicated by an oppositional desire to avoid overwhelming the reader, suggesting that, above all, he hopes to achieve fidelity to a representative experience and for fidelity from his audience: he does not want linguistic exuberance to repel the reader from the text. In our discussion of Yap's stories we explore the strategies Yap develops to negotiate this fine line.

When asked to reflect on the role of the artist in society, Yap comments: "if you look at it from one point of view, I would say that if you want to reflect the environment you live in then I think the difference is in the role that you play" (Brewster 2008, p. 102). Here Yap appears to suggest that the writer does yield a societal function. However, to suggest from this evidence that his artistic sensibility accords with the aesthetics of literary nationalism and national-realist proclivities might be pushing things. In the same interview Yap remarks, "The things that really interested me were just ordinary things. Or, perhaps seeing people in a situation, you know, or talking to people or viewing a landscape or something" (Brewster 2008, p. 99). Yap is certainly interested in locality. As he had told Kevin Sullivan (1984) over a decade earlier, "I suppose basically what I write is something which will reflect my environment" (p. 4). In the context of the poems and even the early short stories it is clear that by environment Yap is referring to and privileging the very local over the national. Although the local and the national are difficult to separate, Yap's representations of locality resist development into sustained nationalist rhetoric, evidenced by how many of the poems and the majority of his short stories reflect the distinctively Chinese, partly elite, partly traditional, and partly modern urban milieu of his childhood and early adulthood during the time period 1943–69. Yap has described how in his writing he focuses on what he is familiar with: Chinese "folkways" in Singapore (Sullivan 1984, p. 4), a term coined by American sociologist and anti-imperialist William Graham Sumner (1906) who defined it as "habits of the individual and customs of the society which arise from efforts to satisfy needs" that subsequently "become regulative for succeeding generations and take on the character of a social force" (p. iv). In the context of our exploration of Yap's stories and their ambivalent attitudes to Chinese folkways and Singaporean modernity, it may be pertinent to bear in mind philosopher William Pepperell Montague's (1925) observation that "there are cases when a 'folkway' or social habit becomes actively evil" (p. 142).

Yap explicitly refers to "folkways" in his 1978 story "The Story of a Mask", a work which, written at a moment in which many of those folkways had already or were in the process of passing away, ambivalently explores the survival and subsequent passing of pre-revolutionary Chinese traditions in Singapore: "they [immigrants to Singapore from China] brought with them, among other things, their beliefs, their superstitions and folkways" (p. 38). To explore the traditional folkways of one's own racial-cultural tradition may seem a modest strategy for a writer in Singapore, a city-state often portrayed as a cultural melting pot. Yap's dogged exploration of past and present Chinese folkways that by their nature imply a traditional, ethnic separation from other races and cultures seems tellingly at odds with the immediate context of Singapore's initial social engineering policies in which disparate local and racial communities were rapidly expunged and dissolved to meld a unified nation. Conversely, it might be argued that Yap's monocultural renderings are comparatively more credible than that of other contemporaneous Singaporean writers' attempts to ventriloquize ethnic cultures of Singapore other than their own. Nevertheless, our sense of Yap's exploration of local folkways is also complicated by an ambiguity concerning the extent to which the customs and traditions of the Chinese diaspora in Singapore were identifiably those of the simultaneously Chinese, Anglican and anglophile, abstract painter Arthur Yap. Known up until his university years as "Chior Hiong", Arthur Yap's first language was Chinese, specifically Cantonese rather than Mandarin (Brewster 2008, pp. 104–5). Grounded in traditional Chinese culture he was therefore to some extent spared the crisis of identity Lee Kuan Yew and many others experienced as a student in the west in the 1940s (Chang 2010, p. 11). Born into Chinese folkways, and part of this living tradition (one which many Chinese Singaporeans subsequently struggled to synthetically reconnect with), Yap chose English as his language of communication and embraced other aspects of Western culture, notably literature and fine art. For his generation and class Yap brings a far from commonplace, doubly informed perspective to bear on early modern Singapore and specifically its Chinese folkways.

Yap grew up surrounded by an urban, monocultural environment, the milieu of the elite and almost exclusively Chinese neighbourhood of River Valley Road and Chinatown during the years 1943–70, and it is in this environment that the majority of his stories are situated. As an ethnic Chinese but also Anglican-Anglophile he is both of and not of this community, simultaneously participant and "ethnic social observ[er]" (Lim 2009, p. 176). In focusing on a specific and endangered ethnic environment that is related to the author, it could be argued that Yap's stories bear some similarity to those of mid-twentieth-century short story writers such as Saul Bellow and Isaac Bashevis Singer in their representations of Jewish communities in urban North America. While other ethnic communities and cultures such as the Malay, Indian, and Eurasian do not appear in Yap's short stories, it might be recalled that in the racially charged political atmosphere of the 1950s and after Singapore's independence in 1965, the government enacted an ethnic and cultural policy of selectively emphasizing certain Chinese folkways to shape the dominant rhetorics and identities that make up Singaporean modernity. To some extent Yap's focus on a specifically ethnic Chinese community might be interpreted as a result of this social engineering, but at the same time, even in his first short story, "Five O'Clock at Noon" (1962), we encounter an engagement with racially and locally bound folkways potentially running counter to Singapore's nationalist imperatives.

THE EARLY STORIES (1962–64)

"Noon at Five O'Clock"

When Yap wrote his first short stories, the genre of the short story in Singapore (first as Malayan state, then as an independent nation-state) was not merely marginal, it was unformed and would not take on a distinctive identity for another two decades. In the early 1960s at least, Yap was writing for a very small, elite, academic and local readership which could almost be described as a domestic coterie. An undergraduate contemporary of Yap's at the University of Singapore in the early 1960s, Koh Tai Ann, recalls encountering Yap's early stories on their publication in *Focus* and enjoying "their rather enigmatic, spare quality" (email to Angus Whitehead, 18 November 2009). Writing in 1978, Robert Yeo identified "two categories of short stories commonly written in Singapore: stories of social realism and stories of the inner life. In the former, the characters and actions are always related to the social milieu, whereas in the latter both character and action are individualistic and not easily explored by reference to a social background" (pp. 117–18). Yeo identifies a third category: the short story that is, "part-real, part-allegorical" (p. 118). Although Yap is prominent in Yeo's anthology, as we shall see, it is very difficult to place Yap's stories neatly into any of Yeo's three categories. All three early stories, while clearly related to the social milieu, also share a distinctive non-representational feature, namely the complete absence of direct speech. Yeo also suggests that Singapore's early short story writers represented in his 1978 collection exhibit "no specific influence" (p. 115). However, Yap's first story suggests one identifiable literary forebear. As a schoolboy at St Andrew's School, Yap read all of D.H. Lawrence's work and was especially captivated by Lawrence's prose rather than his poetry (Sullivan 1984, p. 3). Lawrence's influence seems evident in the opening of Yap's first published short story, "Noon at Five O'Clock" (1962). At midday the central character, whom we may assume is a local schoolboy because of a later reference to his "homework" (p. 33), feels impelled to go out even though he has just returned to his family home. Both private and public Singaporean spaces appear deserted but for the most humble inhabitants: the family's amah and some side street hawkers; a neighbourhood *mandore* and boy dishwasher inhabit the central character's memories and imagination. The schoolboy embarks on an urban voyage of self discovery; he first briefly visits a bookstore, then walks up a side street cul-de-sac of decaying old buildings. His initial dislike for the side street appears linked to the "industrious" poster by SATA (Singapore Anti Tuberculosis Association, a private voluntary organization run by expatriates). This poster is the only explicit and identifiable allusion to Singapore in the story, with the "appeal ... for more blood" (p. 32) perhaps reminiscent of the Singapore government's rhetoric that the populace continue to make sacrifices for the nation's sake. By the time the boy reaches the termination of the humble cul-de-sac, the level of descriptive detail increases significantly, suggesting the physical dead end is in fact precisely the opposite. In the process of entering the back of an old, colonial-era terraced building, which he intends to walk through to reach the street beyond, the boy encounters a time defying, aesthetically pleasing view.

The story begins:

> The sun seems to dazzle everything it touches. And however acclimatized, no one can be impervious to its seeping heat. He was going home, and suddenly he felt sick. Perhaps it wasn't very wise to have walked that distance under the noon sun. But this is one of the things one does. Without having to see if it's wise or otherwise, that is. ("Noon at Five O Clock", p. 31).

In Lawrentian style, Yap begins sentences with the conjunctions "And" and "But", and the passage is marked by authorial indeterminacy. The hesitancy of "seems" when describing the effect of the sun, an object in material reality, destabilizes narrative authority. Indeed — with the possible exception of "A Beginning and a Middle Without an End", this is the most overtly and self-consciously troubling and literary of Yap's stories. The narrative continually challenges the logic of realism, especially its epistemological certainty, as can be seen from the very title of the story, "Noon at Five O'Clock", that seems logically and temporally (if not subjectively) impossible. In the deserted back of the house viewing the shaded courtyard the schoolboy imagines it is five o clock: "[t]he view looked five-o'clockish" (p. 32). However, outside again and returned to "the brightness" he realizes and remembers, "[i]t wasn't past one o'clock" (p. 33). Indeed, in the immediate context of the plot of the story, the title "5 O'Clock at Noon" might to a careless reader seem more appropriate. Yap's challenge to our commonsensical ordering of the world according to the hands of the clock manifests itself in an appropriated synaesthesia, the visualization of time as a physical entity that transcends the tenets of conventional realism.

Two narrative voices appear to operate in the story: a sometimes overt, sometimes ambivalent voice in the first person and present tense that resembles the schoolboy (perhaps an expression of Yap's younger self); another more understated, yet authoritative voice in the third person and past tense (an omniscient narrator, perhaps Yap's slightly older self viewing his younger schoolboy self in ironic hindsight). The schoolboy's often aestheticized constructions of reality are continually undercut by the narrator's repeatedly ironic commentary. Both voices bear a resemblance to the perverse lenses identified by Lim (2009) in some of Yap's poems (p. 140). On occasion the voices in the short story are indistinguishable: the third-person narrator begins to articulate the thoughts of the schoolboy. The sometimes seamless, sometimes jarring alternation between these two voices and viewpoints, as well as the quotidian-micro-topographical plot, recall another modernist writer, James Joyce. This nod towards early twentieth-century modernist fiction suggests that the two alternating temporal voices and viewpoints produce an abstract, painterly quality that is overlaid on the story's straightforward action, thereby questioning the concept of central narrative authority by representing the same moment in time from objective, subjective, and merging perspectives.

Despite its ostensible simplicity, the narrative is saturated in ambiguity and marked by an unspecified and disorientating locality, partially demonstrated by rapid movement between implied locations: "He reached home. No one was in. His father would be at work. Not sweating perhaps. For there must be some air-conditioners around the place. He didn't know where the others were" ("Noon at Five O'Clock", p. 31). Initial seemingly factual statements in the story are subsequently proved wrong and revised. On arriving home the schoolboy concludes that "No one was in" (p. 31), but a moment later he remembers "the amah was in. Anyway she always is ... [h]e had come home rather flustered" (p. 31). Later, as the schoolboy first enters the back of the old house, he does not "think he [is] going to meet a ghost" (p. 32) but a few lines on he reflects people "leave the back [of the house] to the family ghosts" (p. 32). In the latter quotation we encounter the only explicit reference to Chinese folkways in this story, here already firmly located in the abandoned back of the house representing a hurriedly forgotten past. What is significant here is that the schoolboy's expressions of firm belief or factual certainty are constantly revised as he moves through the spaces he should be familiar with, thus developing a tension between the schoolboy's knowledge of his relationship to these spaces and other unexplored or forgotten aspects of his immediate physical and cultural surroundings.

We encounter early indicators of a disorientating linguistic playfulness more common in Yap's later stories. For example, the schoolboy's imagining of the act of washing up is described in a detailed, laboured way: "He had rather expected a bleary-eyed boy to be clanking and whacking and sousing saucers in the process called washing" (p. 32), a description that breaks down a simple household chore into a vivid cacophony of noises and actions represented by the three adjectival gerunds. Seemingly innocuous phrases also take on ambiguous connotations. The schoolboy visits a bookstore (not bookshop) and considers it as "one of those places where one can look nonchalantly around and be taken as putting on a becoming sceptic attitude" (p. 31).

The behaviour exhibited by customers in the bookstore is also ambiguous, as the initial indifference expressed in "look[ing] nonchalantly around" can easily be construed by others as "putting on a becoming sceptic attitude". The word "becoming" may serve as both an adjective (in the sense of "fitting") or a potential verb (in the sense of "changing into"), suggesting that the bookstore is, on one level, a cultural, but also hypocritical space in which the schoolboy is expected to put on an air of indifference and scepticism to fit in, but, on another level, this experience of acting sceptical is itself instructive, enabling Yap's older narratorial self to reflect upon and subtly deride such pretentious behaviour. Just as the schoolboy earlier experiences a palpable, flustering tension between his apparent knowledge of a place and what he discovers about it, so too there exists a slippage between the older, wiser voice of experience and the younger self who looks nonchalantly around a bookstore and is unaware of the implications or connotations of his actions. In addition, when the schoolboy walks down a side lane he encounters "obscure hawkers" (p. 32). Are we to interpret the narrator as meaning that the hawkers are "in the shade", "difficult to see", "difficult to understand", or "of limited understanding"? The precise meaning of the description of the hawkers' imagined customers using the compound adjective of

Yap's own coinage, "anonymous-loving", is also unclear. One would expect the schoolboy to be puzzled and perplexed by these unclear figures, but what is important here is that even the third-person, seemingly omniscient narratorial voice of experience does not elucidate or clarify the obscurity or anonymity surrounding the street hawkers and their customers. Yap's older and supposedly wiser narrator omits to supply a definite answer or explanation that ties together the various experiences and impressions given to us by his younger self; he perhaps deliberately leaves certain physical spaces in the neighbourhood outside the ken of his own narrative authority and the reader's apprehension. Other aspects of this story intimate that such ambiguities have been carefully thought out. In the first line of "Noon at Five O'Clock" Yap describes the effect of the sun: "The sun seems to dazzle everything it touches." While at first glance the statement seems straightforward, approaching an everyday cliché, a closer examination reveals that the linguistically sensitive Yap is using "dazzle" in a far from everyday, straightforward sense. In applying dazzle to objects rather than individuals, he employs a curiously archaic use of the verb that, according to the Oxford English Dictionary, has fallen out of modern usage — namely "to outshine, dim, or eclipse with a brighter light". Through this unorthodox use of a commonplace word, Yap conveys, paradoxically but effectively, that Singapore streets appear dim and poorly lit when they are dazzled by the sun at its midday height. Yap's knowing use of "dazzle" in this context hints at how carefully "Noon at Five O'Clock" and later stories were constructed as well as the equal care with which they need to be read. Yap's stylistic and linguistic innovation often involves using apparent outworn clichés or antiquated words and phrases from "classic" literature or common parlance for what Lim (1993) in another context has described as "syntactically perverse" (p. 137) purposes. For example, the schoolboy anticipates (but fails to encounter) a "bleary-eyed boy". A moment later he thinks of a "helpless maiden" (a phrase used to describe Rebecca in Walter Scott's *Ivanhoe*, still a popular schoolboy classic during the 1950s) who quickly becomes a "sprawling maiden":

> He didn't think he was going to meet a ghost. Or a helpless maiden. He toyed with the idea of the sprawling maiden. But somehow didn't like it. The sprawling maidens he had read of and heard tell always appeared as if they were waiting their cue. And this could be frightening. Really, he didn't think. ("Noon at Five O'Clock", p. 32)

This rapid shift from the register of gothic fiction ("a ghost") to chivalrous romance ("a helpless maiden") and finally into something that hints of sensual eroticism and abuse ("the sprawling maiden") might suggest the schoolboy's unresolved problems concerning female sexuality. The last section of the passage quoted above also appears to suggest the schoolboy's mental response to opinions and statements not articulated in the text and not his own; perhaps he is parroting comments made by his male friends and schoolmates that mock and degrade women as sexual objects. The boy's imagining of a helpless maiden, momentarily "toy[ing]" with the idea of a sprawling maiden and his subsequent discomfort recalls negative representations of female sexuality in Yap's poetry identified by Lim (1993, p. 155) and points towards other such representations in later stories. But, the schoolboy's fright and discomfort when the image of the sexually suggestive sprawling maiden flashes across his mind might also imply an unarticulated resistance towards the norm of heterosexual desire that is represented in mainstream advertising and pornography, a plausible reading if we take into account Yap's gay identity that he kept publicly undisclosed but expressed in poems such as "gaudy turnout" and "your goodness".

"Noon at Five O'Clock" can be read as an affirmation of the personal, individual, and private in the context of the increasing incursion and predominance of collective, public, and national concerns on everyday Singaporean life. Even in this early, largely personal, story, elements of personal and social satire are evident. The story operates as an affirmation of the personal (different, idiosyncratic) over wider, national contemporary interests. Although published in 1962, before redevelopment and later nation-building policies fully impacted upon Singaporean life, it is interesting that the story represents a schoolboy as an individual, peculiar, idiosyncratic persona in contrast with the invisible owners of the terraced residence reflecting a significant section of the rest of the nation: "But sometimes people just live in the front. And leave the back to the family ghosts. And never look back" (p. 32). While the story progresses, via the colonial landscape of early 1960s Singapore city the schoolboy appears to travel back in time, ultimately finding meaning in an already abandoned local past. The story can also be read as a personal satire of an earlier self, a portrait of the undergraduate artist as a student at Saint Andrew's School. The schoolboy is represented as continually restless, precocious, opinionated, scholarly, Western influenced, semi-elite and frustrated with his too-familiar local surroundings, especially Singapore's sun, heat, food tastes, industry, repetition and order. In his peregrinations, the schoolboy increasingly takes on the role of the *flaneur*, a pedestrian who saunters or idles around different city spaces, relishing the scenes of urban life but seldom participating in them. The schoolboy *flaneur* relishes the old city's infrequent obstruction of and resistance to "improvement" and state regulation: "Engineers and architects may scheme and "city-plan" but there are always (to him rather delightful) accidents" (p. 32). However, as we have seen, the schoolboy has hitherto been proved wrong in several assumptions. His hope therefore seems not wholly reliable, perhaps ironically framed. The former schoolboy self's optimism is deflated by the older voice's experience and hindsight in the context of (by 1962) ongoing redevelopment. At this point of transition there is a poignant irony in the younger schoolboy finding ultimate satisfaction, rest, peace located in a nationally neglected past, symbolized by the house that is clearly doomed if not already demolished. Yet, the schoolboy himself may also share less palatable Singaporean characteristics. In attempting to pass through one of the houses in the terrace blocking his way, the boy chooses the "creakiest-looking" (p. 32) back door. The terrace is reminiscent perhaps of the "demented buildings" referred to in Yap's later story, "The Effect of a Good Dinner" (1978, p. 29). The boy assumes that the oldest door at the back of the row of houses blocking the side street will lead him through the oldest shophouse kept by a socially inferior, and therefore unquestioning, owner and out into the street the other side. Aside from the issue of trespass, his reasoning resembles a mean-spiritedness, a *kiasu* mentality that is a widely accepted but not wholly admirable Singaporean trait (Lim 2009, pp. 175–76).

The schoolboy instead discovers that the old building contains surviving architectural anomalies that are ignored peculiar traces of Singapore's past. He encounters within the rear of the old building a first-storey panoramic view of an interior courtyard. As the schoolboy ascends the stairs and discovers the view of the inner courtyard, the narrative takes on painterly qualities: on ascending the staircase, the boy encounters "a single window, paneless. In clear chiaroscuro to its surroundings" ("The Effect of a Good Dinner", p. 32). The introduction of the term "chiaroscuro", suggesting the visual play of black and white, light and shade, lends an aestheticized quality to the scene. In addition, the bright window, momentarily and starkly framed against its dim surroundings, is reduced to an abstraction. An earlier description of the dead end street also bears some resemblance to an abstract painting, "The two blocks of building had been blocked by another lying sidewise" (p. 32). The repetition of "block" as first noun then verb provides an "abstract" sense of the old terraces reduced to blocks, elements. Within the old shophouse, as the boy walks to the window, it in turn frames a far more representational image that marks the end of his journey and the climax of the story: "He saw the court-yard, encased by two walls. The sun could not get in directly. The view looked five-o' clockish" (pp. 32–33).

Although the schoolboy subsequently and periodically returns to this panoramic view of the courtyard "after doing his clever and neat homework" (p. 33), he never enters the courtyard itself and is content to experience it at one remove via the framed panoramic view where time literally stands still. While mandatory daily homework may signify an incursion of the state's expectations and values in educating its citizens, the schoolboy's intermittent negotiated communion with the courtyard suggests a clandestine and uniquely individual enjoyment of aesthetic experience: "Sometimes when there was a breeze, he could see the little clinging plants vibrating. Once there were so many little plants that during a breeze, the walls did not look solid" (p. 33). The old house, a momentarily surviving shady refuge in "a hot country", fuses local antiquity with nature in an increasingly urbanized city. Yet, at the climax of the story the second narrator's deployment of "just for larks" (p. 33) (another antiquated phrase suggestive of late nineteenth-century boy's adventure stories) to describe the reasons for the schoolboy's returns to the house again retrospectively trivializes the schoolboy's experience. In the light of this close reading we might be closer to an interpretation of the didactic but initially ambiguous concluding sentence of the story that is both expressed in the negative and conveys a sense of enjoyment and satisfaction: "But he didn't make a religion out of his OWN view. Which was why he enjoyed it" (p. 33). At one level it suggests a resistance towards institutionalizing personal experience into a larger, formally regulated system. The pleasurable and nurturing view that the schoolboy enjoys is one he visits only sporadically and out of genuine personal desire, in contrast to grand visions of social integration or nation building. Unlike the midday sun, Yap's narratorial presence does not intend to outshine or eclipse everything it touches; instead, the ambiguities of his prose cast his narrative voice in clear chiaroscuro to its surroundings, and the contrast points towards the existence of other perspectives and world views that are not exhausted or completely elucidated by his own, such as those of the obscure hawkers and their anonymous customers in the side lane.

"A 5-Year Plan" (1962)

While "Noon at Five O'Clock" stands out among Yap's stories both for its overt and peculiar literariness and its principal focus upon an individual's as opposed to a wider Singaporean experience, the title of Yap's second story, "A 5-Year Plan", contains a telling allusion to contemporary Malayan-Singaporean government policy for economic development, namely the first and second Malayan Five Year Plan (1956–65). This may suggest that Yap's story operates as a form of allegory. Through an everyday domestic setting, Yap attempts to satirize contemporary developments at the national level. The story foregrounds an aspiring unnamed couple of indeterminate ethnic background whose humdrum downfall is connected to and completed by a seedy and ruthless underworld. Although Singapore is not explicitly mentioned, some details of the couple's financial predicament suggest that they have become entangled with criminal elements among the Chinese community who populate Singapore's underworld. First, debts incurred by the man's momentary lapse into "fierce" gambling put the "meagre" salaried couple and their child in debt, and "obnoxious and terrible" money lenders' interest rates make the predicament terminally irredeemable ("A 5-Year Plan", p. 20). Despite initial resolute ambitions to repay the loan the couple remain in debt and gradually become resigned to their shabby, desensitized lives, labouring at monotonous minor "blind-alley" jobs to stay afloat. All earlier indicators of material-cultural aspiration (such as their bedroom carpet-square and cut-glasses) drop away. Similarly, during the late 1950s and early 1960s Singapore's pragmatic social and economic policies initiated a national leap forward but also subjected the majority of its citizens to a regulated life dominated by long hours of hard, modestly paid, work. In this story the ethic of hard work, traditionally deemed the slow but steady path towards achieving material comfort and spiritual reward, is paradoxically associated with failure, illness, and wasted life. "A 5-Year Plan" then operates as an indirect interrogation of a restricting authoritarian social policy that promotes labour and sacrifice to the exclusion of leisure and culture, as well as the insidiously deadening effect of such a policy on its citizens: "It was a stifling routine, for there was always a sense of the frantic, of rush and ant-like industry" (p. 20). While

"A 5-Year Plan" exhibits less of the ambiguities and linguistic subtleties evident in Yap's other stories, it nonetheless draws on some of the techniques we see in "Noon at Five O'Clock" to establish the contrast between a grand scheme of economic development and the grinding costs exacted on those caught up in the scheme's implementation. The story thus serves as a veiled political allegory as well as an incidental indictment of the less savoury but enduring Chinese folkways of gambling and money lending that, again, stand in contrast to the virtues of community cohesion and consensus building often extolled by authorities as distinctively Chinese or Confucian cultural traits.

"A Silly Little Story" (1964)

"A Silly Little Story" (1964) represents Yap's first explicit and sustained exploration of Chinese folkways using the genre of the short story. While Yap rarely if ever overtly engages with the issues and challenges surrounding Singapore's postcolonial experience, this short story is significant for two reasons: first, it was written and published at a historical moment in which Singapore's nation-building policies involving the dismantling of much cultural and ethnic differences were coming into effect; second, the story marks a shift from a depiction of an urban but not overtly culturally identifiable social environment to an explicit and exclusive portrayal of Chinese folkways, thus going against (but also anticipating developments in) the grain of the social and cultural currents of its time.

Wong Loo, the central character (like Yap's paternal grandfather) is a first-generation Cantonese immigrant, evidently Buddhist (see Angus Whitehead's essay "go to bedok" in this volume for a discussion of Yap's representation of his grandfather in his poetry). The name Wong Loo is reused, along with generous extracts from this story, almost two decades later in another story that explores the passing of traditional Chinese folkways, "The Story of a Mask", published in 1978 and discussed later in this essay. Through Wong Loo, Yap explores and comments upon the milieu of the first-generation exogamous Chinese in Singapore. As in "Noon at Five O'Clock", the informal, matter-of-fact, even anecdotal style of this story veils important ambiguities. The story begins, "Wong Loo was one of those persons who could not possibly have lived anywhere else except in Singapore" (p. 14). Yet, by the end of the story the narrator opines: "But also I think [Wong Loo] could have been happy in, say, the

Chinatown of San Francisco" (p. 16). As in "A 5-Year Plan", there seems to be wider social commentary or interrogation raised through domestic scenes: If Wong Loo, "adher[ing] quietly but stoutly to his little area of animation" (p. 15), would indeed have been as happy in the Chinatown of San Francisco as that of Singapore, what does this suggest about Singapore's identity as a postcolonial nation, or of the Chinese diaspora generally in the late twentieth century? What does the insular and undynamic Wong Loo's aversion to Communism reveal about his liking for Singapore, three years after the formation of the left-wing Barisan Socialis political party? Ironically, post-independence Singapore's policies, like Mao Zedong's in the People's Republic of China, will "greatly disturb ... Chinese traditions and turn ... the social order topsy-turvy" (p. 16). Although the narrator describes Wong Loo as "an ignorant man", it is unclear to the reader whether it is the traditional Chinese immigrant Wong Loo or his young, modernized and Westernized sons who are really ignorant.

"A Silly Little Story" rehearses a more general dialogue between two generations of Chinese Singaporeans in the early 1960s on the cusp of radical national change. The slippage between Wong Loo's use of English in relation to his family and the established Cantonese milieu of his home can be seen from the phrase he uses to describe his "unredeemable" son, "the debased son-of-a-pig" (p. 15). This seems to evoke some stock phrases in Cantonese, namely *"zyu zai"* (piglet) and *"ceon gwo zek zyu"* (stupider than a pig — hence very foolish), with the latter phrase commonly used by Cantonese-speaking Chinese parents to describe their children. Wong Loo's peculiar concatenation of "debased" and "son of a pig" suggests an uncomfortable yoking of East Asian and Western idioms, with the term "debased" here also implying a wider traditional Chinese Singaporean disapproval of apparently Western-influenced material progress and modernization. The narrator appears to sympathize with Wong Loo's sons who see meaningfulness in American pop songs that they describe as "witty". On the basis of this information, Wong Loo who "knows some English", but is "not very bothered about [what English words] actually mean", equates "witty" with "silly, loud and noisy and perhaps, in a plebeian sort of way, amusing" (p. 15). We may assume that Yap himself, a poet and scholar, is very much concerned with and aware of what English words actually mean. If that is the case, how are we to read the use of "silly" in the story's title? Yap seems to be turning us away from the conventional meaning of the word — "being irrational" or "lacking good sense" — and asking us to consider a possible connection between silliness and wittiness. In other words, what appears on the surface as silly or irrational might actually turn out to harbour some keen insight or wit, and these insights, although seemingly little or trivial, should not be ignored in the face of larger social and economic forces such as nation building or material progress.

The narrator appears to frame Wong Loo's view of Singapore as flawed and unreliable: "In an unreasonable frame of mind, [Wong Loo] always thought Singapore was a no-man's land: his reasoning was most illogical — Singapore, a Malaysian state; he himself, originally a Chinese, every one speaks some English; and his unredeemable son hopped about to American pop-songs" (p. 15). But is Wong Loo's reasoning illogical, his description of Singapore in the early 1960s unreasonable? Or is there a different sort of change that Wong Loo, for all his resentment and resistance towards an apparently Westernized modernization of Singapore, admits and accepts? Wong Loo embraces Chinatown selectively, accepting that which is unique and handcrafted while shunning the increasingly prominent mass-produced manifestations of progress and modernity emanating as much from the East as the West. Wong Loo deems French films an acute example of the Western influence that somewhat obscures his enjoyment of Singapore: "Sometimes, an odd French film is shown in one of those cinemas" (p. 15). While expressing distaste for signifiers of modernity and change, Wong Loo acknowledges change in himself while resident in Singapore. His attitude to his grandmother's maxim — "the world was like one big, happy family" (p. 15) — has shifted. In the past when he was of the "unprogressive order" — an archaic phrase from nineteenth-century high Empire English denoting the recalcitrant peasantry who obstruct progress — he "believed" his grandmother; however, now "in tranquility", Wong Loo feels that "his grandmother had been rather morbid" (p. 15). What is important in this passage is that Wong Loo's use of "morbid", which denotes both an air of gloominess and bodily illness, interrogates the concept of human society as a filiative body or family, which is what his grandmother tries to impart to him. Yap, through Wong Loo, may be asking us to think of social relations — whether at the communal, national, or international and "worldly" levels — not in terms of kinship or blood. An alternative to such filial bonds seems to be suggested through the allusion to the English poet William Wordsworth's famous phrase, "emotion recollected in tranquility" (p. 151), suggesting a need for strict regulation of feeling and emotion through intense reflection and recollection. The allusion to Wordsworth points towards a state of mind where one does not directly experience the world in all its force and immediacy, but rather remembers past experiences and recreates those experiences selectively. Wong Loo's desire for an authentic, non-Westernized Chinese cultural heritage for his family and society is therefore undermined by his own (largely unacknowledged) resistance towards a strictly filiative or familial conceptualization of human relationships, as well as his unintended allusion to late eighteenth-century English letters. This selective recreation of Chinese tradition is brought out more overtly in Yap's later reworking of this story.

In this first section we have discussed Yap's first three short stories published while Yap was an undergraduate at the University of Singapore. In the next section of this essay we will explore Yap's five later stories, all of which were written during the first three decades after Singapore's independence and all (save one) published after an extended period of residence outside Singapore. In these later stories Yap, while utilizing much of the linguistic play, undermining of textual authority, social criticism via satire and ambiguity of the early stories, engages more fully and more exclusively with Chinese Singaporean folkways. Alongside the obscured ambiguities already evident in the earlier stories, we argue that Yap's short fiction exhibits ever more complex responses to those folkways and their demise, often reflecting the swift, jarring changes accompanying the ongoing development and identity of the nation-state.

INTRODUCTION: THE LATER STORIES (1969–82)

During the fifteen years following Singapore's expulsion from the Federation of Malaysia on 9 August 1965 and the forging of a new nation out of this geopolitical crisis, Arthur Yap published five further stories. "Soo Meng" appeared in Edwin Thumboo's anthology, *The Flowering Tree* (1970); "The Story of a Mask", "The Effect of a Good Dinner", and "None the Wiser" were published in Volume II of Robert Yeo's anthology, *Singapore Short Stories* (1978); "A Beginning and a Middle Without an Ending" was originally published in the 1982 issue of the Malaysian literary journal, *Tenggara*. In these later stories, elements of the earlier stories are evident, notably Yap's trademark linguistic play that undermines textual authority and his use of satire and ambiguity for social critique. However, in these later stories a fuller, more culturally exclusive engagement with Chinese Singaporean folkways is evident. Against a backdrop of swift, jarring changes accompanying the ongoing development and identity of the Singaporean nation-state from 1970 to 1982, Yap exhibits ever more complex responses to such folkways and their rapid demise, questioning the complacency of official state rhetoric of national identity and multiracialism. The socio-political climate in Singapore during the period of 1970 to 1980 was arguably one of greater authoritarianism and censorship than that in which Yap wrote his first stories. In his later stories, especially the four published on his return to Singapore from the United Kingdom around 1975, Yap prefigures a later generation of Singaporean writers who are also invested in "eschewing bare polemic for more nuanced political commentary" and who "offer a view of history and politics often through the prism of the personal and the familial" (Poon 2009, p. 365).

"Soo Meng" (1970)

"Soo Meng", published five years after Singapore's independence, reflects a continued concern with Chinese folkways, but in an evolving modern context rapidly brought about by recent government policy. Shirley Geok-lin Lim (2009) observes that such "[m]odernisation includes changing traditional social characteristics to those amenable to industrialization, high technology and globalization; for example inculcating attitudes of efficiency, nationality, high achievement, flexibility, and so forth" (p. 174). In "Soo Meng" such modernization is evidenced in the topics covered in female neighbours' conversations. This is the first story in which Yap utilizes direct speech — we overhear a group of women who are neighbours talking — therefore suggesting a more representative style (and his gift for caustic mimicry) and a more direct engagement with the local milieu than he previously exhibited in his writing. As well as the more traditional themes of the neighbourhood women's concern about their children and their excitement over local gossip, the story reflects how modern popular Singaporean conversation now comprises of "recounting television programmes" (p. 149). Singapore Television broadcasts began in 1963, and Lee Kuan Yew's tears when he announced the political separation from Malaysia were televised on 9 August 1965. Between 1965 and 1970, Singaporeans had access to Radio Television Singapore channels in English and Chinese, Channels 5 and 8 respectively. But in this story, talk of TV programmes is juxtaposed with spheres of conversation unforeseen and unsanctioned by the architects of the new republic. These include "topical subjects such as which diplomat has taken a holiday with which showgirl" (p. 149), which probably refers to a historical event involving Singaporean Minister Lim Yew Hock's disappearance and subsequently emerging details of his scandalous affair with a nineteen-year-old Australian stripper ("The Diplomat and the Samaritan", *Time*, 1 July 1966). Through the voices of neighbourhood housewives and his juxtaposition of recent and identifiable local political scandal with TV plots, Yap engages with and expresses a plebeian fascination with and cynicism towards the country's political elite, who are perceived as simultaneously authoritarian and self-indulgent.

Three paragraphs into the story, the voices of two neighbours break in unannounced. Here we encounter Yap's first sustained representation of local speech patterns. However, rather than the demotic or vernacular "Singlish" suggested in the poem "two mothers in a hdb playground" Yap wrote ten years later, we encounter the standard and studied English of an upper-middle-class urban Singaporean neighbourhood of the 1960s, quite possibly an echo of the River Valley Road neighbourhood where Yap grew up:

> Could be a spastic case ... and I said to her, just between the two of us, why don't you take your baby out ... fresh air has never been known to kill anybody...
>
> You shouldn't, that's crude. But I really wonder ... I remember saying to her once, no offence meant, my little boy's just beginning to crawl, so why don't you let him keep your baby company? For reasons of health, she says, but Ho! Her other two kids tumble in and out of the house without so much as a sign of exhaustion. ("Soo Meng", p. 149)

The neighbours are discussing Lim Soo Meng, neighbour Mrs Lim's "idiot" (p. 150) infant son, who is the focus of the story. During a period of transition in Singapore's development, the Lim family appear trapped in a liminal space between two worlds: "The Lims live in the kind of house that most people live in: the sort that one would move out of when, plonk, comes a windfall; the sort that the poor would be very glad to move into" (p. 150). As with the couple portrayed in Yap's earlier story, "A 5-Year Plan", the neighbours have their eyes fixed on upward mobility. However, five years on from the nation's independence, such aspirations seem a remote hope. By placing the child's name in the title of the story, Yap immediately foregrounds a mentally disabled child as the central character. Disability becomes an indicator of Singaporean attitudes at both local and national levels in the second half of the 1960s, a period in which the state prided itself on its limited welfare assistance. The story represents a society unable to adequately support the disabled and entirely reliant on traditional methods of care located in the home. The story implicitly challenges both traditional and modern Singaporean society's preconceptions and attitudes towards the disabled. In the late 1960s, at least, the mentally handicapped in Singapore were part of a larger marginalized and neglected section of a nation-state in which a comprehensive social infrastructure was far from a priority. A neighbour's use of the phrase "spastic case" used in its offensive rather than its medical sense (Soo Meng does not appear to have cerebral palsy) is suggestive of unnuanced attitudes to disability even among the elite, and foreshadows a state that would later experiment with a mild form of eugenics in its anxieties concerning the future prosperity of the nation.

Consequently, Soo Meng's parents, following traditional Chinese beliefs and attitudes to the disabled, initially hide the infant as a shameful secret. Yet, neighbourhood pressure, influenced by apparently emerging modern sensibilities of curiosity and sympathy, forces his parents to let him out into the local open. Soo Meng's pleasant placidness, regarded by the neighbours as the hallmark of an idiot, appears to exercise a positive, humanizing influence on the neighbourhood during the short year between his initial public exposure and his death running across a busy road. The figure of Soo Meng suggests that accidents and other contingent events that cannot be carefully planned or scheduled genuinely cement together neighbourhoods, communities, something which the state's nation-building and social-engineering policies have only had checkered success in beyond the cosmetic. Ironically, the narrator cites the transient communal curiosity and sympathy of Soo Meng's neighbourhood (which the narrator appears to attribute to the "emerging tempo" of Singapore "surging forward" into modernity after 1965) as an indirect cause of the child's death. Indeed, the narrator appears to approve of negative aspects of past folkways as opposed to modern sympathies concerning the mentally handicapped: "At one time, people might have laughed at an idiot; mothers might have plucked their children away from his breathing distance to leave him alone" (p. 151). Such traditional unsympathetic attitudes to the disabled, ensuring he was hidden in the home, would have saved Soo Meng's life.

Soo Meng's fatal accident — being struck by a lorry while running across a road towards an Indian balloon seller — seems poignant and touches on a sensitive if usually unarticulated tension in Singapore.

During the 1960s balloon sellers were not exclusively Indian and were usually found in amusement parks and fun fairs rather than peddling their wares in residential neighbourhoods though such itinerant hawkers were then common. Yet, in representing the balloon seller as Indian and taking him out of the fun fair and into a local neighbourhood, Yap touches on an ethnic tension of the period in Singapore. Kevin Tan recalls that in the 1960s, "very young Chinese kids tended to be afraid of ... Indians", and many Chinese parents of the period used Indians (particularly Sikhs) to frighten their children into good behaviour, telling them, for example, that if they did not finish their vegetables they would be kidnapped by Indians (email to Angus Whitehead, 2 July 2010). A typical Chinese Singaporean child of the period might therefore have been too frightened to approach an Indian man on his own. Soo Meng's apparent idiocy suggests a racial colourblindness. In this context the last line of the story seems as puzzling as the last line of the earlier story, "Noon at Five O'Clock": "Which balloon would Soo Meng have received?" (p. 151). The narrator's conservative tone may suggest the line should be interpreted as pragmatic and derisory. However, it also raises questions about Singaporean perceptions regarding the mentally handicapped. Indeed, the narrator of "Soo Meng" may strike readers as unreliable, just like the narrators of the earlier stories "Noon at Five O'Clock" and "A Silly Little Story". But, while in the earlier stories linguistic strategies are used to destabilize narratorial authority, in "Soo Meng" it is the unnuanced, old-fashioned, and unsympathetic stance to both contemporary progress and mental disability that occasion our unease and distrust.

"The Effect of a Good Dinner" (1978)

"The Effect of a Good Dinner" is the first of three stories published and probably written after Yap's postgraduate studies at the University of Leeds in Britain (during the years 1974 to 1975) before he took up the position of lecturer in linguistics at the University of Singapore. During this year away from Singapore, Yap also spent some time in London and Wales, and his travels may have contributed to a noticeably more detached quality in his writing. It seems likely that the stories were written expressly for inclusion in his former schoolmate Robert Yeo's anthology, *Singapore Short Stories*. Taken together, the three stories represent what might be described as an early post-independence triptych representing the introduction, presence, and passing of traditional Chinese folkways in Singapore. All of them feature the motif of an important dinner central to the action of the stories. While "The Effect of a Good Dinner" and "The Story of a Mask" paint broad pictures encompassing almost half a century of Singapore's recent history (from around 1930 to 1980), "None the Wiser" could be described as a late 1970s domestic portrait in miniature. The stories' shared underlying theme is not the immediate death, but rather the slow and relentless haemorrhaging or wearing away of Chinese Singaporean traditions in past and modern Singapore. Indeed, the reference to "haemorrhage" at the beginning of "The Effect of a Good Dinner" foreshadows the climax of "None the Wiser": "Custom and heritage are the easiest things to kill; even if they are not killed, they are easily jolted into a haemorrhage" (p. 26). Yap's use of the words "jolted" and "haemorrhage" also implies that custom and heritage are unlikely to be sensitively handled by the city-state's pragmatic administrators during Singapore's ongoing redevelopment. During a heated discussion between the Tan siblings and their respective spouses regarding who will take care of their elderly mother, Mei Ching and Teng Soo first suggest placing Mrs Tan in a "home for the aged" (p. 35). "Homes for the Aged" that specialize in "providing basic shelter and care for the aged destitute" were started in Singapore during the 1970s and they are often regarded as a Westernized solution taken up by uncaring children who lack the care and compassion to look after their elderly parents and relatives themselves. For many Chinese traditionalists the homes signified a betrayal of filial piety. Indeed, Mei Ching and Teng Soo's suggestion shocks the other siblings. Shortly afterwards the eldest son discovers that the festive red banner sash, hung over the door to ward off evil but left in the rain despite Mrs Tan's warning, is bleeding red dye. As the traditional Chinese door sash symbolizes good fortune, there is an implication that both material and spiritual prosperity as well as cultural tradition are slowly but steadily bleeding or haemorrhaging away in a rapidly developing Singapore.

"The Effect of a Good Dinner" explores a traditional Chinese folkway situated firmly in Singapore's past and practiced only by the wealthy elite: bigamy, or the taking of a second wife. The custom had come to an end completely by 1961, at the time of the passage of the Women's Charter (Kevin Tan, email to Angus Whitehead, 28 June 2010). The first paragraph frames the story:

> Custom and tradition are the easiest things to kill; even if they are not killed, they are easily jolted into a haemorrhage. Sometimes they appear

comic or ludicrous, or they are grim. When you cease to believe in them, you would seem to have come a long way. Sometimes, you may ask yourself: a long way from what? Then you may want to assert that, now you do not have to tip-toe or kneel your way to where the angels and your ancestors were told to tread. ("Effect of Good Dinner", p. 26)

From the outset, the narrator's passive ambiguity quietly problematizes the idea that discarding tradition or excising oneself from it can be unequivocally described as progress. In the final line, Yap appears to be making a sustained but by no means straightforward allusion to Alexander Pope's (1765) famous line from his *Essay on Criticism*, "For fools rush in where angels fear to tread" (p. 22). In juxtaposing "angels" and "ancestors", Yap signals the coexistence of two belief systems within twentieth century Chinese Singaporean folkways. At the same time, Yap may be slyly aligning Singapore's relentless march to modernity with Pope's loud, ignorant "fools" that "rush in" to even the most sacred spaces.

As in his earlier story, "Noon at Five o'clock", in "The Effect of a Good Dinner" Yap deftly manipulates the chronology of the story in complex ways that challenge readers, such as constantly alternating between tenses. In the third paragraph, for instance, the story shifts abruptly from past to present tense: "Year by year, something gives and fizzles out" (p. 27). This detail throws up an ambiguity: even though he is communicating in the present tense, is the narrator making a general remark about Singapore from the perspective of a specific (past) moment in time? A historicized reading of a subsequent sentence suggests that the speaker is reflecting on Singapore at the time of independence: at the Moon Festival, "[t]he children no longer rise very early to bathe and put on their new clothes" (p. 27). The passing away of this minor ritual in Singapore during the mid-1960s can be seen as an indirect effect of redevelopment, specifically the mandatory movement of Singapore's working- and middle-class citizens from traditional to HDB (Housing Development Board) housing and the subsequent fragmentation of traditional Chinese extended families. The narrator compares the *gradual* and almost unnoticed erosion of tradition in colonial Singapore during the first half of the twentieth century (represented by the granduncle exchanging his singlet or Mandarin coat for a modern shirt fit for all occasions, and the grandaunt having her hair waved a la Jean Harlow) with the explicit, mandatory, and systematic excision of tradition and folkways that are part and parcel of the ongoing, crisis-driven creation of the contemporary nation state: "They acquired new habits and gave over their old ones. But still they did not give away everything. There wasn't any need to. In their heyday, Singapore wasn't so instant" (p. 28). If the characters in this story are types that represent their generation rather than fully fledged individuals (Brennan 1990, p. 33), then the central figure of the granduncle could be seen as articulating emerging tensions between tradition and modernity experienced by numerous Chinese Singaporeans a generation or so before national independence.

Yap, writing during the 1970s, might also be suggesting that, ironically, aspects of the prevalent modernity of post-independence Singapore, framed by the state as a "forward-looking teleological story of orthodox nationalism and nation-building" (Poon 2009, p. 365), actually derives much from traditional Chinese folkways evident in Singapore in the decades preceding independence. Before World War II, the granduncle works hard in order to purchase, in addition to a jade bangle for his wife (a traditional Chinese symbol of wealth and prosperity), various objects redolent of modernity and material prosperity such as a portable radio, a bike, and a car. The granduncle, in many ways a traditional figure of a lost past, is also presented, like Wong Loo in "A Silly Little Story", as changing along with society and the times. He also prefigures post-independence Singaporeans in his work ethic and material acquisitiveness: "work[ing] to keep his family very fully alive" (p. 26). This work ethic is so persistent that it seems to be unaffected by the trauma and violence of World War II, during which Singapore was invaded and occupied by the Japanese: "During the war, they did not suffer unduly. (They had friends who did).... After all, during the war one had to make sacrifices" (pp. 28–29). The reference to sacrifices seems to prefigure the PAP's rhetoric of the population having to "make sacrifices". The "quickening" pace provoked by the end of the war is represented simultaneously as the source of both the old man's desire for a new younger wife and the national desire for independence from the British, but it ultimately leads to both domestic and social changes that the granduncle is unable to accept.

On the one hand, as Frank Brennan suggests (p. 31), the narrator of the story patently disapproves of the old custom of matchmaking, through irony, dark humour, and the tellingly gendered observation that the custom would still be used in the present "if there was an ugly girl or an idiotic boy in the family" (p. 27). But the narrator's position is actually more nuanced: after remarking that *"things would have been slightly different* if there was an ugly girl or an idiotic boy in the family", the narrator adds a further qualification: "But usually, by a family's own standards, there are simply no such things" (p. 27, italics added). The sentence is doubly ambiguous: it is unclear whether the second "things" refers to ugly girls and idiotic boys or circumstances that might "have been slightly different". The ambiguity suggests the narrator's detachment and refusal to overtly criticize the ritual of matchmaking that, as a Chinese Singaporean folkway, had by the 1970s become more or less obsolete (Kevin Tan, email to the authors, 24 June 2010). What Yap seems to be asking us to consider is the ways in which Chinese folkways in Singapore were not merely denigrated and stamped out by the heavy-handed intervention of the state. Rather, from the early 1960s onwards, a younger generation of Singaporeans influenced by Western modernity and popular culture and represented by the narrator's coolly detached voice, began resisting and turning away from Singapore's unlegislated domestic traditions. The narrator of this story talks about the past matter-of-factly without identifying with his granduncle or grandaunt and with little or no emotional investment or attachment to the question of bigamy involving his extended family. To the narrator, such an incident or issue appears to be a thing of the past, literally a matter of fact to be recounted but not dwelled upon.

"None the Wiser" (1978)

While "The Effect of a Good Dinner" explores disappearing Chinese folkways, "None the Wiser" presents contemporary, surviving, and arguably more fundamental folkways threatened by Singaporean modernity. The story is set in the midst of Singaporean redevelopment during the 1970s. The Tan family's surviving members have moved from their original traditional "terrace-house" ("None the Wiser", p. 33) and have dispersed across the island to newer kinds of residence already available to the upper-middle class in modern Singapore. Mrs Tan's three siblings' households can perhaps also be read as representatives of early post-independence Singapore.

The story begins in the Queenstown HDB flat of insurance clerk Teng Soo and his wife, elite kindergarten teacher Mei Ching. Teng Swee Kheng observes that "Mei Ching holds a respectable job as a private kindergarten teacher, and although she is less well-off than the others, she is happily married to a respectable insurance clerk, and they have their own flat" (p. 35). But, at dinner Mei Ching describes her life here as far from "a whale of a time" (p. 36), and describes her home as "our cubicle" (p. 35). In Singaporean parlance of the period this indicates a one-room HDB flat, housing of the most rudimentary and basic variety, principally built for low-income families. Mei Ching seems to be stressing the smallness of their home as an inadequate residence for Mrs Tan. The detail also indicates a genuine economic inability to assist their mother, compared to her more affluent brothers. Her and her husband's relative poverty, despite the fact that she works for an elite kindergarten, may suggest the wide socio-economic discrepancies in the early years of Singapore's economic development. If, as details in the story imply, the couple have children, life for the family is less rosy than Teng suggests.

As Mei Ching raises her hands to slide open and secure the window at the beginning of the story, "Teng Soo ... thought for one amusing moment that his wife was extending her arms into the sky to help the weather" (p. 32). On the one hand, "[t]he rain sets the depressing tone for this story, and the image of Mei Ching with arms outspread in an effort to help the weather proves to be as misleading as Kok Lian's hopes that she and Teng Soo will help with his mother" (Brennan 1990, p. 36). But, on the other hand, the rain that Mei Ching attempts to assist is also the rain that, after the climax of the story (the angry discussion provoked by Mei Ching and her husband's suggestion of an old folk's home for her mother), is discovered to have caused Mrs Tan's birthday sash to bleed its red dye ("None the Wiser", p. 32). The detail retrospectively suggests not merely malicious but also malevolent witchlike qualities in Mei Ching, who, despite her nurturing role as a teacher, is cast as a source of unfilial piety in the story.

Mei Ching's older, more successful brother, Kok Lian, director of Lucky Advertising, exhibits both his wealth and his expensive (if poor) tastes in the "chandelier-like", "costly", "garishly-fashioned" and "ornate ceiling lamp" (p. 32) in his detached "house" (p. 34). Teng Soo and Mei Ching's discreet, conspiratorial mockery of this "pretence" may be linked to aesthetic considerations, but it is primarily concerned with his ostentatious display of wealth, which provokes jealousy and sibling rivalry. In Kok Lian's choice of the hideously expensive lamp, we catch a glimpse of an unhealthy national attitude that combines conspicuous consumption of material goods and the flaunting of these goods in the face of one's family and friends. Another brother, Kok Beng, a Sydney University chemical engineering graduate, lives with his Australian wife, Phyllis, in "one of the new flats quite close to the Katong Park" (p. 33). In the eastern region of Singapore, located not far from the sea, Katong Park was from 1930 to 1960 a popular park open to the public, known for its police and military band concerts. A decade or so later, the time in which the action of "None the Wiser" is set, the recent redevelopment of the East Coast area has left the park landlocked, reduced and neglected. Nevertheless, the location of Kok Beng and Phyllis' new flat, coupled with the fact that they own a car, suggests they have done well, perhaps representing a happy medium between the fortunes of Mei Ching and Kok Lian. Although we learn least of this sibling, Kok Beng seems the most sympathetically portrayed, with his university education, moderate success, and cosmopolitanism signified by Phyllis, his Australian wife. Kok Beng, unlike his siblings, makes no proactive attempt to push the matter of caring for his mother on to someone else. He is annoyed at Too Seng's suggestion that none of them need have Mrs Tan come to stay with them: "You mean she's to live alone? Or perhaps you'll lend her your cat?" (p. 35). Kok Beng and Phyllis appear on the brink of being forced into looking after Mrs Tan when Teng Soo first raises the idea of "some institution" (p. 35). Although Kok Lian ultimately refuses to consider placing Mrs Tan in a retirement home for elderly people, it is Kok Beng who seems, at least initially, most shocked at the idea: "You mean — gosh! You mean we should send mother to the Home for the Aged?" (p. 35).

The issue of "the Home for the Aged" highlights a topical dialogue between traditional and modern Singaporean points of view. Teng Soo and Mei Ching's discreet criticism of Kok Lian's ostentatious displays of wealth (p. 32) seems to go hand in hand with their desire to see Mrs Tan settled in "some institution" (p. 35). Such a position echoes an early post-independence Singaporean pragmatism in which both culture and domestic folkways such as filial piety appear to defer to expedience and practicality. It is significant that the option of the retirement home comes not from Kok Beng, the son educated in Australia, but Mei Ching, who remained in Singapore and has not fared as well financially as her two brothers. The emergence of an unfilial mentality amongst some Chinese Singaporeans in the 1970s may be connected to the lack of a substantial, personal dimension beyond the everyday mundaneness of their own work-life in the nation-state. This is suggested by the boredom of Mei Ching's husband, Teng Soo, and his snooping into his insurance customers' private lives. Teng Soo's belittling vision of Kok Lian's refusal to send his mother to a home for the aged — "For one amusing moment, he had the idea that Kok Lian was going to rip off the sash, girt it round his waist and brandish a sword in defiance of the home" (p. 36) — underlines the couple's dismissive attitude to traditional filial obligations. It is also noteworthy that Teng Soo and Mei Ching and Kok Lian and Li May's children are curiously absent from the story and this family gathering, thus underscoring the fragmentation of the traditional Chinese extended family consisting of three or more generations living under one roof.

The title of the story, "None the Wiser", suggests deception and ignorance, and refers no doubt to Mrs Tan's obliviousness to her fate being plotted by her children. But the title may also raise questions concerning her children's wisdom despite the veneer of material wealth and economic progress in early post-independence Singapore. Mrs Tan, sitting placidly content in her blue vinyl armchair, seems to be a satisfied elderly matriarch who believes in the comfortable life her children will provide for her during her twilight years. As an elderly grandmother she appears to stand for a nurturing tradition increasingly in danger of being discarded by modernity. Brennan (1990) has suggested that Yap's portrayal of Mrs Tan is wholly sympathetic: "We are made to feel sympathetic towards old Mrs Tan which, of course, will make our lack of sympathy for her children all the more pronounced" (p. 36), suggesting a simple dichotomy in which tradition is seen as desirable and to be championed while modernization is regarded as unwholesome and to be condemned. But in Yap's stories things are never that straightforward. The story's focus on a less appealing facet of Mrs Tan's personality suggests that Yap's assessment of the relationship between traditional attitudes and modernizing developments is more nuanced. The traditional, conservative Mrs Tan clearly does not like her Australian daughter-in-law, Phyllis. Indeed, Mrs Tan's lack of sympathy for Phyllis may indirectly feed into her children's attitude towards their mother. To enhance this point, Yap deploys weather imagery to connect the mother's traditional dislike of non-Chinese individuals to Mei Ching's cold and dismissive attitude towards her own mother. The conservative Mrs Tan has a mercurial attitude to her Australian daughter-in-law; her "almost instinctive timidity as well as dislike of Phyllis" causes the older woman to be either "too kind, too generous" or else "totally indifferent and cold", a coldness which the narrator compares to "the winters in Australia" ("None the Wiser", p. 33). Mrs Tan's indifference and coldness towards Phyllis, expressed in terms of temperature and meteorology, seem connected to Mei Ching's pose with her outstretched arm at the beginning of the story, when she appears to "help the weather" and the "rain [that] was pouring down" to wash away traditional beliefs and culture (p. 32). Yap therefore seems to suggest that traditional Chinese folkways, while threatened by modernity, have at the same time influenced Singapore's uncompromising, uncivil, unfilial version of modernity.

"The Story of a Mask" (1978)

In "The Story of a Mask", Wong Loo, the main character of Yap's undergraduate story "A Silly Little Story" reappears, transformed into a significantly more sympathetic character: he is an unmarried, childless, and peripatetic proponent of a traditional Chinese art that he perpetuates in the "Nanyang" — namely, Malaysia and Singapore (p. 37). Wong Loo is also removed from the quotidian reality of the story's fictional world and mythologized as a heroic figure of a modern Singaporean fairytale. He serves a national allegorical role, representing both traditional and modern Chinese Singaporeans who are confronting inevitable changes in a rapidly transforming society, and, unwittingly or not, playing a part in the demise of their own traditional folkways. At the same time, Wong Loo and his immigrant generation recognize, as subsequent Singaporean generations in a pragmatic nation increasingly cannot, the importance of the minute particulars of their cultural history and art:

> They brought with them, among other things, their beliefs, their superstitions and folkways and when they were unhurried, (which was quite often), they looked around and saw that, though they felt unchanged, they were in fact changed. Change was inevitable and it was inevitable for opera actors. They found that these changes had become very much a part of their lives, and it was by recounting the things of the past that they were able to trace the differences between themselves then and themselves now. ("Story of a Mask", p. 38)

However, although spiritual beliefs, folkways, and a sense of history are represented as enriching the life of the immigrant Wong Loo, the tragic ending troubles any simple reading of the story as a championing of Chinese folkways over modernity.

As in "None the Wiser", "The Story of a Mask" features telling topographical references. "[T]he Great World, the New World and the Happy World" (p. 38) were amusement parks opened by Chinese businessmen in the 1920s and 1930s. In these public spaces Singaporeans of all classes mingled freely, and Cantonese and Malay opera were also very popular in Singapore during the prosperous late colonial period from the 1930s all the way to the 1960s. The amusement parks provided platforms for Chinese opera, but paradoxically they were in themselves a manifestation of the very modernity that contributed to the demise of this art form, commonly known as wayang, in Singapore. As a study of this performing art form suggests (Lee 2009), in the amusement parks, traditional Chinese wayang competed with a myriad of other, newer, amusements, such as *gewutuan* (literally "song and dance troupe"), a kind of variety show originating in China in the 1930s, as well as taxi-girls (women who would dance with paying customers), fair rides, theatrical revues, and cinema.

In representing the period from 1930 to 1969 as a period of prosperity, Yap troubles the blandly progressive trajectory of official national history following Singapore's independence in 1965. In his short story this time period becomes the location for a moral tale about contemporary Singapore. The period immediately preceding national independence is presented as the first time in Singapore's modern history that "people could afford some culture" (p. 38). There is clearly some irony in this phrase, as it suggests a popular Singaporean conception of "culture" as a luxury commodity for those who could afford it, a conception that emerged in the first half of the twentieth century and is present even today. The fad for fabrics and traditional Chinese medicine that physically replaces traditional theatre in the amusement parks caters to the treatment of "a host of ... little illnesses" symptomatic of the comparatively comfortable, sedentary modern urban life of Singaporeans living in the mid-twentieth century (p. 39).

Wong Loo and his colleagues' professional past in China and subsequent working life in Singapore is described as "a difficult one but they had not savoured enough ease to want to strive for a life of comfort" (p. 37). In this gnomic sentence Yap again uses the past as a mediated critique of material improvements in Singapore that result in the paradox of a simultaneously wealthy and materialistic but also overworked and culturally arid existence. But, the story also reveals a development in Yap's story-telling technique, as he skillfully blends modern Singaporean quotidian reality within traditional Chinese folklore and belief. At the end of the story, the narrative mode shifts and the hitherto omniscient and modern narrator suddenly enters the world of Wong Loo's traditional beliefs: "His soul, as usual, left to wander. In the early hours, with the slow intrusion of light, it flittered back and hung quiveringly over the bench, and then retreated" (p. 41). Wong Loo, a practitioner of a traditional Chinese performing art, transforms into a figure out of a Chinese folk myth or ghost story in this prose fiction about modern Singapore. Through this narrative experimentation, in which a modern short story suddenly shifts into a traditional folk tale or ghost story, Yap not only shows the ebbing of Chinese folkways and art forms but also suggests that the eradication of these folkways and art forms will eventually, like Wong Loo's wandering and quivering soul, haunt Singapore's cultural imagination. We may, by extension, understand that the short story qualifies the official narrative of Singapore's unequivocal progress and development after 1965. Wong Loo and his fellow Chinese wayang performers appear to be professionals who can barely make a living from their art; they only perform during two major festivals and spend the rest of the year creating traditional objects. Their once daily but now rare performances are set in the context of the New Year and Moon festivals. These occasions seem to Wong Loo "frantically real" (p. 40), which implies that during the rest of the year, life in Singapore is numbingly surreal or uniformly dull. Wong Loo's frantic seizure of reality through the cultural medium of Chinese wayang seems intimately connected with the departure of his soul from his body at night, and this plot twist also reflects a traditional Chinese belief that dates back three thousand years to the Zhou dynasty. According to Chinese legend, a human being has two souls: a superior, spiritual soul (*hun*) and an inferior, material soul (*po*). The superior soul can wander while the latter is asleep and stays with the body. If the superior soul becomes detached from the body through death, it wanders the world till it finds a body it wants to enter. This out-of-body experience seems to have an invigorating effect on Wong Loo, whose soul "returned" faithfully "each morning" and made him feel "a little cheered" (p. 40). That Wong Loo is cheered by this night-time sojourn of his soul elsewhere suggests the benefits of this momentary metaphysical escape from the restrictions of a material and materialistic world — perhaps an analogy with the artistic power of Chinese opera to engross and transport its viewers into another world of traditional folk tales and myth. But at the end of the story, Wong Loo dies because his soul cannot re-enter his body; the exhausted Wong Loo goes to sleep "without having removed his mask" or thick make-up he wore when he was on stage, thus making his own body "not familiar" and "not as usual" to his soul, but "a mockery of the real thing" (p. 41). The most obvious conclusion we can draw from this tragic ending is that Wong Loo is a victim of a modernizing society that no longer values his art and exhausted his physical and cultural resources as a Chinese opera practitioner; at the same time, his soul's inability to recognize and re-enter his body due to the mask-like Chinese opera make-up on his face may be Yap's way of considering how an art form like Chinese opera also needs to adapt to and change with the times, making itself understandable and appealing to a modern-day audience. Authenticity in a complex performing art like Chinese opera need not only be measured by how well its practitioners guard and preserve its traditions, which, if it becomes an obsession, may end up making "a mockery of the real thing" instead of staying true to the spirit and soul of the culture and society in which the art form was created and in which it must continue to exist.

"A Beginning and a Middle Without an Ending" (1982)

"A Beginning and a Middle Without an Ending" should be read in the context of a Singapore in many ways materially transformed beyond recognition from its earlier guise in the 1970s. The year 1982 marked seventeen years since Singapore's independence, a decade since the country began its rapid modernization and economic development, and the period in which Prime Minister Lee Kuan Yew's prediction of the city's transformation from colonial town and swamp to metropolis had occurred. However, by this date almost two decades of government social engineering policies had begun to wear away at the traditional and local community values that had initially survived the mandatory country-wide relocation from village and urban neighbourhoods to elite private houses and condominiums (for the privileged few) or HDB housing estates (for the majority).

The story portrays a sophisticatedly urban, identifiably modern Singapore that appears to exclude the island's traditional local folkways and topography. Writing in firmly realist prose, Yap presents two snapshots of women's lives in Singapore. The first is set in a domestic milieu in the early post-independence period, around the years 1969 to 1975; the second takes place "thirty-five years later", specifically at the time the story is supposed to be written, which is an imagined twenty-first century future. That speculative future vision appears to derive from Yap's imagined trajectory based on contemporary government policies in the early 1980s; the story thus fast-forwards late-twentieth century Singapore in order to show what the effect of these policies will be on a generation of Singaporeans in the early twenty-first century who have grown up under their aegis. In this society, individuals not only fail to help and sympathize with one another; they also appear to take an almost sadistic pleasure in the disappointment and discomfort they cause others as well as in the power they can exercise over their subordinates. In this story the central character, Betty, moves from initial idiosyncrasies and an idealistic, aspiring personality to what might be described as a conformist attitude to hard-nosed *kiasu* Singaporean pragmatism.

The title of the story, "A Beginning and a Middle Without an Ending", draws attention to the story's distinctive structure, which is divided into three sections. In the first, Yap shows us a reunion of female school-friends. Betty, the younger sister of one of the women and a girl of rather vacant serenity, is urged to give her interpretation of a song in Mandarin she once heard performed by a female Taiwanese singer. In her performance, the "sensational" Taiwanese singer "ended the song with tears hosing down her face" (p. 75). For Betty, listening to the song was like "having access to an entire vista of human understanding" (p. 75), which suggests another salutary representation of popular culture as meaningful rather than simply entertaining. Twelve-year-old Betty sings her version "in obedience to the mannerly deployment of her heart" (p. 75). Yap's curious phrase foreshadows middle-aged Betty's later poise, while suggesting genuine feeling in her youthful performance. Betty attempts to "extend the Taiwanese singer's interpretation" by ending her performance falling "onto the floor in a heap" (p. 75). Her elder sister, quickly realizing that the "crumble" is due to artifice rather than faintness, is overcome with "admiration, shame and anger" and gives Betty "a resounding slap" (p. 76). The performance and consequent violence causes the formerly "dull" female gathering to end "on a merry note" (p. 76). Leng Eng's mocking suggestion that Betty should perform her Mandarin song on *Talentime*, a local talent show televised on Radio Television Singapore, confirms the time period of the story's setting as sometime in the late 1960s to mid-1970s.

The second section portrays Betty's professional, public life "thirty-five years later" as "the executive director of a modelling school"

(p. 76). This suggests that, although Yap was writing sometime in 1982, the second section is set sometime in the early twenty-first century, and we are therefore reading his representation of an imagined, futuristic Singapore. In this futuristic, chic Singaporean interior setting, Betty's colleague Vicki's hand is described as "a nubile technological extension" of an "elegant white telephone" (p. 76). Betty's "eggshell" office denotes not only elite commercial taste, but also physical as well as symbolic fragility. It is clear that events recounted in the earlier snapshot have had consequences on Betty's character thirty-five-years later. Betty is now a successful woman; the twelve-year-old girl who was once made a laughing stock by her older sister and her schoolmates is now a forty-seven-year-old executive director of a modelling agency and school, and her transformation is related to Elaine's confused and Leng Eng's heartless treatment of her in the first section. Betty remains committed to poise and etiquette, but a role reversal has taken place. In middle age, Elaine, the older sister, is poor and estranged from Betty. But Betty herself now mirrors the cruel and abusive aspects of her tormentors, relishing in the failure of others, and unable or unwilling to help younger and hopeful prospective applicants such as Miss Zatika enroll in her school's courses. For Betty, elegance and charm are both an almost religious path to happiness and an ethical solution to world problems: "There is so much unhappiness in the world. If I could educate every woman to be elegant and charming, half the troubles of the world would be gone" (p. 76). "[L]evitat[ing] from her chair" (p. 76), "her hands describ[ing] quarter-circles of beatitude" (p. 77), Betty resembles a spiritual teacher, if not an artistic representation of an Indian *guru* or Christ himself. However, Betty's secretary's mistranscription of her school's forthcoming course as "cent meditation" is unwittingly nearer the mark than Betty's original title, "Zen meditation" (p. 77). Commercial and commodified perceptions of female beauty are repackaged as keys to spiritual wisdom and global salvation. The narrator's tongue-in-cheek tone suggests that, despite Betty's pretensions, she is merely imbuing her modelling agency with undigested scraps of wisdom that are in accord with the Singapore state's pragmatic and economically driven logic of success rather than spiritually and culturally rich religious and literary texts.

The third section of the story is a brief, one-paragraph conclusion that is characteristically ambiguous. The title phrase "without an ending" has two possible meanings: first, that there is no conventional, formal end to the story; second, Singapore's cultural history beyond the two snapshots presented has reached a state of stagnation, ossified to the point where it cannot surpass its bureaucratic authoritarianism and mass commercialism. The authoritarian climate of the early 1980s may have constrained Yap to this ending, which is arguably more elliptical and ambiguous than his earlier prose:

> An ending must be found. Without it, Betty Wong could only go on rejecting the Zatikas. The Zatikas are abundant. Somewhere in between the rejection and the realization that the Zatikas were being rejected for nothing, for things that weren't there; somehow, in between the chuckle and the choke, Betty Wong drew a conclusion. It was the collapse before the song started. And poor Elaine, the face, the recollection of the face that could not launch Betty Wong's hand. (p. 78)

The final sentence is a parodic reworking of Faustus' paean to Helen of Troy in the English dramatist Christopher Marlowe's famous play *Doctor Faustus* (Romany and Lindsey 2003, p. 390). That Betty's face launched Elaine's hand to strike her in youth, while Elaine's face in middle age cannot launch Betty's hand to write a cheque for her now-impoverished older sister, may gesture to Yap's verdict on the negative effects of unnuanced authoritarianism, harsh power, but also about a culture motivated by superficial beauty rather than need. Betty is initially portrayed as an original, visionary, aspiring talent. Yet, the discouragement and mistreatment she suffers at the hands of others turns her into a powerful and abusive agent who puts down the talent of other younger people like Miss Zatika, whom she rejects for her course. The initial cruelty inflicted on Betty by her sister causes her desire to snub the masses of Zatikas who apply to her courses. Betty's modelling school purports to run courses on "Inner Poise and Zen meditation" and "The Externalization of Inner Light" (p. 77). The first course sounds characteristically Singaporean as it fuses terms from distinctively Indian and Japanese religions. The second sounds as nonsensical as her "Beauty Edification Project" file, which is inscribed:

> DhPP/II/16A
> Physiognometrics — Within and Without
> Beauty, the Art and the Science of, and the
> Philosophy of

For Betty, it seems the Zatikas, like her sister Elaine, do not understand the meaning of true poise, beauty, outward grace. By transferring her anger to these faceless applicants, Betty wreaks revenge on her sister. Her school's outward shows of beauty and philosophical reflection are shown to be hollow, underscored by the metaphor of the nearby file that is, as Yap concludes, "empty, without" (p. 78). The file, with its verbose inscription but empty interior, seems a commentary on Betty's purported philosophy. Physiognometrics is a discredited nineteenth century pseudoscience concerning the study of physical, and especially facial, characteristics to identify superior and inferior members of society. Betty's ill-conceived attempts to fuse eugenics and spirituality could be interpreted as a comment upon Singapore's attempts in the 1980s at eugenics and social engineering in the name of nation building, such as the regulating of marriage through segregation in matchmaking and the Graduate Mother Scheme (Mauzy and Milne 2002, p. 60).

In this story, more than in any of his earlier pieces, Yap deploys Singaporean patois to effect. Only here does he deploy overt Singlish rather than the slightly stylized version of this demotic language we encounter in his poems. Singlish, it seems, has survived well into Yap's projected twenty-first-century Singapore: Betty's new secretary's "got two more enrolled this morning. Want to accept or not?" (p. 76) echoes Leng Eng's "Want some more coffee or not? Better say so, if not no time to make some more" (p. 76). Betty's "You have to speak correctly" appears to echo contemporary elite and state anxieties in Singapore concerning linguistic correctness and purity. Despite Betty's pontifications to others, she makes her own grammatical slips, such as "very brand new", and misquotes idiomatic phrases, using "poetry of motion" instead of "poetry in motion", and, in a moment of genuine excitement with her intimate young colleague, Vicki, also utters a typically Singlish exclamation: "all expenses paid for. What!" (p. 77). Betty's "What!" echoes the bullying Leng Eng's earlier unequivocally Singlish "What's there to mind? Sing what?" (p. 75), where "what?" is not a question but an imprecation. This is the kind of supposedly ungrammatical and improper English that gives grounds for Betty to fire her new secretary. Yap here appears to satirize an enduring Singaporean obsession with purifying or sterilizing all forms of English used in Singapore to adhere to a strict but imagined standard form, a form that approximates an ossified version of the English language used in Singapore during the late colonial period of the 1950s and 1960s and that no one can practically live up to.

CONCLUSION

In a discussion of Arthur Yap's poems, Shirley Geok-lin Lim (2009) draws a dichotomy between his representation of tradition as good and modernization as bad (p. 176). However, in Yap's stories things seem much more ambivalent and nuanced. In the context of Singapore in the early post-independence era, Yap employs embedded ambiguities as a strategy to explore with minimal controversy the erosion and persistence of local folkways against the wider background of politically engineered social change. This ambiguity derives from an ambivalent and often seemingly uneasy response to Singapore's progress towards modernity. Such a response seems shaped both by Yap's own attempts to come to terms with radical and implacable change and his attempts to negotiate the potential political minefield of authoritarian censorship. While raising questions about the effects of societal modernization and cultural Westernization penetrating Singapore from above and below, the stories also interrogate the idea of Asian values as a cohesive set of traditions championed by the legislators of the nation-state. Taken together the stories represent a telling commentary upon post independence Singapore's selective retention of Chinese tradition and a similarly selective acceptance of modernity and Western values. In these stories Eastern traditional values are potentially as suspect as Western modern ones. The condensed, enigmatic and perplexing nature of Yap's short stories, the rich polysemous nature of apparently mundane and clichéd words and phrases used, as well as their particularly difficult endings, recall the ambiguous and ambivalent quality of his poetry. In writing prose only superficially resembling — and sometimes parodying — the pragmatic plain speaking encouraged by state authorities, Yap appears to be using a maverick's linguistic trickery to subvert prevalent rhetoric. In his short fiction Yap displays an eclectic, tolerant, erudite, and culturally mature artistic sensibility, derived from a lifelong immersion in both Chinese folkways, Western art and popular culture that could accommodate Singapore's colonial past, a history composed of different ethnic and cultural traditions, and a contemporary modernity. Significantly, such a sensibility may have eluded many of the first-generation forgers and legislators of the nation-state.

Note

We would like to express our thanks to Jenny and Fanny Yap, Cyril Wong, Patricia Wong, Angelia Poon, and Kevin Tan for their invaluable advice and help during our research for this essay.

References

Brennan, Frank. *Notes on Singapore Short Stories*. Singapore: Heinemann Asia, 1990.
Brewster, Anne. "An Interview with Arthur Yap". *Asiatic* 2, no. 1 (2008): 97–107.
Chang, Rachel. "[MM Lee on Mother Tongue Weighting]; 'No equal status' for English, Chinese". *Sunday Times*, Singapore, 27 June 2010.
"The Diplomat and the Samaritan". *Time*, 1 July 1966 <http://www.time.com/time/magazine/article/0,9171,835866,00.html> (accessed 14 July 2010).
Lee, Tong Soon. *Chinese Street Opera in Singapore*. Urbana: University of Illinois Press, 2009.
Lim, Shirley Geok-lin. *Nationalism and Literature: English Language Writing From the Philippines and Singapore*. Quezon City: New Day, 1993.
——— . "Introduction". In *Writing Singapore: An Historical Anthology of Singapore Literature*, edited by Angelia Poon, Philip Holden, and Shirley Geok-lin Lim. Singapore: NUS Press, 2009.
Mauzy, Diane K. and Robert Stephen Milne. *Singapore Politics Under the People's Action Party*. London: Routledge, 2002.
Montague, W.P. *The Ways of Knowing or the Methods of Philosophy*. London: Unwin, 1925.
Patke, Rajeev and Philip Holden. *Southeast Asian Writing in English*. London: Routledge, 2010.
Poon, Angelia, Philip Holden, and Shirley Geok-lin Lim, eds. *Writing Singapore: An Historical Antholgy of Singapore Literature*. Singapore: NUS Press, 2009.
Pope, Alexander. *An Essay on Criticism*, edited by John Churton Collins. London, 1765.
Romany, Frank and Robert Lindsey, eds. *Christopher Marlowe, The Complete Plays*. Harmondsworth: Penguin, 2003.
Sullivan, Kevin. "Achievement: The Poet with an Artist's Touch — Arthur Yap Talks with Kevin Sullivan". *South East Asian Review of English* 8, no. 2 (1984): 3–20.
Sumner, W.G. *Folkways: A Study of the Sociological Importance of Usages, Manners, Customs, Mores, and Morals*. Boston: Ginn, 1906.
Tan, Swee Kheng. *Singapore Short Stories: 'N' Level*. Singapore: EPB Publications, 1991.
Wordsworth, William. "From Preface to *Lyrical Ballads*". *Norton Anthology of Literature*. Vol. 2, 6th ed. New York: Norton, 1993.
Yap, Arthur. "A 5-Year Plan." *Focus* (1962): 19-23.
——— . "Noon at Five O'Clock". *Focus* (1962): 31–33.
——— . "A Silly Little Story". *Focus* (1964): 15–16.
——— . "The Effect of a Good Dinner". In *Singapore Short Stories*, edited by Robert Yeo. Singapore: Heinemann Asia, 1978.
——— . "None the Wiser". In *Singapore Short Stories*, edited by Robert Yeo. Singapore: Heinemann Asia, 1978.

———. "The Story of a Mask". *Singapore Short Stories*, edited by Robert Yeo. Singapore: Heinemann Asia, 1978.

———. "A Beginning and a Middle Without an Ending". In *S.E. Asia Writes Back! Contemporary Writings of the Pacific Rim; Skoob Pacifica Anthology, No. 1*. London: Skoob Books, 1993. 75–78. Originally appearing in *Tenggara* 14 (1982): 17–20.

Yeo, Robert, ed. *Singapore Short Stories*. Singapore: Heinemann Asia, 1978.

Index

"1-2 MIN.POEM", poem, 90
"2 mothers in a HDB playground", poem, 35, 45–46, 104
"10th floor song", poem, 82–83, 105
"12-Times Table", poem, 69
1984, novel, 110
50,000 Up: Homes for the People, 81
"& the tide", poem, 50, 87

A

"A 5-Year Plan", short story, 152, 164–66, 170
"absolute", poem, 58
abstraction as resistance, 43–47
"aesthetic experience", 7, 163
"afternoon nap, an", poem, 35–36
Aichele, Kathryn, 57, 62
Alfian bin Sa'at, 97, 99, 104, 111
Anglo-American modernist poetry, 15, 23
Ang Siang Hill, 80–81
"another look", poem, 61
anthropocentrism, 7, 114, 116, 125
anti-establishment, and poetry, 97
antiromantics, 115, 125, 132
Arnold, Matthew, 20
Ashbery, John, 137
Asian identity, 19–20
"at nagoya", poem, 123
Au, Alex, 134, 136, 142–43, 148

Auden, W. H., 61–62
authoritarianism, 169, 186

B

Bakhtin, Mikhail, 31, 33, 35
Barisan Socialis, 166
Barlow, Adrian, 84
Barrell, John, 74
Barthes, Roland, 8
Baudelaire, Charles, 98
Beckett, Samuel, 100
Bedok, residential area, 87–92
"Beggars All", poem, 78
"Beginning and a Middle Without an End, A", short story, 157, 168, 183–87
Bellow, Saul, 155
Benjamin, Walter, 98
Beowulf, 115
Bhabha, Homi, 116
bigotry, 88
Bishop, Ryan, 6, 111
black & white paintings, 57, 60, 62
"black and white", poem, 63
Blake, William, 42
Blunt, Alison, 101
Boey Kim Cheng, 5, 9, 77, 134
Book of Genesis, 116–17
Bowen, Elizabeth, 9
Braque, Georges, 64
Brennan, Frank, 175, 179

Brewster, Anne, 80, 92, 131, 146, 152
Brown, Bill, 15, 17, 26, 28, 30–31, 39
Brueghel, Pieter, 62
Bryson, J. Scott, 115, 118, 132
Bryson, Norman, 65, 68
Buell, Lawrence, 131
"Building Dwelling Thinking", essay, 109
Bukit Ho Swee fire, 78

C

camp, 138–39, 141–42
censorship, 136, 169, 188
Cézanne, Paul, 64–65
Chakrabarty, Dipesh, 5
Chinatown, 76, 78–82, 84, 86, 155, 166–67
Chinese diaspora, 155, 166
Chinese folkways, 154–55, 159, 165, 169, 172–76, 180, 182, 188
  see also folkways
Chinese opera, 85, 181–83
Chinese painting, 67–68
Chinese University of Hong Kong, 97
Chinese wayang, 181–82
Chior Hong, see under Yap, Arthur
Chua Beng Huat, 103
Chulia Street, 78
"citizen journalism", 148
CNN, 140
code-switching, 35
colonialism, 6, 10, 19, 111
Commonplace, 2, 44, 48–49, 57, 60, 67, 82–83, 87, 91, 135, 147
  Zen and the art of, 63–71
"commonplace", poem, 66, 127, 129, 146–47, 152
communism, 166
"conceptual art", poem, 53
cosmopolitanism, 76, 123, 178
Cotán, Juan Sánchez, 68
critical theory of objects, 15
Cubist, 55–56, 64–65

"Cultural Dances of Malaysia", mural, 85
cultural identity, 4–5, 39
cultural geography, 96, 101
Cultural Medallion, award, 2
cultural places, 82–86
Culture and Anarchy, 20
Cummings, E.E., 21, 23
Cuscaden House Hotel, 82, 89

D

Davies, W.H., 84
de Certeau, Michel, 101
defenestration, 28
Delaunay, Robert, 55, 57
de Souza, Dudley, 76
Dickens, Charles, 137
disability, 170–72
Doctor Faustus, 186
Down the Line, 2, 48, 54, 57, 98, 104, 147
"down the line", poem, 22, 57, 104, 108
"dramatis personae", poem, 54–55, 103, 126

E

East Coast Reclamation Scheme, 87
ecocriticism, 4–7, 101, 103, 106
ecopoetry, 2, 7, 114, 118, 120, 131–32
  definition of, 115
Ee Thiang Hong, 67, 87
"Effect of a Good Dinner, The", short story, 162, 168, 172–76
Elden, Stuart, 107
elite civic spaces, 82–86
Eluard, Paul, 43
English language
  economic mobility, and, 19–20, 29–30
  function of, 34
  multiculturalism, and, 18–21
  registers of, 31

Index

environ, definition, 7
environmental literature, 131
Essay on Criticism, 174
ethnic identity, 19
Ethnic Integration Policy, 87
eugenics, 187
Evernden, Neil, 7

F
Faber Book of Modern Short Stories, 9
Fall of Icarus, The, 62
Federation of Malaysia, 84–85, 152, 168
female sexuality, 161
filial piety, 80, 173, 177–78
"fire off Kim Seng Bridge", poem, 78
Flowering Tree: Selected Writings from Singapore/Malaysia, The, 80, 84, 168
Focus, 78, 152, 156
folkways, 78, 82, 86, 91–93, 154–56, 171, 178, 180, 183, 188
 see also Chinese folkways
Formalism, 74
Foucault, Michel, 18, 74, 137, 138
Frankham, Steve, 140
Frost, Robert, 115

G
"gaudy turnout", poem, 139, 143–48, 161
gay promiscuity, 144
globalization, 6, 111, 169
Goh, Robbie B. H., 76, 79, 100
Gordon, Jan B., 19–20
Graduate Mother Scheme, 187
Greenblatt, Stephen, 74
Gris, Juan, 64
"group dynamics I", poem, 88
"group dynamics II", poem, 87–91, 93

H
Haskell, Dennis, 87–88

HDB (Housing Development Board), 77, 79, 81, 86, 90, 103–4, 174, 176–77, 183
Heidegger, Martin, 109–10
Helen of Troy, 186
Hesse, Herman, 42
"heteroglossia", 31–33, 35, 39
historicism, 74–75
historicity, 6–7, 111
history, as narrative, 6
Hokkien Mee, and poetry, 3
Holden, Philip, 92
home for the aged, 173, 178
homoeroticism, 143, 148
homophobia, 136–38, 142
"Homosexuality and the Problem of Scale", article, 134
Housing Development Board, *see* HDB
humanism, 114, 153

I
identity politics, 8–9
IndigNation, event, 8
"in passing", poem, 84–86
"in the quiet of the night", poem, 99
Ismail Talib, 88
"i think (a book of changes)", poem, 104
"it rains today", poem, 56
Ivanhoe, 160

J
James, Henry, 137
Japanese occupation, 175
Jeffers, Robinson, 115
"Jobweek 1992", poem, 104
Jones, David, 42
Journeys, Words, Home and Nation, 76
Joyce, James, 158
"june morning", poem, 56

K
Kandinsky, Wassily, 43

Kantor, Martin, 144
Keats, John, 68
kiasu mentality, 162, 184
Kim Seng Bridge, 78–82
Klee, Paul, 42–44, 46, 51–52, 55, 57, 62
Koh Tai Ann, 75, 80, 156

L
landmarks, demolition of, 75
land reclamation, 50–51, 106
"landscapes", poem, 47–48
Langbaum, Robert, 115
language, and cultural values, 19
language policy, 19, 25, 36
"late-night bonus", poem, 98, 106
Lawrence, D.H., 42, 156
Leeds University, *see* University of Leeds
Lee Kuan Yew, 140, 155, 169, 183
Lee Tzu Peng, 75, 97, 99
Lefebvre, Henri, 7, 97, 107–8, 112
"lesson on the definite article, a", poem, 98
"letter from a youth to his prospective employer", poem, 33
Lim, Shirley Geok-lin, 20–21, 35, 77, 82, 88, 116, 169, 188
Lim Yew Hock, 170
linear motif, 49, 53–55
"list of things: A MARKET AT UENO, a", poem, 124, 139, 141
"local colour", poem, 46
local spaces, and poetic map, 77–78
"location", poem, 24, 26, 29
Lo, Joseph, 139
Loke Wan Tho, 85

M
Malayan Five Year Plan, 164
"Malayness", 90
"Malaysian Rural Scenes: Occupations, Pastimes, Conveyances", mural, 85

"Man of Few Words, A", article, 134
Man, Snake, Apple and Other Poems, 2, 10, 29, 64–66, 98–99, 116, 135, 147
"man, snake, apple", poem, 116–21, 126, 131
Mao Zedong, 166
Marina Bay waterfront, 6
Marlowe, Christopher, 186
"mensnakesapples", 121, 123, 125, 131
migration, mandatory, 79
"mixed shots", poem, 83
modern art, 45
Modernist, 43, 58, 64
Montague, William Pepperell, 154
Montblanc-NUS Centre for the Arts Literary Award, 2
Moon Festival, 174
Moonrise at St Germain, 52
"Mother and Child", sculpture, 83
"mother tongue", 18–20, 37
Motherwell, Robert, 46
multiculturalism, and English language, 18–21
multiracialism, 18, 169
Mundy, William P., 85–86
mural, 84–86, 93
"Musée de Beaux Arts", poem, 62
"My Country and My People", poem, 97

N
Nagaoka, Miyuki, 66
narcissism, 144
National Book Development Council, 2
national identity, 4–5, 134, 169
nationalism, 3–4, 92, 154, 175
National University of Singapore, 2, 97
nativism, 4
"nature poetry", 115
"nature study" poem, 48, 106
"nature writing", 131

Index

New Criticism, 74
New Historicism, 74
Newspeak, 110
"new year '75 leeds", poem, 60
Ng Eng Teng, 83
No. 1, 61
No. 12, 61
No. 15, 61
"None the Wiser", short story, 168, 173, 176–81
"Noon at Five O'clock", short story, 152, 156–65, 172, 174
"north hill road, leeds", poem, 59, 61

O

objectification, 16–17, 26, 29, 32, 34, 38
objects and things, distinction between, 17, 22
"Ode to a Grecian Urn", 68
"old house at ang siang hill", poem, 2, 37, 45–46, 80, 82, 86, 105–8, 110
One Fierce Hour, 104
Ong Sor Fern, 134
Only Lines, 2, 10, 15, 24, 46, 49–50, 80, 84
"open road", poem, 53
Orwell, George, 110

P

"paired stills", poem, 69, 98
"Panoramic View of Singapore Skyline in the Evening", mural, 85–86
Pang, Alvin, 77
Papineau Studios Advertising, 85
"paraphrase", poem, 98, 101, 105
"pastoral poetry", 131
Patke, Rajeev, 21–22, 92, 98–99
penal code, 139–40
"peony display, ueno park, a", poem, 123
People Like Us (PLU), lobby group, 139

People Like Us: Sexual Minorities in Singapore, 8
People's Action Party (PAP), 85, 175
Peranakan, 81
Perloff, Marjorie, 23–24
personification, 27, 30
Philips, John, 6, 110
Picasso, Pablo, 43
pink dollar, 140
poetic map, and local spaces, 77–78
"poetic painting", 46
poetics of "indeterminacy", 23
poetry
  anti-establishment, and, 97
  Hokkien Mee, and, 3
  perceptions of, 5
  spaces and places in, 101–7
poetry prize, 2
poets who paint, 42
politics of the closet, 136
Pope, Alexander, 174
postcolonial criticism, 4–5, 10
postcolonialism, 6, 111
Pound, Ezra, 43
Pratt Lecture, 52
"precedence", poem, 56
Production of Space, The, 97, 107
public housing, *see* HDB
Puroshotam, Nirmala, 18–20

Q

Quarterly Literary Review Singapore, 83
queer community, 8
queer literary theory, 9

R

Radio Television Singapore, 169, 184
racism, 88, 142
Raffles Village, 83, 89
rapidizing, 31
Raya Art Gallery, 83
realism, 153, 156–58

"recurrent event, a", poem, 79
Rothko, Mark, 47, 51–53, 60–61, 63, 69

S
Sago Lane death houses, 79–80
Said, Edward, 4–5
Saint Andrew's School, 2, 156, 161
"samson & delilah", poem, 104
SATA (Singapore Anti Tuberculosis Association), 157
Savage, Victor, 77, 79, 87
Scott, Walter, 160
"seasonal", poem, 122–23
"Second Coming, The", poem, 14
Second Tongue, The, 19
Section 377, penal code, 139–40
Sedgwick, Eve, 137–38
sexism, 142
Shamsuddin H. Akib, 85
"Silly Little Story, A", short story, 152, 165–68, 172, 175, 180
Singapore
 airport, 84–86
 colonial past, 6
 English language and multiculturalism in, 18–21
 ethnic identity in, 19
 immigrants to, 154
 Japanese occupation, 175
 language policy, 19, 25, 36
 penal code, 139–40
 separation from Malaysia, 169, 181
 social engineering policies, 155–56, 171, 183, 187
 street names, 77
Singapore Anti Tuberculosis Association, *see* SATA
Singapore English, *see* Singlish
"Singapore Night", 83
Singapore Short Stories, 168, 172
Singapore University, 2
Singer, Isaac Bashevis, 155

Singlish, 31, 35, 46, 88, 170 187
social engineering policies, 155–56, 171, 183, 187
"sociality", 8, 10
social satire, 3–4, 161
Sontag, Susan, 141
"Soo Meng", short story, 168–72
Southeast Asia Write Award, 2
Space of City Trees, The, 2, 50, 87, 90, 102, 131, 135, 146
spaces and places in poetry, 101–7
Standard English, 4
"statement", poem, 32, 34
Stein, Gertrude, 14, 21, 23–24, 43
Stevens, Wallace, 42–43, 49, 64, 115
still life, 64–66
"still life I", poem, 66
"still life II", poem, 99
"still life IV", poem, 109
"still life V", poem, 108
"still life VII", poem, 110
"still life: woman with birds at Richmond", poem, 64
"Story of a Mask, The", short story, 154, 165, 168, 173, 180–83
straits born, 81, 105
Straits Times, 79, 83, 85, 134
"street scene I", poem, 98, 109, 127–28
"street scene II", poem, 98, 127–28
"subject-object relation", 18
Sullivan, Kevin, 77, 154
Sumner, William Graham, 154
"Sunday", poem, 56
"sunny day", poem, 56
SQ21: Singapore Queers in the 21st Century, 8

T
Tagore, Rabindranath, 5
Talentime, talent show, 184
Tan, Kevin, 172
Tan, Paul, 77
Tay, Eddie, 7

Index

"Tender Buttons", poem, 23
Tenggara, journal, 168
"The Eye", club, 83
"the grammar of a dinner", poem, 98
"The Shisen-Do", poem, 97, 123, 125
"there is no future in nostalgia", poem, 58, 106, 107
"thing-like" approach, 15–16, 31, 33
"things", poem, 27–28, 58
"thing theory", 5, 15–18, 31–32
Thrift, Nigel, 102
Thumboo, Edwin, 4, 10, 21, 45, 51, 75–76, 80, 97, 99, 111, 134, 168
Toh Chin Chye, 85
"traffic", poem, 127, 129–30
travel poems, 65
Troika, restaurant, 89, 92
"tropical paradise", poem, 29–30, 116, 121

U

"Ulysses by the Merlion", poem, 97, 111
United Overseas Bank, 84
University of Hong Kong, 97
University of Leeds 2, 58, 172
University of Singapore, 78, 89, 152, 156, 168
Unnamable, The, 100
Untitled, 51–52
Untitled No. 3, 47–48
upward mobility, 170
urban studies, 4–7, 10, 107

V

View from a Window, 57
Vincent, John Emil, 137
"Void Deck", poem, 104

W

Watson, Keith, 8, 134–36, 148
Wei Wei Yeo, 76
"Western" language, 20

Williams, William Carlos, 43, 58
Window, 57
window motif, 57, 59–60
Women's Charter, 173
Wong, Cyril, 8
"words", poem, 66
Wordsworth, William, 167
World War I, 4, 22
World War II, 175
Writing for an Endangered World: Literature, Culture, and Environment in the U.S. and Beyond, 131
Wu, Daven, 84

Y

Yap, Arthur
abstraction, and, 43–49
awards, 2
born, 2
childhood home, 78
Chior Hong, also known as, 155
death, 133
growing-up environment, 155
literary trademark, 15
modernist poetry, and, 21–24, 43–44
paintings, and, 2, 43–44, 51–54, 57, 60–62, 64, 67, 70–71
published works, 2
reclusive, as, 73
sexual identity, 8–9
short stories (1962–64), 156–64
short stories (1969–82), 168–87
Singaporean space, and, 76–93
social commentary, 31–39
solipsism and reflexivity, and, 97–101
"thing-like" perspective, and, 24–31
windows, and, 55–62
work, analyses of, 3
Yawning Bread, website, 134, 148
Yeats, William Butler, 14, 21

Yeoh, Brenda, 77, 79, 87
Yeo, Robert, 10, 45–46, 75–76, 147, 156, 172
Yeo Wei Wei, 6, 111
"your goodness", poem, 140, 146, 148, 161

Z
Zen aesthetic, 69, 124
Zen, and the art of *Commonplace*, 63–71
Zhou dynasty, 182
Zhou Xiaojing, 7–8

Plate 1. *Untitled*.
Reproduced with permission of Ho Chee Lick.

Plate 2. *Untitled*.
Reproduced with permission of Ho Chee Lick.

Plate 3. *Untitled*.
Reproduced with permission of Jenny Yap.

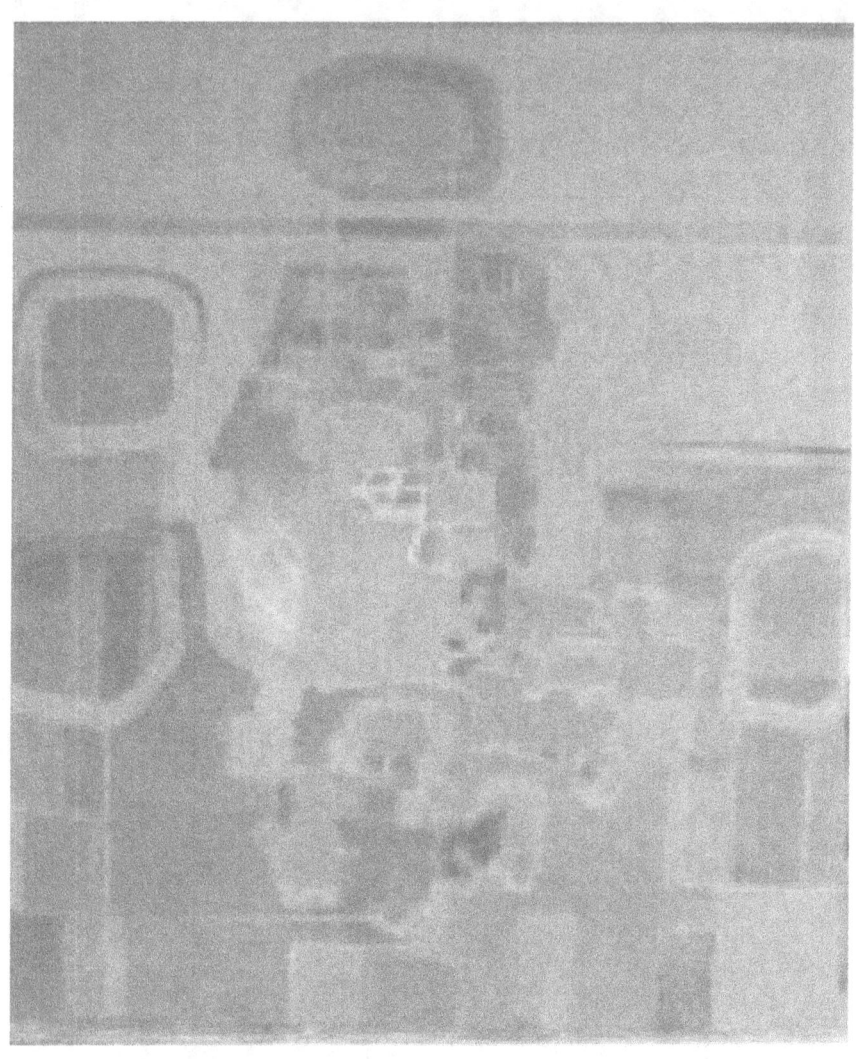

Plate 4. *Untitled*.
Reproduced with permission of Jenny Yap.

Plate 5. *Untitled*.
Reproduced with permission of Jenny Yap.

Plate 6. *No. 1.*
Reproduced with permission of Jenny Yap.

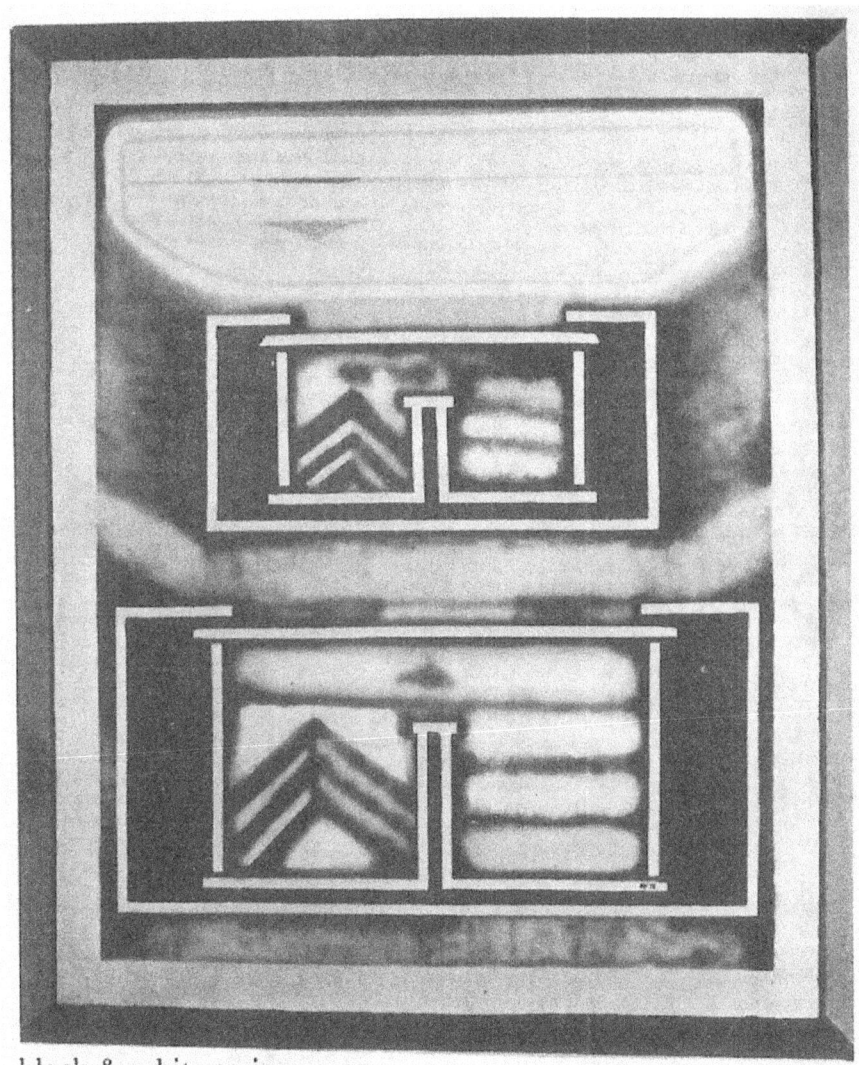

black & white series no 15
acrylics on canvas 112 cm × 92 cm

Plate 7. *No. 15.*
Reproduced with permission of Jenny Yap.

another look

About suffering they were never wrong,
The Old Masters: how well they understood
Its human position.

     Musée de Beaux Arts, W.H. Auden.

how an adaptation
between canvas & the hand:
an old masterly breath
dispensed sectorial suffering,
here, where it all is going on
is not the locus; but further
up or down are the spatial reactions
for surprise or sadness.
never level, the locus, this suffering
has to be watched carefully.
the stabbed figure in convulsion
has a destiny to go into,
an explanation, an appraisal,
a catalogue-listing.

never level, this suffering, this locus:
what it is, the literal size
incorporates, & larger or smaller
than life, this resinous suffering,
less frenetic, keeps pace
with or without contemporaneous occurrence.

black & white series no 12
acrylics on canvas 117 cm × 127 cm

Plate 8. *No. 12*.
Reproduced with permission of Jenny Yap.

Plate 9. *Mother and Child*. Sculpture by Ng Eng Teng.
Photograph by Peter Schoppert.
Reproduced with permission of Peter Schoppert.

Plate 10. Three Murals from Paya Lebar Airport Passenger Terminal. Image from an informational brochure owned by William P. Mundy. Reproduced with permission of William P. Mundy.